Praise for

# Ahead
# of the
# Curve

"Brian Kenny's passion for the game jumps off the page to tell a great story about how the game is being watched and analyzed in the age of information and technology."

—Billy Beane, executive vice president, Oakland A's

"Traditions are built on wisdom and experience, but learning from the past helps us challenge conventional thinking. Brian Kenny does just that."

—Buck Showalter, manager, Baltimore Orioles

"Illuminative and surprising, respectful and rebellious. You won't agree with all of Kenny's conclusions—now, what would be the fun in that?"

—Kostya Kennedy, *Sports Illustrated*

"Brian Kenny gives you (and yes, a few holdout managers) one last chance to join baseball in the 21st century."

—Rob Neyer, author of the Rob Neyer's Big Book of Baseball Series

"A delight for baseball lovers but also a useful parable about the power of habit and tradition, barriers to accepting answers hiding in plain sight for years."

—*Kirkus Reviews*

# Ahead of the Curve

## Inside the Baseball Revolution

## Brian Kenny

Simon & Schuster Paperbacks

New York   London   Toronto   Sydney   New Delhi

Simon & Schuster Paperbacks
An Imprint of Simon & Schuster, Inc.
1230 Avenue of the Americas
New York, NY 10020

First Simon & Schuster trade paperback edition July 2017

SIMON & SCHUSTER PAPERBACKS and colophon are
registered trademarks of Simon & Schuster, Inc.

For information about special discounts for bulk purchases,
please contact Simon & Schuster Special Sales at
1-866-506-1949 or business@simonandschuster.com.

The Simon & Schuster Speakers Bureau can bring authors to your live event.
For more information or to book an event, contact the Simon & Schuster Speakers
Bureau at 1-866-248-3049 or visit our website at www.simonspeakers.com.

Interior design by Ruth Lee-Mui

Manufactured in the United States of America

1   3   5   7   9   10   8   6   4   2

The Library of Congress has cataloged the hardcover edition as follows:
Names: Kenny, Brian, 1963–
Title: Ahead of the curve / Brian Kenny.
Description: First Simon & Schuster hardcover edition. |
New York : Simon & Schuster, [2016] | Includes bibliographical references and index.
Identifiers: LCCN 2015039474 (print) | LCCN 2015046188 (ebook) |
ISBN 9781501106330 | ISBN 1501106333 |
ISBN 9781501106361 (ebook) | ISBN 9781501106361 ()
Subjects: LCSH: Baseball—United States—Miscellanea.
Classification: LCC GV867.3 .K46 2016 (print) |
LCC GV867.3 (ebook) | DDC 796.357—dc23
LC record available at http://lccn.loc.gov/2015039474

ISBN 978-1-5011-0633-0
ISBN 978-1-5011-0635-4 (pbk)
ISBN 978-1-5011-0636-1 (ebook)

*To the love of my life, my girl, my wife—*
*Nicole Jacqueline Kenny. I love you with all my heart.*

# Contents

# Preface

Somewhere along the line, we just stopped thinking. In the most basic ways we all spoke about baseball, a purposeful ignorance set in, reflecting a fascinating part of our own nature. We are all too easily stuck in our own habits, swayed by bias, allowing emotion and laziness to overrule our intellect. Inertial reasoning is a powerful thing. We have received considerable baseball wisdom from the early days of childhood. We have also received it from powerful forces: our adult role models, our peers, the media, and the baseball industry itself.

What is so fascinating is that all this nonsense survived in spite of the following:

1.  Baseball is played in the most public forum possible, in front of a wide audience.
2.  Baseball discussion and analysis have been encouraged, not discouraged, for decades.
3.  The sport itself is an extremely competitive endeavor, with heavy incentives for winning.

So we have something happening right in front of us. Something we think about and discuss on a daily basis at least six months a year. An industry where strategy and information are vital. And yet for nearly a century, no one ever bothered to think about it deeply enough to give themselves an incredible competitive advantage, even when presented with the information.

Batting average, errors, pitchers getting their own "wins" to take home with them like prizes—it once did make sense. At a certain point—about the time we discovered penicillin—it was time to evolve past these 19th-century town-ball relics. Instead, our collective thinking calcified and then endured decades beyond its point of usefulness.

How did this happen?

# 1

# The Herd

"The group mind does not think in the strict sense of the word. In place of thoughts it has impulses, habits and emotions."
—Edward Bernays, Father of Modern Public Relations

There is safety in the pack. One must understand this to completely understand why it is so difficult to act independently. To adopt new methods is not just to stray from the pack, but to mock the herd itself. For this, there are repercussions. The herd—large, powerful, belligerent—has ways to deal with rogue operatives.

In football, a sport seen as a quasi-military exercise, innovative head coach Bill Walsh was routinely called a "genius." It was done as a tribute to his creative play calling. In baseball, a sport laden with tradition, innovative manager Tony La Russa was also referred to as a "genius." It was done to mock him.

Football culture, unlike baseball culture, has welcomed the idea of "intelligence" as a tactical practice. It's seen as necessary, even manly. Coaches are lauded for "attacking" in new ways, like a brilliant general. Yet even in football, the herd mentality is difficult to shake. ESPN.com's excellent columnist Gregg Easterbrook once asked Don Shula if there was an innovation left in football. Shula said, "Someday there will be a coach that doesn't punt."

Over the last decade, the practice of mindless punting has decreased. Patriots head coach Bill Belichick, though, has been able to maintain an almost automatic advantage over other clubs by frequently going for it on fourth down.

David Romer, an economics professor at the University of California at Berkeley, churned out a mind-blowing study on the folly of incessant punting in 2005. Studying NFL data, Romer concluded you should go for it on fourth down in the following circumstances:

1.  Inside your opponent's territory, on fourth and seven or less.
2.  Inside your opponent's 33, on fourth and 10 or less.
3.  Fourth and four or less, anywhere on the field.

So, given the statistics, why do NFL coaches keep punting? Because that is what has always been done.

In life and in sports, it's easier to stay within the herd and fail than go out on your own and succeed. An innovative coach can insulate himself from a herd backlash by winning, but woe to him when the pendulum swings. If he begins to lose, he will not be "one of the guys." Going against the herd is not a career path for the timid.

Reverential of its tradition, the baseball culture eyes innovation even more warily. The baseball equivalent to punting is bunting. Both are seen as automatic moves.

Let's set the scene. The leadoff man gets on. You have a choice, let your next batter hit away or have him bunt. The manager stands on the top step, giving the sign to bunt. The batter squares up, the fielders are in motion, and the runner is primed to move. Here is the skipper, the leader of men, taking matters into his own hands, initiating a lot of action, with his players fully engaged. Unfortunately he'd be much more productive if he just sat on the bench and did nothing.

Here's why: With even a successful bunt, you are giving up an out. It feels good—you can actually see your base runner move closer to scoring. What you don't see is that one third of your resources have been spent.

Here's what bunting actually does in this situation:

**Run Expectancy—Based on 1993–2010 Scoring Environment**

| Situation | Runs Expected |
| --- | --- |
| Man on 1st, no outs | 0.94 |
| Man on 2nd, one out | 0.72 |

With a man on first and no outs, you will, on average, score .94 runs. Move that man over on a bunt? You now, on average, will score .72 runs. So let's be clear: Even with a successful bunt, you score fewer runs.

Of course, you often bunt not to maximize the scoring, but to score one, single run. Surely, the successful bunt increases the chances of that happening, right?

**Run Expectancy—Based on 1993–2010 Scoring Environment**

| Situation | % of scoring |
| --- | --- |
| Man on 1st, no outs | 44.1% |
| Man on 2nd, one out | 41.8% |

With a leadoff man on, a team will get that manager that one precious run 44 percent of the time. When the manager or player lays down the bunt successfully, that team will score a run 42 percent of the time.

Keep in mind this doesn't take into account the times the bunt fails, which is not an insignificant percentage. But even when the bunt moves the runner over, it lessens your chances of scoring a run. You are working against your own goals.

Think of the psychology of this for a moment. If it's late in the game and your team is trailing, there is an expectation that you will bunt. When a team doesn't bunt, the manager is playing the percentages correctly. But if the next three hitters fail to drive in the run, the manager "sat on his hands," failing tactically. When a team bunts, and the next two hitters don't drive in the run, it is the players who failed.

Conversely, if a run scores after a successful bunt for *any* reason, it is seen that the bunt "worked." Sometime after a sac bunt, you'll see back-to-back hits, or something that'll bring in 2 runs. Even then it's seen that the bunt "sparked" a rally. Perhaps. You should also ask, "How many runs *would've* scored had they not given the defense an out?" This, of course, is not asked.

It should also be pointed out that the object of bunting a man to second base is it gives you two chances to score that run on a single. In the dead-ball days, this may have made sense, given that the simple single—the base hit—was regularly seen throughout a game. These days, however, players do not hit many singles. Players currently have a risk/ reward swing, which results in high strikeouts but hard contact. 2014 saw the fourth fewest number of singles in baseball history. The returns on bunting continue to diminish.

Yet managers have bunted mindlessly for decades. Think of the benefits:

1.  Avoid all blame for failure.
2.  Get all credit for success.
3.  Look manly and competent while doing it.

Given the culture, it's understandable. Most managers are better off giving the bunt-happy fans what they want.

## Blame-Free Failure?

You might not be convinced that failing conventionally has great benefits. If so, do you remember all the heat on Angels manager Mike Scioscia in

2014? Did you miss that controversy? Of course you didn't. There was no controversy.

Game 1, 2014 AL Division Series. The Angels had the best record in baseball, and are opening their postseason. Tied 2–2 with the Royals, LA gets their leadoff man on base in the 7th, 8th, and 9th innings. Each time they bunted, giving up an out. Each time they failed to score a run. Angels manager Mike Scioscia took virtually no criticism. Why?

By bunting all three times, he put the next two batters in the spotlight—there's the man on second, waiting to be driven in. When he doesn't score, it's those two hitters that didn't get it done. Failure is there *visually*—in the hitter slinking off field, having left a man on base. The manager walks off scot-free, even though *he is the one* who traded three chances for two.

This is a simple point that seems to be lost until you look for it. Anytime a team bunts, and the next two hitters end the inning, look to the on-deck circle; that's the guy who should be hitting, but isn't.

Not to dog-pile, but it's also one thing to scratch away for a run when your offense stinks. But where do you think the Angels ranked among offenses in baseball that year? The correct answer is number one. The Angels led both leagues in runs scored, and had MLB's deepest lineup. They were the only team that year in which *every* regular was above league average (above 100 in OPS+) (see Glossary). By bunting three straight innings, Scioscia took the bat out of the hands of Erick Aybar twice (103 OPS+), and Kole Calhoun (123 OPS+). The on-deck hitters who didn't bat were Chris Ianetta (123 OPS+), Calhoun (123 OPS+), and David Freese (104 OPS+). That's a lot of quality hitting lost—by both being ordered to bunt, and by having at bats exchanged for outs.

The Angels, with the best record in the major leagues, would lose that game, and the next two. They wouldn't win a game in the postseason.

In mainstream-land—the national broadcasters and national columnists were focused only on Ned Yost and his plucky little band of Royals. Other managers that postseason took immense heat—Nationals manager Matt Williams for taking out his starter with two outs in the 9th for a fresh reliever, and Dodgers manager Don Mattingly for a variety of offenses. Scioscia, though, was covered. Moving within the herd, he and his best-offense-in-baseball moved safely out of the postseason.

Of course, herdlike thinking in baseball is not limited to bunting.

# Closer by Committee —
# The Scourge of the Age

The 2003 Red Sox had new owners, a 28-year-old GM, and had hired the Godfather of Sabermetrics himself, Bill James. This new assemblage of brainpower was committed to a radically logical approach in its bullpen usage. Yale-trained GM Theo Epstein tried hard to explain it while not "scaring the straights":

> I'll leave it up to Grady [Little] to find usage patterns in the pen . . . the way we've built the pen is with versatility and flexibility in mind. On any given day, we want Grady to have lots of options to attack game situations and opposing lineups.

Versatility? Flexibility? Seems like a reasonable fellow. Burn him!

Remember, this is pre-Curse-busting Theo. He would soon find out that being innovative can get you whacked in certain industries.

Unfortunately for the Sox, their bullpen wasn't just bad, it was if they were dead set on creating the worst possible impression. Blowing a 5–1 lead in the ninth on Opening Day is definitely a way to lock in the perception of failure.

The failure snowballed, with the bullpen finishing April with a 5.68

ERA. Not good. The blame fell not on the pitchers or their short-term performance, but somehow on these pitchers being so dang-gummed confused.

Troy Percival, closer for the Angels, was asked what he thought of the Boston experiment: "Anybody who thinks the 7th inning is like the 9th, should go get a uniform and experience it for himself." If only we could take Percival up on it. I've never seen Bill James throw, but I'm willing to bet he would be just as bad pitching in the seventh as he would in the ninth.

The bullpen heresy was being linked to the man seen as the wizard-behind-the-curtain. Here is how A's pitching coach Rick Peterson put it, "Tell Bill James to come into a clubhouse that has just blown a 3-run lead in the 9th inning. It's a horrific experience."

True, but could Bill also come in and gloat over a boring 5–2 win where Ortiz, Millar, Mueller, and Walker—all acquired in a three-month stretch upon his hiring—all got hits?

Theo initially hung tough: "I think if it was any other city but Boston, where they ask you a thousand questions about why you don't have a bullpen, it would just be a bullpen waiting for someone to emerge. We'll be fine. The success or failure of any bullpen will come down to how your relievers pitch. Usage patterns might affect a game or two."

But reliever Chad Fox, who struggled early, could smell the fear: "We are going to get a lot of heat on the bullpen by committee, because no one really does it like this."

For those of us who never have had to hole up in a castle while mobs assemble with torches and pitchforks, it is easy to dismiss public pressure. The Sox stopped commenting publicly about their new philosophy, and traded for Byung-Hyun Kim in late May.

After starting several games, Kim was put into the pen, pitched 44 games, working 50 relief innings with a solid 3.18 ERA overall. The Sox traded for Scott Williamson, Todd Jones, and Scott Sauerbeck, and eventually brought up rookie Bronson Arroyo.

By early July, Kim was being called the "newly named closer." In late

July, Epstein was quoted as saying, "We are extraordinarily happy with the job Byung-Hyun Kim has done as closer." The white flag was up. Theo had learned to keep his Ivy League mouth shut, and Bill James was never formally charged with being a witch.

The club won 95 games and the AL Wild Card. What's remembered is that the Sox shut down the stupid closer-by-committee nonsense, and added some "established closers." Men who knew the difference between the seventh and ninth innings and who weren't a bunch of gutless pukes about it. Here are the bullpen pitchers added after April:

|                    | IP    | ERA   |
|--------------------|-------|-------|
| Byung-Hyun Kim     | 79.1  | 3.18  |
| Todd Jones         | 29.1  | 5.52  |
| Scott Williamson   | 20.1  | 6.20  |
| Scott Sauerbeck    | 16.2  | 6.48  |

Is it me? Or did all these guys except Kim stink?

Kim, Jones, and Williamson had all been "closers" before. While they all may have given sportswriters a warm, confident feeling when they took the mound, this group—with the exception of Kim—made things worse. Jones and Williamson finished with a combined ERA of 5.42 in 66 innings. What actually led to the staff turnaround was that two bullpen-by-committee-of-doom members straightened themselves out after May 5:

|              | IP    | ERA   | K/BB  |
|--------------|-------|-------|-------|
| Mike Timlin  | 63.1  | 3.27  | 53/9  |
| Alan Embree  | 50    | 3.24  | 41/13 |

So it wasn't the traditional "roles" that saved the Red Sox, it was the acquisition of a quality reliever coupled with other pitchers returning to their normal levels of production.

For Manager Grady Little though, it came down to the labels: "The biggest factor was when Kim went down there to become the closer for us. It defined all those people's roles down there, and they've been very productive." It's amazing, everybody has to "know their roles." The role of "get outs when we call you" doesn't seem to have been defined sharply enough.

The team that would win 95 games and the AL Wild Card would meet its end in one of the most spectacular failures in baseball history. Ironically, their postseason would end because they *didn't* go to their bullpen.

# The Grady Little Game

Game 7 of the 2003 American League Championship Series was a classic case of stunningly poor decision making.

I was at this game. I can tell you firsthand, Yankee Stadium—the old rocking and rolling Stadium—was dead quiet. Down 4–0, Roger Clemens KO'd, and Pedro Martinez on the hill. This one was over. The Bronx crowd was facing the likely prospect of the Red Sox dancing on the field, celebrating an American League title and the end of the Curse. As Mandy Patinkin said in *The Princess Bride*, "Humiliations galore." It was a feeling of deep dread.

Seventh inning, 4–1 Boston. With two outs, nobody on, the Red Sox win expectancy is 91 percent. The win expectancy, by the way, doesn't know Pedro is pitching. If it did, it would have shut down the lights and called it.

With two outs, Jason Giambi clubs his second solo homer of the game, and it's 4–2. Win expectancy goes from 91 percent to 84 percent, a big swing. What happens next is of particular interest: Enrique Wilson and Karim Garcia both single. Not Derek Jeter and Bernie Williams, but Enrique Wilson and Karim Garcia. If the greatest starter inning for inning is giving up back-to-back hits late in a game to the opponents' two weakest hitters, it's time to starting thinking about your options.

Pedro then went six pitches before striking out strikeout-prone Alfonso Soriano on a 2-2 pitch. Martinez was at 100 pitches. The Red Sox' win expectancy had dipped to 78 percent before the strikeout, and Pedro, the league leader in strikeouts per nine innings, was fortunate to have faced a low-contact batter (Soriano fourth in the AL in strikeouts).

Boston had escaped with a comfortable lead, but I'll give you my own "eyeball test" on Pedro at that moment: He was done.

If for some reason my untrained scout's eye doesn't convince you, there's always data: It's not a secret that Pedro was not the most durable of pitchers. The Yankee MO on Pedro for a good part of a decade was to grind out at bats in the hopes of getting him out, and the bullpen in. To back that up, here is what the AL did against Martinez in 2003:

| Pitches | BAvg/OBP |
| --- | --- |
| 1–25 | .183/.232 |
| 26–50 | .210/.290 |
| 51–75 | .213/.243 |
| 76–100 | .232/.303 |
| 101 | .298/.365 |

You don't need Bill James or Theo Epstein to tell you that the American League hit like a washed-up bench player against Pedro *until* he got to 100 pitches. At that point, at least in batting average and on-base, they began to hit like American League All-Stars.

Unfortunately for Boston, somebody *did* need to tell Grady Little.

I still remember looking toward the Red Sox dugout and bullpen to see who might be coming out to pitch the eighth. I recall being absolutely incredulous when I saw Pedro coming out of the dugout. I exchanged stunned looks with the guys sitting next to me in the stands. Something along the lines of "You gotta be kiddin' me" was uttered in a Bronx accent. I hadn't even thought of the *possibility* Pedro would be back out there for another inning.

Pedro gets Nick Johnson to pop up, but it's a seven-pitch at bat. Boston's win expectancy is a solid 94 percent, but Pedro is at 107 pitches.

Jeter doubles. Pedro stays.

Bernie Williams singles in Jeter, and it's 5–3. Pedro stays.

Where's Grady? There he is! He's come out to . . . *talk* to Pedro? Pedro stays.

Hideki Matsui doubles. Second and third, one out. Okay, that's it, right?

Nope. With the Red Sox win expectancy down to 65 percent, Little leaves Pedro in to face Jorge Posada.

The ship hasn't sunk, but water is pouring in. Posada has just had one of his best years—which is saying something: a .405 on-base, slugging .518. This is an extremely dangerous hitter, and Martinez is at 118 pitches.

I'm convinced that somewhere in Grady Little's mind there was some bullpen-by-committee bruising that hadn't healed. He could not have been oblivious to the obvious fatigue. He had to be aware that his ace fades—and fades fast—at 100 pitches. One hundred pitches is not some obscure stat, but the number for "has reached his pitch limit." If you were playing *Jeopardy!* and got the clue "Starting pitcher tires at this number," you would answer, "What is 100 pitches?" Yet, Little would not go to his bullpen.

The mainstream thought is still that Little didn't trust a shaky pen. I've heard people say that. Yet Little had used the pen liberally in those playoffs, going five games against the A's, and now seven against the Yanks. He had used nine pitchers out of the bullpen. The regular bullpen core had worked 30 innings, giving up *three runs*. That's a 0.90 ERA.

Could Little have hesitated to go to the bullpen because he didn't have a designated "closer" to go to? Byung-Hyun Kim was not on the ALCS roster. Kim had put base runners on in Game 1 of the Division Series against the A's, which led to a Sox loss. After he gave the finger to a booing Fenway in the Game 3 introductions, he was banished, leaving Little with an effective, but closer-less bullpen.

So there we were; a gassed Pedro vs. Jorge Posada. When Posada drops in his double to tie it up, you could not hear yourself yell. Yankees are whirling around to the plate, Red Sox center fielder Johnny Damon doesn't have a play home, and it's a 5–5 ballgame.

It's not only deafening; the stadium itself is shaking. The fans' delirium came from the improbability of the moment—timely Yankee hitting and historically bad Red Sox management.

The Yankees had come back from 4–0 and 5–2 deficits to tie it 5–5. Most of the night, the crowd was coming to grips with the end of the Curse. That the Curse was still very much in place, and actually more painful to the Red Sox than ever, was too awesome to contemplate.

The Red Sox' win expectancy, still a decent 65 percent before Posada batted, cratered to 35 percent by the time Little came to take Pedro out. You know the rest—an Aaron Boone home run off Tim Wakefield in the 11th, and the Yankees vanquish the Red Sox again.

Remember the pressure that forced the Red Sox to name a closer? Years later, Epstein would say, "It was bad execution because a few of the guys we got didn't perform early, so it became a huge controversy. In hindsight, we were a little naive how big a story it was going to become and how it was going to take on a life of its own in a detrimental fashion."

And yet, before Grady Little refused to take out Pedro in Game 7, he had, in the playoffs, used four different pitchers in the ninth inning: Alan Embree, Derek Lowe, Scott Williamson, and Bronson Arroyo.

Sounds a little like bullpen-by-committee, doesn't it?

Yet when Pedro Martinez was sputtering to the finish line in Game 7 of the American League Championship, Grady Little looked to the bullpen and didn't see his "proven closer." He saw a "bullpen-by-committee" and could not, in the biggest moment of the season, pull the trigger. Historically, Little takes the hit on this. But he is not solely to blame.

The most forward-thinking club in the majors boldly stepped into a new era and then backed away. Their fear of the herd had delivered the Yankees a chance at a reprieve on an old-school, data-hating platter. Little would be fired, but only after insisting to his bosses that had he a chance to play Game 7 over again, he wouldn't change a thing.

# The Shift

Opening Day 2012, I'm at my meeting for *MLB Tonight*, and I'm telling everyone there the theme of the early season had already been set: The Shift was on. The Tampa Bay Rays were taking a major step forward in innovative baseball thinking.

The Yankees, stocked with big-money hitters, were hitting it right at fielders with a stunning regularity. Watching a game on TV, we'd all been trained to see the ball hit back up the middle and think "base hit." Against the Rays, the sequence would be like this: Yankee ball hit up the middle, shortstop moves two steps to make the easy out, close-up of perplexed Yankee wondering what just happened. Clearly the Rays had taken a leap forward in the tactical battle. We would make it a major talking point on the program.

Still, though, there was resistance. I was told by one of our analysts that "teams had been shifting for years," and that it "goes back to Ted Williams." This was true, but what was unfolding in front of us, I argued, was quite different. At a network that goes to nearly every game—live— every day, this back-and-forth would be a daily drama. You're ad-libbing for hours with two or three other analysts. Since I'm the host, it's usually me and two other former Major League players. These were men who had spent a good part of their lives preventing runs, and they made it clear; they did not dig The Shift. Former infielders thought the slight "shading" from the coaches' scouting reports was enough. Ex-pitchers said it would be demoralizing for a hurler to have a ball hit to a traditionally occupied spot, only to see it dribble through for a hit. Either way, all this shifting was too cute for its own good.

Understandably, they had trouble believing they had been misled all these years. When a ball would roll through the hole where the shortstop would normally be standing, one of our analysts would yell out, "Doubleday put 'em there for a reason!"

For the next two seasons, there would be on-air cackling at the sight of a ground ball that would slip through an open spot. Taking the bait, I would point out, "You know that there is always going be open ground *somewhere*, right?"

Abner Doubleday didn't actually put them there, but thousands of coaches did for a century of baseball. Could they *all* have been wrong?

The visual evidence of a shift's failing was powerful, and in another era, the trend toward shifting might have rolled back. But it happened as the data on hitters was increasing exponentially, being implemented by teams that had fully staffed analytics departments. It was the last days of defense without thinking.

One thing seemed certain to me: This was only the beginning. Yankees outfielder Nick Swisher was impressed by the Rays' work, telling MLB.com: "That's the first time I've seen a shift like that. Righties, lefties, it doesn't really matter. It feels like there's 15 guys on the right side of the infield or the left side of the infield."

The Rays were already shifting more than anyone in baseball. Manager Joe Maddon had been going after David Ortiz with new wrinkles since 2006. The use of spray charts in applying defensive alignments was hardly a secret. The Rays just believed in it the most.

Maybe their shift would have been ignored if it they hadn't gone whole hog on Opening Day, which gets big exposure. Or against the Yankees, who draw a sizable audience. Maybe it would have been more easily dismissed had they not swept the $200 million Yankees in that opening series.

For at least that opening series, the Rays must have felt the way the Yankees felt when they had Babe Ruth in 1923: You are not prepared to play us.

Yankees hitting coach Kevin Long, representing the Herd, insisted there was plenty of luck involved in the Rays' defensive show: "They're not above the game by any means. . . . They were in the perfect spot. Come on, man, that's not going to happen all year."

Maddon wasn't above the game, but he sure was *ahead* of it.

By early May, the Rays had *twice* as many shifts as the team with the second-highest total. They had won the American League four years earlier, and had won 90 games in three of the past four seasons, despite a bottom-five payroll. With so many smart people in major league front offices, and with so much more data becoming available to track hitting tendencies, this particular innovation was about to reach what Malcolm Gladwell famously called "the tipping point." The Rays had embarrassed the team with the highest payroll and the team armed with what was likely the largest analytics staff in the sport.

Within two years, the Yankees themselves would be shifting more than the Rays. And they wouldn't even be leading the league. There were 2,358 shifts employed throughout MLB in 2011. In 2014, the number of shifts would top 13,000.

## The Boudreau Shift

If you give it about 30 seconds of thought, you realize why, for about 130 years, professional baseball players stood where they did on the field:

1. It seemed to make sense.
2. That's where they always stood.

Which is fine when the sport is 20 years old. Or you're just playing softball with your Burger King co-workers (we were really good).

Realize there *had* been effective shifting before. Ted Williams was an extreme left-handed pull hitter. Lou Boudreau, the Indians' shortstop player/manager, decided to try *something* to slow down baseball's best hitter. You have to give him credit—he did not go halfway:

It's something else, isn't it? I mean, Boudreau, the team's shortstop, is playing the second base position, and the third baseman is playing up the middle. *There's no one on the left side of the infield.* The one player on the left side is a short left fielder. Boudreau had guts—this was a massive change for 1946. It would have been a massive change in 1996!

The shift did, in fact, frustrate Williams. Exact data is not available, but Williams was famously stubborn and chose not hit to the opposite field. Fast-forward to the 1946 World Series, Cardinals manager Eddie Dyer put up his own shift, which held an injured Williams to a .200 batting average in his only World Series. Williams finally bunted up the third base line in one of the games.

So you'd figure the shift would come into play in force in 1947. And you would be wrong.

With this brief exception, everyone at the professional level of baseball stood in the same defensive positions for 130 years. Then—in a span of four years—everyone decided that defensive shifts were an effective strategy.

With this inability to evolve it makes you wonder: How do we even survive as a species?

# The *National* Pastime

While baseball is an international sport, American baseball has been the dominant culture, strong enough to repel any challenge to its cultural norms. The Nippon Professional Baseball organization is a high-level league, but has operated, until recently, within its own sphere. Hideo Nomo, the first Japanese star to play in the U.S., landed stateside in 1995. When Ichiro Suzuki came over in 2001 to great fanfare, his chances of success were openly questioned. A Japanese hitting star had never flourished in the U.S.

Ichiro could have been an excellent example of how a different sporting culture can influence another. Coming over in the height of the rocketball/juiced player offensive era, he was completely different from the American prototype: He hit for contact and average, not power, didn't strike out, and didn't look to walk. An excellent runner and fielder, he was not only an outstanding player, but was outstanding in a completely different way.

There were once plenty of players like this. In the 1920s and 1930s, even with home runs being in style, there were still players who slapped at the ball, just trying to get on base. Players like Lloyd Waner and Sam Rice hit for high average, didn't walk, and didn't hit for much power. There were some parks back then that were so vast that they lent themselves to a guy succeeding by hitting doubles and triples. But it was more than that.

I remember writing a story about Stan Musial a few years back. Musial was an all-time great in many ways. I had the good fortune to meet him at various Cardinals games and the Hall of Fame Induction Weekends, and he was an absolutely delightful person, as the many glowing features written about him suggest.

If you're a fan of baseball, you've heard a lot about Musial, but have you ever seen him swing? We have gotten so used to one type of swing—the basic offshoot of Mark McGwire's one-handed uppercut—that Musial's swing, seen today, is stunning.

He was famous for his "peek-a-boo" stance, his back turned to the pitcher with only the corner of his eye peering out. When he swung, he would spin his whole body with the bat toward the pitch. This was described as a corkscrew swing. It was the type of swing you might expect if you went to the Hall of Fame vault and they showed you some rare Wee Willie Keeler film; a level swing, with the bat plane through the zone for a long period. It looked like a dead-ball swing.

Musial, though, hit 475 home runs. When he retired, that was sixth on the all-time home run list. He also had a .331 lifetime batting average, and drew his fair share of walks. At different times he led the league in doubles, triples, walks, and of course batting average (seven times). When he retired, he was number one in total bases. He was both versatile and sensational.

But if a kid out of high school today goes to a minor league camp swinging like *Stan the Man Musial*, a squadron of coaches will descend upon him to change that funny swing.

At any given time, the herd says you have to swing a certain way to succeed, even when one of the greatest hitters ever showed us there used to be a different (swing) path to success. By 2001, bats had become lighter, home runs were everything, plate discipline was highly valued, and strikeouts were no longer a cause of shame.

So in comes Ichiro, not having gone through the local (U.S.) training. Year one, he hits for a .350 batting average with only eight home runs, and the eighth lowest strikeout rate in the game. He slaps 242 hits, with enough doubles (34) to slug a respectable .457. I opined immediately that this would start a new wave of players who could succeed the "Ichiro Way."

It's not as if he wasn't noticed. He played for a team that won 116 games with him leading off, and he even won the AL MVP.

Yet there has been no wave of Ichiros flooding MLB. Ichiro was seen as an anomaly, and maybe he was. Not many can come into the major leagues and hit .372, as he did in 2004. But couldn't more young players hit .300 if they adopted a singles-hitting approach?

The game's emphasis on power was incentivizing the single out of existence. The year 2014 saw the fourth lowest rate of singles in baseball history. This at a time when defensive shifts were stifling left-handed power hitters, batting averages were plummeting, and the diverse offense attack was dying.

I'm not saying Adam Dunn should have styled himself after Ichiro, but where had all the 5'9" singles hitters gone? I had this conversation with Randy Winn, an All-Star with the Rays. Randy was on *MLB Now* with us one day when I asked him about shifts and the lack of spray hitters who could adjust. He said, "Those players exist, but they're not being promoted." Organizations are looking for players with power—that had been the emphasis for generations. The goal is to get big-time talent to the majors, not maintain a diverse attack for the betterment of Major League Baseball.

Eric Byrnes, also an analyst at MLB Network, says singles hitters face a rougher path through the minors. "No question. And then good luck once you get to the majors. Check out my walk rates in the minors; I was patient. But when you get to the majors and you're not a power hitter? You're not a big investment for them? You'd better deliver right away. And that means hits. Next thing you know you're pressing, next thing you know—you're gone."

Byrnes brings up a good point. A club will have patience for a slugger who hit 30 bombs at a high level, but for a non–power hitter, any slump can be taken as a sign that "his swing doesn't translate." This is the Herd Mentality manifesting itself physically, affecting not just strategy but player development.

Both Winn and Byrnes are not examples of a win for the "little guy." Both are 6'2", 200 pounds, and in top shape. But both broke through despite not being sluggers. Winn for example averaged just 11 home runs a year, even during his peak (2001–2009). He also hit .298 and averaged 37 doubles a year. While this made him a slightly above average hitter (103 OPS+), his baserunning and defense made him a 3-win player, on average, according to WAR (wins above replacement—see Glossary). This is an extremely valuable player.

Byrnes scrapped around for years before getting comfortable, and then in 2007 erupted for a 50 stolen base season with a .353 on-base and .460 slugging percentage. Injuries derailed him from there, but he peaked as a nearly 4-win player. There are ways of playing baseball other than taking your base and occasionally crushing the ball into the seats. There is a good chance these players just aren't given the same opportunities, leading to a homogenized one-dimensional American player.

American baseball didn't adjust to Ichiro because it didn't have to. If a Japanese team filled with singles hitters was regularly challenging U.S. teams in international competition, things would be different. Japan won the first two World Baseball Classic tournaments, but that didn't seem to bother the United States fan base the way it did in Olympic basketball. With the WBC being played during MLB's spring training, it's not seen as a true test of baseball strength. Even with the United States never finishing in the top three, we just don't seem to care how we perform internationally.

Soccer is an example of what the open cauldron of world competition can produce. Unlike baseball, soccer has nations of competitive equals with different cultures and styles of play. Brazil played ball control, with lots of dribbling. England played the long game, sending the ball deep into the offensive zone to be chased. The Netherlands played Total Football, sending its backs on deep runs up the field. Italy had its signature defense.

This all began to change in the 1970s and 1980s as the world got smaller. Technology and travel triggered a cross-pollination in style of play. Countries were no longer isolated. The UEFA Champions League was just one of the international tournaments that had teams crossing borders and comparing notes.

There was a convergence of tactics, where best practices took over. Passing would be short, dribbling kept to a minimum. Players in the backfield would be freed up to make runs upfield, like the old Dutch teams. Clubs started moving as one, with the ball.

In the terrific book *Soccernomics*, Simon Kuper and Stefan Szymanski describe this shift in the soccer world: "Most countries on the fringes of Europe had dysfunctional, indigenous playing styles. The ones on the southern fringe—Greece, Turkey, Portugal—favored pointless dribbling, while the British and Scandinavians played kick and rush. Gradually, they came to accept these styles didn't work ... You need to play continental European soccer."

Dutchman Guus Hiddink would become the prime exporter of the new way to play. After a successful stint coaching the Netherlands, he began taking his ideas to the third tier of soccer nations: South Korea, Australia, and Russia.

Hiddink's culture crash in South Korea is fascinating. He would bring a combination of tactics honed in the cauldron of high-level European soccer, and he would also challenge the very class system of the nation. He had the simple notion that he would form his national team roster with the best players. This sounds simple, but this was not, as we often hear, "how it was done" in Korea. Selection policies were "based on personal, family, education, and social class affiliations."

Hiddink is an example here of diversity overcoming groupthink. Those who study the "Hiddink Syndrome" note that a coach from South Korea would likely not have considered breaking the existing cultural system, nor would he have been given the power to do so. In Korean soccer, a "results over process" mentality led to a cycle of failure. A Korean coach who suffered a lopsided defeat would be expected to hand in his resignation. It didn't matter if the team had been winning, was making progress, or had just run into an excellent team. The coach would be out, and the whole system would start with a new national coach. Hiddink twice suffered 5–0 losses early in his tenure, but was allowed to continue. This gave him time to work his transformation.

At the 2002 World Cup, having never won a single World Cup game, South Korea advanced out of group play, won two knockout round games against Italy and Spain, and lost close to Germany in the semifinals. Hiddink became a national hero in South Korea, with his philosophies branching out far beyond that of sport.

"Hiddink's recognition is also linked to his ability to demonstrate that success could be achieved through hard work, skill, and merit rather than inherited social standing or political connections," write Kuper and Szymanski. "Beyond this, the fact that Hiddink, a foreigner, was able to chal-

lenge the authorities and even operate outside traditional cultural protocols
signaled that Korean society was changing and perhaps, more important,
needed to change in order to be successful in the new global economy."

All teams—national or club—that didn't adapt would be left behind.
Being lazy or stubborn in the old ways—whatever they happened to be—
was becoming a losing option.

Baseball has never had a Guus Hiddink, an outsider challenging the
authorities and operating outside traditional cultural protocols. Japan
might slash at the ball and save their pitchers for once-a-week starts, but
the U.S. doesn't have to worry that Japan has found a better way. No one
else—Cuba, the Dominican Republic, or Venezuela—has a league that is
big enough to challenge Major League Baseball. The U.S. has enormous
advantages: a head start in creating the game and culture, a huge population, and a powerhouse economy. That counts a lot in global competition.

So we can leave a starter out on the mound long after he's exhausted.
We can play defense without any thought to where a batter has a tendency to hit the ball. We can give away outs bunting even when it lowers
the chances of scoring a run. We can keep our best pitcher in the bullpen
for the ninth inning even if the game is on the line in the sixth. We can
do all sorts of things that don't make any sense because there isn't anyone
else forcing us to get better.

The pattern is not likely to hold. U.S. hegemony will not last, even
in baseball. As we will learn, with the influx of data and new front office
talent flooding the game, the Herd may be forced to change from within.
It's been a long time coming.

## What You Don't Know *Will* Hurt You

Herd mentality is only one reason we resist good information, but it is
a powerful one. In *Thinking, Fast and Slow*, Nobel Prize–winning economist Daniel Kahneman writes that inertial (old school) thinking can
survive when it's "supported by a powerful professional culture," adding,

"people can maintain an unshakable faith in any proposition, however absurd, when they are sustained by a community of like-minded believers." Like-minded believers are not limited to baseball, nor are we merely limited in our thinking when it comes to baseball.

There are times when a culture needs to step back to see clearly how to do things better. I recall attending two very different seminars I could describe as mind-blowing—where I sat listening to an expert who had studied an issue I had barely considered. One was a nutritional seminar by Dr. Joel Fuhrman, the other an interview seminar at ESPN by interview guru John Sawatsky. In both, there was insightful, life-changing, and in my opinion, irrefutable information. Yet during both presentations, there was vehement resistance by the audience. Whether being told they needed to eat more vegetables or ask better questions, people at both seminars seemed to be downright angry.

"Humans are a social animal, a herd animal," said Fuhrman. "We have beliefs based on what the herd believes. It's uncomfortable to believe things other than what your herd believes." The bestselling author says it's more than just the taste of junk food that leads to a poor diet. "You need societal approval. We all belong to a societal group. It's hard to go against it. People have been trained, indoctrinated, *not* to think."

I told Dr. Fuhrman what I do in my study of baseball, how I challenged conventional baseball thinking in the mainstream media. He said, "So people are annoyed by you, right? We have a lot in common. People are infuriated by me."

Sawatsky had studied the art of interviewing for years and was passing along easily applicable lessons to ESPN anchors and producers. Most were fighting him at every step. "People are resistant to change instinctively," says Sawatsky. "We're conservative by nature. It goes right back to the reptilian brain—you have to conserve your energy, in order to have energy to get food. That instinct is still there."

There may be an evolutionary component to holding on to information. Listening to a parent telling you not to eat certain berries or get too close to fire can help you survive your childhood. "People are weak at being able to weigh consequences and facts," says Furhman. "It's inherently primitive to still believe what we learned when we were young, despite what's right in front of us."

Why can't we override these impulses with our intellect? We have more information available to us than ever before, but that is a very recent phenomenon. Much stronger inside our personal system is the belief that listening to received wisdom will insure our survival. The instinct that makes us wary of an animal baring its teeth may also make us hold tight to believing the numbers on the back of a baseball card.

Bill James says a major shift in baseball will happen only when the information reaches down far enough demographically. "The orthodoxy still believes what they were taught to believe when they were eight years old. You have to change the orthodoxy in order to permeate to the level of the high school coaches. Once you permeate to the level of the high school coaches, you change what the players believe, and eventually you get to the eight-year-olds." It is an internal fight against the evolutionary tools of human nature. Kahneman says we are hardwired to avoid doing the math. Thinking causes actual physical exertion, requiring glucose. We recognize that we will often avoid physical labor, but we need to recognize we all avoid hard thinking for the same reasons. Kahneman calls it the "law of least effort," writing, "The law asserts if there are several ways of achieving the same goal, people will eventually gravitate to the least demanding course of action." He adds: "Laziness is built into our nature." It's more than fighting off laziness, it's fighting the evolutionary tools of human nature.

In Furhman's case, the information he gives out—to eat nutrient-dense food—is actually life-saving. Do people listen? "I'm still, after all these years, staggered by nonsensical beliefs. You hope, in time . . . well, you just help the people you can help, and do what you think is right."

Is it different when it's just interviewing skills? Sawatsky says most will try, but eventually revert to their old ways. It's a truth that transcends this issue: "It's one thing to change your mind," Sawatsky says. "It's another to change your habits."

# 2

# Good Looking Beats Good Pitching

"Trust not too much to appearances."

—Virgil

"Kid, you're too small, go get a shoeshine box."

—Casey Stengel to future Hall of Famer Phil Rizzuto

The day before the 2014 All-Star Game, I walk right into John Farrell. Now of course I know John Farrell, he's the manager of the defending World Series champion Red Sox and as such the manager of the American League team. Yet, I'm frozen, I can't think of his name. I say a muddled "Hi, how are . . . you?," which is a coded response for "Hi, I can't think of your name."

It could've been worse. What I was thinking—and what I was this close to actually saying—was "Hi, Mike."

As in, Mike Matheny, manager for the National League team, who I would run into a moment later. I stepped away, embarrassed, but relieved I didn't come off as a complete idiot.

Why did I mix them up? Put them side by side, they don't look much alike. But there was something deeper to my flash of confusion—they each fit a certain archetype. The major league managerial archetype of what someone in that position is *supposed to look like.*

# The World Series

I do remember confusing the two before, at the 2013 World Series. They share similar characteristics; tall, handsome, big-shouldered, rock-jawed. For one game of that World Series, I sat in a seat on the third base line, and had a good view of both dugouts. Both Farrell and Matheny stood at the top step in a similar way; one step up, one down, like a sea captain. Like Washington crossing the Delaware. Or Captain Morgan in the rum commercials. More than just standing and watching, they stood and *projected solidity.* They exuded leadership. Their physical presence sent a message. *We're in charge. Everything is okay.*

When it came to decision making, however, everything in that World Series was *not* okay.

Farrell had a number of tactical issues. Entering the World Series, he scuttled his righty/lefty platoon of Daniel Nava and Jonny Gomes, going with Gomes, even with right-handers on the mound. In the regular season, Nava crushed right-handers, while Gomes did better against left-handers. A perfect platoon.

Citing a "different club personality" when Gomes started, Farrell gave Gomes the starting job in left field for the Series. The Red Sox were 7–0 in games Gomes started in that postseason. Perhaps they did *seem* to have a better personality, since all of us act happier when we're winning. But to directly connect "Gomes starting equals winning" is to flagrantly ignore the contributions of 24 other players involved in the larger dynamic. A sportswriter writing up a story might think it's connected, but a manager must have a greater understanding of causation and correlation. Meaning, the difference between something that happened *because*

Gomes was starting, versus something that happened *while* Gomes was starting.

After Gomes went 0-for-7 in the first two World Series games, Farrell went back to data, or tendencies, over the "club personality." Nava started Game 3 against a right-handed starter and drove in two runs.

There were other issues in Game 3. With no DH in the National League city, David Ortiz—Boston's best hitter—moved to first base, and Mike Napoli hit the bench. Over the previous three seasons, Napoli had the 20th best OPS+ in all of baseball. With one of the best hitters in the game sitting on your bench, a manager must know that one of the most important decisions of the day is: "When do we use Napoli?" It needs to be on the to-do list that afternoon, right after "Make sure wife and kids get tickets at Will-Call."

Yet, in the ninth inning, in a tie game, in a World Series tied up 1–1, Mike Napoli sat on the bench, while Farrell sent relief pitcher Brandon Workman to the plate. Workman, who had never batted as a professional, stood in against 100-mph throwing Trevor Rosenthal, and struck out on three pitches.

You don't need win probability added (WPA—see Glossary) to tell you just how big a spot this is. Tied 1–1 in the ninth, in a Series where the winner goes up two games to one, it is an absolutely pivotal moment. Farrell threw away the at bat, never got Napoli into the game, and ended up replacing Workman the next half inning anyway.

Farrell may have contributed mightily to the Red Sox winning 97 games over the six-month grind. I'm not minimizing that. The game also happens quickly, and mistakes can happen. But the difference between winning and losing a World Series is worth tens of millions of dollars. How is an organization with a payroll of nearly $200 million allowing its on-field decision making to be made this way?

# Race to Four

Joe Torre, during the Yankees' championship run, was asked if it's okay, relatively speaking, to lose a certain game in a best-of-seven. Torre waved it off and cut to the bottom line: "No. It's race to four. Whoever gets four first, wins."

Each loss is crippling. Things do *not* have to even out. You need to fight and scrap, and give yourself the best chance to win in every half inning of every game. Burn this into your own mind: You cannot give away a game.

Back to the 2013 World Series. Game 1, Fenway Park. I'm up in the MLB Network suite up the right field line (You should be happy for me—I worked 11 years in UHF) where you can look directly into the Cardinals bullpen. Second inning, Adam Wainwright is struggling. Already down 3–0, the bases are loaded, with Dustin Pedroia and David Ortiz due up. It's early, but the normally dominant Wainwright just doesn't have it, and the game is about to be blown open. I looked to the Cardinals bullpen, wondering who might come in first, and what left-hander could be used against Ortiz. I was stunned.

There was nobody warming up.

*It's a race to four.*

Pedroia singled, and Big Papi hit a sac fly. It was 5–0. A few moments earlier, the Cards still had a fighting chance. The game was on the line, with the game situation calling for a team's best relief pitcher. Yet Matheny had not even considered bringing in one of his available players. Now the Red Sox' win expectancy was 91 percent. It was all but over. The Sox took Game 1 8–1.

Jump ahead to Game 6. Red Sox lead three games to two, with a chance to win the Series at Fenway. Even conventional wisdom says *All Hands on Deck*.

It starts badly. Down 3–0 in the 4th, on the road, the Cards' win expectancy is already down at 14 percent. The Cards cannot allow much more damage and have a reasonable chance to avoid elimination.

Leading off the fourth, Stephen Drew hits a solo home run off starter Michael Wacha. Four–nothing Red Sox, and the win expectancy for St. Louis is down to 8 percent. The window on the season is closing. Matheny has seven pitchers in his bullpen and, more than likely, no game scheduled for the next five months.

Matheny leaves Wacha in. For four more batters. When he does go to the bullpen, it's 4–0 with men on first and third, and he brings in fifth starter Lance Lynn.

There was just no compelling reason to go to Lynn except that it was still the fourth inning, and that's when you'd normally go to your back-end-of-the-rotation starter. Lynn had an ERA near four in the regular season, and an ERA over five in the postseason. The Cardinals had at least four better options to try to get out of the inning with no more damage. Your season is ending. It's time for your best pitcher—your relief ace.

Single, walk, single. It's 6–0 Red Sox. Fenway is rocking, the fans are singing, and this thing ... is o-vah.

I'm not judging the decision by the result. Anyone could've given up two more runs in that situation. The point is, the best percentage play to stop the disaster was not made, and it wasn't made because of a manager not grasping the dire immediacy of the situation.

The fourth inning, by 2013 norms, is too early to bring in either one of your two best pitchers. *Even facing elimination.* Think of how powerful conventional thinking is when a manager goes directly against his own best interests in plain sight with the championship being clinched, and is not given a bit of guff by the media or fans for it.

Carlos Martinez and Trevor Rosenthal, Matheny's relief aces, would still pitch in that game. Martinez in the seventh, and Rosenthal in the eighth. The Cardinals' two top relief pitchers at the time were brought in when their club had a 1 percent chance of winning.

I later asked a member of the Red Sox staff what the team was thinking when they saw Lynn coming into the game. He said, "I thought he [Matheny] was conceding."

Both Farrell and Matheny are given high marks for what they did over the six-month regular season. This should not be overlooked. Both were in their first year managing their clubs, and both teams had a high number of players performing at peak levels that season. This could partly be due to the atmosphere set by the manager.

Tactically, though, they were sorely lacking. Fortunately for them, they at least failed using conventional decision making. Failing this way is safer—you're merely following the herd.

And I couldn't help but notice the similarities between the two. They made mistakes, but they sure looked the part.

The question should be asked: Do teams hire managers based on their looks?

# Bobbleheads

For the record, it's not as if my industry doesn't do the same thing. I remember being at a restaurant, looking up to the screen, and wondering what show ESPN was playing back on tape, since it looked like I was doing the hosting. It wasn't me. It was Rece Davis.

My wife once was meeting me at ESPN the Cafeteria (as I called it), and she called out to me as I was walking in, with my back to her. And yep, that too was Rece Davis.

We aren't twins, but we likely fit a certain type; what someone on TV is supposed to look like. Maybe our head sizes combined with hair color and demeanor. But I doubt it was an accident. One year the Hudson Valley Renegades minor league team held a "Brian Kenny Bobblehead Night." I was extremely honored. I had called games for the Renegades years before I got to ESPN. It was a chance to go back to the Hudson Valley with my family, enjoy the game, and see some of the people where I once worked as a local sportscaster. Doesn't get much better than that.

Months ahead of time they asked me for a photo to send to the company that made the bobblehead (you think this stuff is easy?). I did just that. When it came back, I recognized the doll. I showed it to my wife, my kids, and then my co-workers. They all said the same thing: "Hey, that's Rece Davis!"

# Managing

If you told me I would be a NFL head coach tomorrow—taking over on a Monday in the middle of the season—I could pretty much guarantee it would be a disaster. I wouldn't be good at organizing practice, let alone game planning and play calling.

Same thing if you gave me an NBA team. I could preach ball movement all I wanted, but defending the pick and roll, setting up an effective zone defense, and drawing up offensive sets are all beyond me. Beyond that, I am aware, just from calling college basketball games years ago, that things on the basketball floor happen *fast*. Very fast.

Now, tell me I'm managing the Cincinnati Reds tomorrow. You know what?

*I'd be fine.*

I'm serious. I certainly understand baseball better than those other sports, but it's also the sports themselves. Putting out a lineup and utilizing the bench is just not that hard. Using their bullpen correctly would be a challenge, but if I had the guts to execute an all-out bullpen attack, I would be better at using my pitchers than almost every manager employed today (there are a bunch of managers who *could* be better than I would be, but they are tied to convention).

Understand the distinction. I'm not saying I could *coach*. I couldn't teach a cutter, or even a good curveball. I couldn't teach a hitter proper mechanics. I would be a bad coach at any level past Little League. But *coaching* isn't *managing*.

I know what you're thinking: "What about being a leader? Managing egos?" What about it? Being on top of any group and managing them takes skill and a grasp of group psychology, but are there really that many managers that do that? Plenty of ex-players who played for successful managers have told me they often didn't have an actual conversation with their managers for *months* at a time. The players eventually just managed themselves. Not everyone needs a pat on the back or a kick in the ass. What they need is to be put into the lineup and have the right pitcher put into the game at the right time. This can be done effectively without wide shoulders.

There are decisions to be made. Players will tire, and players will bitch and moan. You need to be observant and responsive. There is pressure, and your decisions will be scrutinized. But let's not make it out to be more than it is.

My football defense would be exploited by Bill Belichick, and my basketball offense would be stymied by Mike Krzyzewski. But the Reds or Indians would go along for days before you even knew I was there. It's not that hard.

Let me ask you this: If the job was so difficult, how come the recent trend in the game is to hire ex-players with zero managing experience?

This is simply not an option in the NFL. Can you imagine LaDainian Tomlinson going directly from the backfield to head coach? It's just not possible, and not even considered. Football is too intricate; a lengthy apprenticeship is necessary, and a requirement.

In baseball, with its limited amount of strategy and skills that are hard to quantify, it is actually more important to *look* good than *be* good. When I say "look good" I don't necessarily mean be "good looking," as much as "looking the part."

Things like leadership and managing the clubhouse aren't like hitting and pitching. With the absence of quantification, other cues come to the fore. Things we also respond to subconsciously, like size, looks, and charm.

# The Candidate

We make selections based on looks all the time. In multiple studies, people were shown pictures of political candidates and asked about their electability. Only pictures were used—no names, no information about their experience or qualifications whatsoever. The researchers were exclusively interested in determining who looked the part.

Sadly—for democracy's sake—the candidates who were found to most "look the part" went on to win in the actual elections 70 percent of the time. This means that those considering exclusively superficial appearances matched up 70 percent of the time with a general voting body that is supposedly voting based on merit, experience, qualifications, etc. Even when we think we are making an intellectual choice, this experiment suggests that maybe we aren't.

You think Mitt Romney was a presidential finalist because of his grasp of public policy? His knowledge of economics? Please, the man looked like he was chiseled out of Reaganite granite. When party power brokers saw this guy, they said the same thing a scout says when he sees a 6'5" right-hander throwing 95 mph: *Yep, that's what it looks like.*

Another political study focused on a "low-information contest." In this case, it was deciding who would sit on urban development boards. What does an urban development board do? I don't really know, and probably neither do you. Turns out, this lack of knowledge makes our bias toward those that look the part even stronger.

The study asked individuals to rate the looks of the candidates for the board. Contenders whose appearance rated highest had close to a 90 percent chance of winning in the actual race. Nine times out of ten, the best candidate was also considered to be the best looking.

Think of how we would rate a baseball manager's effectiveness. What are their duties by which we can evaluate them? Most of it is nebulous: managing a clubhouse, putting individuals in a position to maximize performance, and communicating group goals. There is such a wide range of required skills that it's difficult to center on any one of them. Looks can end up being a deciding factor.

Even when a manager makes concrete mistakes, like Matheny not using his best relievers or Farrell choosing to keep one of his best hitters on the bench, we don't hear much about how they botched the decisions. Why?

First, failing by conventional means is relatively safe. You're not showing up anybody.

And second, our subconscious bias—based on looks—is likely more powerful than we know.

# The Men in Blue

On the field already there are people who are seemingly hired—at least in part—because of their looks.

For a major league umpires, physical size matters. The reason is— once again—tradition, not necessity.

In the nineteenth century, baseball was a very rough sport. The phrase "Kill the Umpire" was no joke. The game was played by ruffians— working-class types, often immigrants used to having to fight for what they wanted. Society was also just entering the rule of law. These days we all know putting your hands on someone will lead to all sorts of repercussions. This was not the case back then.

One of my first news directors was Brian Madden, a New York television sportscaster in the 1970s. Madden gave me my first full-time gig as a sports anchor at WTZA in upstate Kingston, New York. He used to tell me that whiskey and fistfights were common in the TV and radio newsrooms where he came of age.

Grown men in suits. Brawling.

He told me this in 1986, and even then that type of behavior seemed crazy. These days it's even more verboten. We have become more civilized. We all basically know punching a colleague in the face right there in the office will get you fired.

In 1800s baseball, though, it was a free-for-all:

Umpires were routinely spiked, kicked, sworn at and spit upon by players, while fans ("kranks" as they were then called) hurled curses, bottles,
and all manner of organic and inorganic debris at the arbiters. Mob-
bings and physical assaults by players and patrons alike became commonplace; police escorts were familiar and welcome sights to the men
in blue. . . . In short, a rough-and-tumble, no-holds-barred mentality
dominated the game in the last part of the 19th century.

Larry Gerlach, "Umpire Honor Rolls"
research.sabr.org/journals/umpire-honor-rolls

The man who called balls and strikes in those days needed to be more cop
than ump. Physical size was necessary for an umpire not just to discour-
age violence but also to defend himself and extricate himself from a mob
of angry townsfolk.

This all began to change with the founding of the American League
in 1901. Ban Johnson saw the opportunity to start a new league that
would appeal to a wider part of society. He rightly saw that gambling and
brawling would hold back the sport from greater popularity. The American League was founded with two key founding principles: rule of law,
and respect for the umpires.

One hundred years later, it's obviously a vastly different society and
baseball culture. So what do we have on the field? Umps who still look,
and act, like bouncers.

A modern umpire needs eyesight, judgment, experience, and the
ability to make quick and accurate decisions. Observational skills are
paramount. There are many ways to test this. We already know we haven't
gotten the best umpires from the population pool because only about half
the population pool has been eligible.

I once went to an independent league game in Bridgeport, Connecti-
cut. Behind the plate was Perry Lee Barber. The strike zone was consistent
and excellent, the calls were decisive and correct. Though Perry was what

you call "petite," the players were respectful because of the overall compe-
tence shown. Perry, by the way, is a woman. Within a few pitches, no one
cared. Perry has been an umpire for 30 years, and still calls spring training
games for the Mets. She has been unable, however, to break through to
the majors. She doesn't make a stink about this, nor does she think she
is the only woman qualified for the job. She would just like a woman to
have a fair chance. That has not been the case.

There is no reason a woman cannot umpire a major league game. If
there were no umpires of color—any color—ever to work a major league
game, we would consider it unacceptable. Why is it okay for half the
population to be basically ineligible? Umpires might have to stand their
ground here and there, but they do not have to physically defend themselves. The tiniest bit of contact these days warrants—as it should—a
fine and suspension. And yet our hiring practices are still rooted in the
nineteenth century.

We can recognize this in umpires, but do we also see how it translates
to managers? Athletes today are highly compensated, well-trained professionals. They might not be gentlemen, but everyone knows a physical
move toward a manager would bring severe consequences. It's simply not
tolerated, and absolutely not worth the trouble.

Yet we have managers who still look like and are built like Sgt. Rock.
We're hiring people for the wrong reasons.

## Managerial Qualifications

To become a major league manager, you need to be one or more of these
three things:

1.  Large
2.  A former catcher
3.  Ruggedly handsome

I remember one of the more memorable things Tim McCarver said on TV in the '80s was that catchers made better managers because they were the only players who were always looking at the whole field. (Tim was not sabermetrically inclined later in his career, but broadcasting Mets games in the '80s he was definitely the thinking man's broadcaster.)

Catchers are the only players regularly in on the pitch-by-pitch strategy and flow of the game. This would likely instill a discipline that could elude other players.

Let's go through the 2014 managers, dividing them into two groups:

## Large, Catcher, Ruggedly Handsome

Bruce Bochy, Fredi Gonzalez, John Farrell, Robin Ventura, Brad Ausmus, Ned Yost, Kirk Gibson, Bryan Price, Mike Redmond, Mike Scioscia, Joe Girardi, Don Mattingly, Bob Melvin, Ryne Sandberg, Clint Hurdle, Mike Matheny, John Gibbons, Matt Williams, Bud Black, Joe Maddon, Ron Gardenhire, Bo Porter.

## Not Large, Not a Catcher, Not Ruggedly Handsome

Buck Showalter, Lloyd McClendon, Terry Francona, Walt Weiss, Ron Roenicke, Ron Washington, Terry Collins, Rick Renteria.

Some of the managers in the second group are good-looking men, but not in a rugged-movie-star drill-sergeant way. This might just be junk science, but dammit, I have to make a call here.

The score:

| | |
|---|---|
| Large, catcher, or ruggedly handsome | 22 |
| Not large, not a catcher, nor ruggedly handsome | 8 |

Some of these managers could be in either group, but there was a recent handsome-hiring wave, which tilted the scales.

More than two thirds of the major league managers in 2014 fit a prototype that has nothing to do with their ability to do their job well. Maybe this isn't a fair sampling. Maybe most major league players are large anyway. But if you'd like to be a major league manager, I would advise you to be 6'3", 230 pounds, appear able to physically push around grown men, and have a background in calling pitches as backup catcher. Even if this has very little to do with doing your job.

# The Credibility Game

While players subconsciously respect size and a square jaw, they are, in fact, conscious of membership.

Ballplayers give a fairly clear line of demarcation: To command attention as a manager, you must have at least *played* in the major leagues. You don't have to have been a star. Being an excellent college or minor league player is worth something, but it will force you to command the room in different ways. And not having played at a high level puts you at an extreme disadvantage. Getting to the majors for at least a short period of time gives you legitimacy to eventually lead at this level.

**BREAKDOWN OF 2014 MANAGERS**

| | |
|---|---|
| Major league veteran: | 25 |
| Minor league vet: | 5 |
| No pro experience: | 0 |

The overwhelming majority have played Major League Baseball, and there isn't one manager who hasn't played some level of professional baseball.

This makes sense at one level. Familiarity with a high level of baseball certainly can help you lead a baseball team. But isn't the point to know *baseball*, not Major League Baseball? Why do the major leagues completely preclude the large talent pool of players who have played, say, Division 1 college baseball? Is it really all that different? What major league teams are saying is that to manage in the majors, you have to have played at that major league level, or you have little chance of being hired.

Just to make a quick check, out of the top 25 NCAA Division 1 baseball teams, only one manager had played in the major leagues. To run a major college program, big league experience was not a requirement, and possibly not even an asset.

This holds true in other sports.

And if you think a baseball manager has to have played Major League Baseball to be successful, do you believe an NBA or NFL head coach has to have played *at that level* to win?

**Percentage of Managers/Head Coaches
with Top-Level Pro Experience, 2015**

| | |
|---|---|
| MLB | 83% |
| NBA | 50% |
| NFL | 19% |

You think Major League Baseball requires some different level of understanding of its sport that the NBA and NFL don't? It's just not the case.

It is more likely that the more complicated the game, the less likely it is you can just use the existing talent pool of ex-players and get away with it.

A club executive told me, "The biggest holdup in the game is the lack of intellectual capacity of the people in uniform. We pick from the same talent pool again and again. Ex-players—no college. They coach and teach the same way they were coached and taught. It's the unending cycle of the game."

## The Best of the Best

If you are looking for a manager, there is some wisdom to looking outside of the former major league player. If you do *not* have this automatic legitimacy, it means you must earn it in other ways. Your ideas must win the day.

Your strategies and utilization of personnel must make sense on their own, and not because the skipper "must know what he is doing." By having a manager who is not granted automatic legitimacy, you can have a leader whose ideas and actions speak for themselves.

Let's examine the managers who are routinely spoken about as the best in the major leagues and see if there is anything to this. They are: Joe Maddon, Buck Showalter, and Bruce Bochy.

Showalter and Maddon were at a disadvantage. Both were excellent players. Showalter broke hitting records at Mississippi State, Maddon played in college and in the minors. Neither though, would break through to the major leagues, so they had to rely on their ideas, principles, and ability to maximize performance from their players. In short, the skills of an actual manager.

Bochy is an example of how the obvious traits that seem to appeal to our subconscious can translate into success. A backup catcher in the big leagues for nine years, he is not only large, but has a very large head—conveying power and dominance. A strange thing usually occurs to those who meet Bochy for the first time; they will walk away from him saying, "I didn't know he was so big." This is because on TV, his head, shoulders, and hands give him the proportions of a squatty catcher. But he is a full 6'3". He also happens to be an excellent manager, proving that you can be hired for the right reasons or the wrong reasons and still turn out great. I wouldn't bet that way, but it sure did happen for the Giants.

# The Manager Effect

I don't want to overestimate the effects of a manager's decisions. But even if you believe—as most who study this do—that a manager means at best two to five wins a year, that's still often the difference between making a Wild Card, and missing one. Or winning a playoff game and losing one. This means millions of dollars to an organization.

Yet we seem to be hiring people because of what they are signaling to us emotionally rather than on the basis of the skills they can bring to the job.

Likely, this will change. Decades ago, a general manager could be hired if he was a former star player or married into the owner's family. This is not being done now—the job is much too important. GMs are hired after a lengthy climb through an organizational structure. Not only after an apprenticeship at the side of an older executive, but frequently after years of being involved in player development. It could take years, but it stands to reason that this same mind-set of professional hiring would move to the dugout as well. In Chapter 16 we will discuss how this is just beginning to happen.

More than most industries, baseball is a meritocracy. On the field, we think a player is judged on his record alone. But physical appearance affects our perceptions of more than just managers.

# Player Perception

Players, unlike managers, have a much more valid statistical record, and players with long careers should be much more easily judged. Yet bias confounds even the large sample size of two Hall of Fame pitching candidates. One just missed Hall of Fame induction from the Baseball Writers Association of America ballot, while one barely avoided falling off the ballot for a lack of votes. Yet the only thing I can find separating the two is their looks. I'm talking about Jack Morris and Mickey Lolich.

Quick, what jumped to mind when I mentioned these two? Go ahead, admit it. For Morris, it's his big-game pitching. For Lolich, it's his big gut.

Here's an example of sportswritery pieces on Jack Morris:

"Baseball's Last Gunslinger" (Forbes.com)
"Coming at Ya: Winning Is Everything for Ultra-Competitive Morris"
   (*Minneapolis Star-Tribune*)
"The 100 Manliest Moustaches in Sports History" (Brobible.com)

Here are a few for Lolich:

"Fat Man on the Mound" (*Sport*, 1972)
"When Fat Is Beautiful" (*New York Times*, 1989)
"Carrying Their Weight" (*Washington Post*, 2006)

Umm, detecting a pattern?

Here's a bit of "When Fat Is Beautiful" by Ira Berkow in the *New York Times* in 1989:

> Fat was getting a bad rap. This came from no less an authority on the subject than Mickey Lolich, who was once one of baseball's plumpest pitchers, and one of its best.
>
> From his business establishment, Mickey Lolich's Donut Shop, appropriately enough, in Lake Orion, Mich., the one-time Tiger, Met and Padre hurler said: "Throughout my 16 years in the major leagues, whenever things weren't going right, people always looked for reasons. For some, it was 'Maybe they're staying out too late at night,' 'Maybe too many outside interests,' 'Maybe their head's not screwed on right.' For me, it was 'He's too fat.'"
>
> *New York Times*, August 1989

The impetus behind this piece was Kevin McReynolds of the Mets facing criticism because he had gained weight. Even a writer of Berkow's stature went right to Lolich—and like manna from writer's heaven, the big guy had opened a donut shop!

Despite the reputations, and the difference in perception, Morris and Lolich had essentially the same career. I mean, they are, in a baseball historical sense, the same guy:

|          | IP    | ERA+ |
|----------|-------|------|
| Lolich:  | 3,638 | 104  |
| Morris:  | 3,824 | 105  |

Looking pretty similar. Long career for both. Lot of innings. Essentially the same pitcher.

Let's look at both for the bulk of their careers—their best 12 years:

|         | Avg IP | ERA+ | AVG WAR |
|---------|--------|------|---------|
| Lolich: | 268    | 104  | 3.9     |
| Morris: | 241    | 109  | 3.1     |

Morris is still a bit better inning for inning, but for 27 innings fewer per year. Lolich is still more valuable, but it's reasonably close.

If you had to choose between the two, you would likely pick Lolich. Yet it's Morris who was close to Hall of Fame induction, and is still a good bet via the Veterans Committee. Lolich is not even being considered.

Two similar players, for various reasons, are remembered very differently. It happens all the time in baseball history.

But in this case, one guy looks like a cowboy, and the other one looks like this:

NATIONAL BASEBALL HALL OF FAME LIBRARY, COOPERSTOWN, N.Y.

Mickey Lolich

I'm sorry to go fat bias on you, but if you have a better reason, I'm all ears.

# The Early Vote

Not that I put much stock in what the HOF voters say, but it is an indication of how the player was at least *perceived* at the time. Check out how each player started on the Hall of Fame ballot:

|          | Morris | Lolich |
|----------|--------|--------|
| Year 1:  | 22.2   | 19.7   |
| Year 2:  | 19.6   | 20.2   |
| Year 3:  | 20.6   | 20.3   |
| Year 4:  | 22.8   | 25.5   |

Four years into their 15 years on the ballot, Morris and Lolich were viewed very much the same way. Lolich had even gotten more votes as of the fourth year. They both started about 20 percent, far below the 75 percent required for induction. That's a long climb, but players as recently as Bert Blyleven and Bruce Sutter have been down around 20 percent, and still made it to the magic number for induction.

Funny things happened from there. Morris kept climbing, while Lolich would drop out of sight:

|          | Morris | Lolich |
|----------|--------|--------|
| Year 5:  | 26.3   | 10.5   |
| Year 6:  | 33.3   | 6.1    |
| Year 7:  | 41.2   | 7.4    |
| Year 8:  | 37.1   | 10.5   |
| Year 9:  | 42.9   | 10.2   |
| Year 10: | 44     | 5.0    |
| Year 11: | 52.3   | 5.7    |
| Year 12: | 53.5   | 7.0    |
| Year 13: | 66.7   | 7.2    |
| Year 14: | 67.7   | 8.2    |
| Year 15: | 61.5   | 5.2    |

Even amid the senseless voting patterns of the BBWAA, this is bizarre.

Morris's support steadily grew, even as a new wave of sabermetric writers took turns pointing out the new age numbers. You know, like his ERA.

Morris's earned run average was 3.90. It would've been the highest of any starting pitcher in the Hall of Fame. Writers, though, started coming up with new ways to quantify his career. He "pitched to the score," he was "the winningest pitcher of the '80s," and he "always started on Opening Day." It's true he often started on Opening Day—14 times in all. He also started three All-Star Games. He may have never finished higher than fifth in ERA, but for some reason he was, three times, thought of as the ace of the American League. That would translate into a somewhat heroic profile while on the Hall of Fame ballot.

Why is this? Go ahead and take a look:

Jack Morris

This guy *is what it's supposed to look like.*

Six foot three, 220 pounds. Not exactly a matinee idol, but tall, with big shoulders. Rugged. He looks like a cowboy.

Morris was not some fraud. He was extremely durable. Six times he was in the top three in innings pitched. He led the league in strikeouts once. But even in pitching WAR, which takes his impressive innings workload into account, he was never higher than fifth in the league. He was in the top 10 six times, which is excellent, but it just doesn't make up for the fact that in his prime, he was just a bit (8 percent) above league average when it came to preventing runs.

But what was sticky for Morris? Durable. Reliable. Big-game pitcher. A fucking cowboy.

Memories fade. Nuances and specifics are lost, and what is left for many borderline Hall of Fame candidates are just select story lines that stick. It's almost as if you need a winning one-line blurb to gain Hall of Fame traction.

Bruce Sutter "revolutionized the game" with a new pitch. Phil Rizzuto, according to writers quoting Joe DiMaggio, was "the one guy the Yankees couldn't win without." Jim Rice was the "most feared hitter" of the '70s.

It's like a screenwriter working on his "elevator pitch": You get on an elevator with a producer—BAM!—you have 10 seconds to wow him before the door opens. Same thing seems to happen to Hall of Fame voters.

Essentially the same pitcher, the Cowboy received 61.5% of the vote in his 15th and final year on the ballot, the Donut Shop owner finished at 5.2 percent.

I didn't mean to ignore Morris's calling card, I was just saving it for last.

# World Series Heroes

Jack Morris of course pitched one of the best games in World Series history. A 10-inning shutout in Game 7 of the 1991 Series. Morris famously outlasted John Smoltz and *his* seven and a third innings of shutout ball.

It was a helluva performance. But was he actually a better postseason pitcher than Mickey Lolich? If you know how to take the test, you already know the answer.

Mickey Lolich only got to start five postseason games. He pitched at least nine innings every time. Nine innings in four of the five games, ten innings in the other. He pitched 46 innings of postseason ball. His ERA? 1.57. Fat man, indeed.

You probably know some of the story, but believe me, this will surprise you. In the 1968 World Series, he went head-to-head with Bob Gibson, then—and now—seen as one of the best postseason pitchers in history.

But hold on, Lolich not only faced Gibson, he came back *on two days rest* to face Gibson, *and beat Gibson*. Lolich did so pitching a shutout up until two outs in the ninth, with a 4–0 lead.

Until Mike Shannon hit a solo home run with two outs in the ninth, Lolich was pitching a Game 7 shutout for a World Series title, *and* his third complete game victory of the Series. The Tigers won Game 7 and World Series title 4–1.

Forgive me if I don't care what Mickey Lolich looked like.

Here's their full postseason record:

|        | IP   | ERA/WHIP   |
|--------|------|------------|
| Lolich | 46   | 1.57/.98   |
| Morris | 92.1 | 3.80/1.25  |

Mickey Lolich was every bit the pitcher Jack Morris was over 15 years, and was clearly better in the postseason.

That he isn't remembered as such has more to do with us, and our biases, than with his performance.

# Epilogue

The effect of one's personal appearance is more powerful than you might think. This goes beyond baseball.

In the United States, being male, white, and heterosexual makes life easier. It doesn't mean a white straight man doesn't have to work for everything he gets, but it does mean there are fewer obstacles built into the power structure. I learned this attending the LGBTQ Task Force Conference in 2015. LGBTQ stands for Lesbian/Gay/Bisexual/Transgender/Queer. The saying that the trainers used for straight white males at Ally Training was "the wind is at your back."

In most of the U.S., being a straight white man means being able to walk wherever you want and not worry that a cop will give you a second look. It means not hearing jokes that diminish your worth in social settings. It means the person that interviewed you for a job probably looks like you and speaks the same language.

Any manager in the major leagues right now would understandably be outraged that someone would think he was selected based on his looks. It's a difficult job, and any former player can look back on his entire career path as the needed training. Becoming a backup catcher in the major leagues is not a gift that is handed out. The position is attained by very few and takes an enormous amount of work and excellence. But for those who reach this level and are looking for employment beyond their playing days, the wind is at their back.

In the United States, privilege means male, white, and straight. In the culture of baseball managing, it's white, male, and straight, plus large, catcher, and ruggedly handsome.

When considering who should manage your team, work for your

company, or who should get your vote for city council, keep these things in mind.

The best person for the job might just be a straight white male ex-catcher with a jutting jaw. But you should be open to the possibility that it is not.

# 3

# The Will to (Not) Win

"Never attempt to teach a pig to sing; it wastes your time and annoys the pig."

—Robert A. Heinlein, *Time Enough for Love*

The three most influential thinkers in the history of baseball are Henry Chadwick, Branch Rickey, and Bill James. Stretched out across a full century of baseball, they did all they could to educate the masses. But the conduit to those fans, the sportswriters, provided an effective blocking action for decades. Chadwick, a sportswriter himself, was the driving force in bringing baseball into the statistical realm and was rewarded with induction into the Baseball Hall of Fame in 1938. His love of small ball and emphasis on batting average was sensible given the station-to-station nature of the game in the 1800s. He died in 1908, fittingly the last year of the true dead-ball.

James was an outsider, opening our minds after decades of dead-ball accounting. Until he was hired by the Red Sox in 2003, he was a baseball anarchist, lobbing his bombs at the closed mind-set of the industry. James's appeal was both in the logic of his thought process, and the glee in which he skewered the sacred.

Rickey, though, is a different entity altogether. An insider through and through, he worked within Major League Baseball—as a player and executive—for his entire adult life. Yet he constantly challenged orthodox thinking and revolutionized the game from within.

While with the Cardinals, he developed the first minor league farm system. While with the Dodgers, he of course famously integrated baseball by signing and promoting Jackie Robinson. After being forced out in Brooklyn, he threatened to open another baseball league, resulting in Major League Baseball expanding in the 1960s. On top of all this, he realized baseball was hopelessly stuck in the past when it came to its treasured statistics. Instead of keeping it to himself and hoarding proprietary knowledge, he decided to let everyone in on his secret.

There were many news publications in the 1950s, but none was bigger than *Life* magazine. It carried world and national news, reflecting American culture to the masses. It was the very center current of the mainstream.

In *Life*, in the middle of the 1954 baseball season, Rickey, then the Pirates general manager, handed the rest of the league the keys to the hidden kingdom. It opened with a two-page spread, with Rickey himself standing in front of a calculation written out in chalk on a blackboard. It was titled "Goodby to Some Old Baseball Ideas."

Rickey could not have been more cognizant of his audience. He knew there might be some resistance, writing, "Baseball people are generally allergic to new ideas. We are slow to change." He knew that for many there was a disconnect between the physical world and data, writing: "Statistics of course cannot tell the whole story. But . . . a man . . . can construct a formula which expresses something tangible."

Rickey, in short, knew he was writing to an obstinate bunch. He didn't just say, "Hey, ever wonder why the Dodgers have been kicking your ass for the last eight years? Would you like to know the best way of quantifying talent and production? Oh, shoot, here ya go!"

He then took the pains to spell out the process by which he and his statistician Allan Roth figured out their ideas. This is probably where his message was lost. By telling people he and Roth had sent 20 years of data to Princeton University, he crossed an invisible intellectual barrier:

> We compiled these figures for both major leagues for each season over the last 20 years ... we took them to mathematicians at a prestigious research university. Did they know baseball? No, but that was not essential. Their job was to take our figures and by process of correlation analysis see what relation one set of figures had to another.

Oh boy. Mathematicians? Didn't know baseball? "Correlation analysis"? No math perfessor ever hit no curveball. Rickey probably thought a country not far removed from winning a world war would have a better idea of the importance of quantifying production—whether building tanks, or improving bombing missions. Maybe he was just cocky after all those pennants in Brooklyn. *I'm Branch Rickey, dammit!*

Rickey wrote the following:

> Batting average is only a partial means of determining a man's effectiveness on offense.

> The ability to get on base, or On-Base Average, is both vital and measurable.

> The correlation shows that OBA went hand in glove with runs scored.

> The next measurable quantity is Extra base power.... My own formula computing power ... is called isolated power, is the number of extra bases over and above singles in relation to total number of hits.

> Runs batted in? A misleading statistic.

> Fielding averages? Utterly worthless as a yardstick.

Somehow baseball's intangibles balance out. They reflect themselves in other ways. Over an entire season, or many seasons, individuals and teams build an accumulation of mathematical constants.

So in 1954, Branch Rickey took a big swing at batting average, errors, and intangibles. Sure, there are intangibles: grit, determination, fortitude, and the like. But they "reflect themselves in other ways," as Rickey writes. Meaning, if a guy keeps good habits and shows staying power, it will reflect in his production. Saying "utterly worthless" for anything was strong stuff back in those days, but 60 years later, when I say tabulating "errors" is a waste of time, I am laughed at. I feel your pain, Branch.

The main contribution, though, is the formula on the blackboard. Like every other bit of early sabermetrics, it looks complicated only when spelled out. What it's saying is that you need to add walks to batting average, and give a hitter credit for his total bases. That's about it. No baseball fan at any part of history would argue against it. Yet this formula, completely spelled out by baseball's most famous executive, *and* written in the country's most popular magazine, was ignored.

Just for the record: Branch Rickey gave all of his competitors his most brilliant insight; invaluable information on what was truly important in the nation's biggest sport—in *Life* magazine—and was ignored.

It's reminiscent of the scene in *Patton*, where Patton routs a German panzer division in Northern Africa led by German General Erwin Rommel. George C. Scott, playing Patton, peers into his binoculars, watching the German's retreat while yelling, "Rommel, *you magnificent bastard, I read your book!*"

But no one in the National League would be able to yell at Rickey, "*Branch, you tightwad, I read* Life *magazine!*"

Says Bill James, "If you look at all of the changes in baseball in his lifetime, they occurred more or less as a direct result of Branch Rickey. Yet people who wrote about him were as negative about him as they were about me. People would write that he was deceptive and a moralizer, but he was a great man."

Indeed, the sporting press would take shots regularly at Rickey, including for his attempt to improve his Dodgers team by adding Roth to his staff:

> President Branch Rickey is quietly patting himself on the back because of a new Rickey idea: that of sending a statistician along with the club on its final western road trip to tabulate every pitch made for and against the Bums.
>
> —Frank Eck, Associated Press

Clearly Rickey deserved a pat on the back for this innovation, but with none forthcoming, he did it himself. This foray into baseball measurement would culminate with the article in *Life*, one where he, as usual, saw things clearly. He finished by writing, "It is the hardest thing in the world to get big league baseball to change anything. But they will accept this new interpretation of baseball statistics eventually. They have to."

The Mahatma was, of course, correct: 60 short years later.

# Fear of a Smart Planet

Baseball has a rich tradition of anti-intellectualism. There was a *Sports Illustrated* feature on the game going to hell with math madness, called "The Numbers Nonsense." This was in 1958, well before sabermetrics. Sports columnists have long been the guardians of the culture, keeping the brainy barbarians at bay. Sportswriting legend Jim Murray once grumped, "It's not a sport anymore, it's a multiplication table with baselines." This wasn't a shot at Bill James. Murray said it in 1961.

In 1964, Earnshaw Cook, a metallurgist out of Princeton and MIT, fired the next major statistical broadside, *Percentage Baseball*. It challenged the accepted traditions of bunting, starting pitchers, and stealing bases. It was a huge breakthrough in what would later become known as "sabermetric thinking":

Baseball offers a completely balanced, highly complicated statistical system, demonstrably controlled in all its interactions of play by the random operations of the laws of chance. As such, it becomes a fascinating illustration of a process readily susceptible to reliable mathematical analysis.

His math may have been off here and there, but his basic theories and beliefs have mostly been backed up decades later. Of course, Cook, according to MLB's official historian, John Thorn, "was widely dismissed as a crackpot."

Cook followed up with *Percentage Baseball and the Computer* in 1971. Having thought many in the sport would have seized on the competitive advantages he was handing them, he was baffled by the rejection: "Baseball also furnishes a classic example of the utter contempt . . . for the scientific method."

Both books, admittedly, are a tough read. Dense in math, with confusing graphs and charts, they will baffle anyone not fluent in college-level calculus. If only Cook could have had a liaison to the fans, someone bright enough to understand his work while also able to communicate with the message. Oh wait, he did. That would be Frank Deford.

Deford, for those of you who missed it, was a sensational sportswriter, a staple for those of us raised on the writing in *Sports Illustrated* in a pre-cable-TV sports age. In March of 1964, he profiled Cook and *Percentage Baseball* for *SI*, tossing subtlety aside by giving his profile the title "Baseball Is Played All Wrong" (Did I tell you Deford was great?).

Deford somehow resisted the temptation to call Cook a nutty professor, and treated his work with respect. Some highlights:

- The sacrifice bunt is a negative strategy, validated beyond reasonable doubt.
- Contrary to all baseball folklore, the time to steal is when there are no outs, not two outs.
- In each game, a reliever should start, go two or three innings and

come out for a pinch hitter his first time up. He would be followed
by a starter type, who would go about five innings.

These radical but sensible ideas had been put into accessible form in the
nation's top sports magazine. First in 1964, and then again by Deford in
1972.

Cook found a receptive audience in Royals owner Ewing Kauffman, but Kauffman did not think he could get these ideas through to
his on-field staff. In a letter to the Baseball Hall of Fame in 1975, Cook
wrote, "Their doubt concerning its acceptance at the present philosophi-
cal level of general and field managers has thus far prevented its adoption
in actual play." Even ownership could not buck the baseball culture. Cook
continued, "At the age of seventy-five, I do not expect to survive to wit-
ness any changes of attitude in this respect!"

Cook, who would live another 12 years, was correct. The revolution
was still decades away.


# When Computer Freaks Attack

There were some managers and general managers who were ready for
percentage baseball. Punished for their impudence, they would find it
was not just their peers who feared knowledge, it was learned members
of the fourth estate—the men famously referred to by Ted Williams as
the Knights of the Keyboard.

When he took over as manager of the A's in 1983, Steve Boros saw
a chance for an advantage, and began to use the Edge 1.000 computer
system. It's hard to know now if the baseball industry hated the idea on
its own merits, or if they hated being ridiculed by the press. The headlines
in the off-season include, "Computerball Is Here" (*Sport*), "The Computers of Summer" (*Newsweek*), and "It's the Apple of His Eye" (*Sports Illustrated*). In his excellent book *The Numbers Game*, Alan Schwarz wrote,
"Steve Boros woke one morning as the standard bearer of baseball's

on-field information revolution. After one year on the job, having been profiled in dozens of publications and all but cast as a circus freak ... he was fired midway through the 1984 season."

Fear of the computer age wasn't limited to baseball in those days, but why were so many connected to the game so threatened by the advancement of knowledge? A handful of sabermetricians were hired though the 1980s, including Steve Mann with the Astros, Craig Wright with the Rangers, and Mike Gimbel with the Red Sox. All were regularly mocked by the press, and most were run out of town.

Gimbel was a classic case. He was a consultant for the Red Sox and GM Dan Duquette whom almost every writer belittled for his eccentricities. Mocked even, for working for the Bureau of Water Supply in New York. For this, he was called "a computer-savvy Ed Norton."

I don't know about you, but I'm wondering why working for the utility that supplies water to eleven million people makes you a nut job. I would *hope* a number of bright, logistical thinkers are actively working to get clean water to the inhabitants of the country's largest city. New England sportswriters, instead of studying Gimbel's process, instead told us of his love of animals, mainly reptiles. I've had small animals running around in my home for the past 20 years—they're called dogs. Who cares? In most pieces written about Gimbel in 1997, though, alarms were going off:

> As the Red Sox were losing 3–0 to the Rangers, word was spreading among the players and coaches that the power behind the throne had been revealed. The Red Sox are being run by a statistics guru.
>
> *Hartford Courant*, 1997

Another way of looking at it would be, "The Red Sox are using a consultant to make data-driven decisions." But I guess this was asking too much of the press in the dark ages of ... oh, 1997. Certainly the article would dig deep into his philosophies and methodology, right?

"Gimbel's credentials? Well, he is participating in a fantasy baseball league run by *USA Today*'s Baseball Weekly."

Okay, I guess not. The writer was shrewd enough to get the keen, scientific insight of the players themselves: "This is the all-time spring training fiasco," one veteran player said.

The article went on to say Gimbel was giving advice on setting the lineups, while also showing up in the press box wearing "heavy clothes," and looking "disheveled." I don't know what this has to do with his decision making, but fashion seemed to matter quite a bit to sportswriters covering the Red Sox. We could use some insight into what exactly Dan Duquette was doing with such an outcast, but instead the writer went back to the grousing veteran players to deliver a nerd death blow: "You cannot evaluate the game on computer," Mo Vaughn said.

Of course, you *can* evaluate the game much, *much* better with a computer, but I can understand a power-hitting first baseman not comprehending that. I cannot, however, understand a sportswriter, with any level of education, putting that quote in his piece as if it had any validity.

Mo Vaughn's job was to hit for power, not evaluate the latest trends in the game. It is, however, a sportswriter's job to help bring the game to a mass audience: to help the interested reader or listener understand the latest strategic innovations, explain the nuances, and keep them abreast of the ongoing evolution of the industry. During the sabermetric revolution, the sportswriting fraternity failed miserably.

Ridiculous anti-intellectual pieces like this one were the norm through the rise of analytics, and that helped delay the baseball age of enlightenment. Even the most progressive baseball executives—Tal Smith, Dan Duquette, Sandy Alderson—had to be aware that the tide was against them. The beat writer and columnist were a direct line to the fans. The Internet counterculture was not yet powerful enough to provide a balance. If you were getting drilled in the papers, you were dead.

It's like Sonny Liston, when asked in the early 1960s if he would join the civil rights marches in the South. The fearsome new heavyweight champion of the world replied, "I ain't got no dog-proof ass." Even the toughest guy on the planet has limitations. Baseball executives who wanted to embrace new ideas not only had to guard against a backlash from jealous peers, they had to be aware of a media that would mock them for even trying.

Through the years you will find plenty of positive reviews of sabermetric work done by Dan Okrent, Peter Gammons, *The New Yorker*, and the *New York Times*. John Thorn says *The Hidden Game of Baseball* was met with universal praise. There were intelligent, receptive voices out there, but the occasional thoughtful message had to compete with the more bombastic local columnist and beat writer.

It is interesting to note that even the most famous of breakthroughs came about after great resistance. Dan Okrent first introduced Bill James to a national audience by writing a piece about the *Baseball Abstract* author for *Sports Illustrated* in 1981. The piece, "He Does It by the Numbers," ran only after a great deal of fighting by Okrent. Fact-checkers and editors for the nation's top sports magazine were so taken aback by James's contrarian ideas that the piece was spiked and shelved several times. Eventually, when James's theories were backed up, the editors fell back on several discrepancies found in some of James's numbers; things like being off by two one-thousandths of a percent on someone's on-base percentage. James had been off on these numbers because the Elias Sports Bureau would not release its statistics to him, and he had to do a great deal of tabulation on his own. Said Okrent, "They told me, "Well, if he's wrong about these things, imagine how off he must be on everything else."

What's interesting here is that these editors and fact-checkers had no vested interest in the old-school baseball status quo. They didn't work for baseball, or a major league team. They weren't players, trying to defend the wisdom of respected coaches or elders. Yet James's mere questioning of accepted baseball folklore was so inflammatory that these outsiders actively tried to keep the piece from being published.

Okrent is the man who founded what was known as Rotisserie Baseball, which triggered a new level of fandom. Keith Olbermann, an early SABR member, was more interested in baseball history than stats, but he says that fantasy baseball was a crucial component of the analytics revolution. "It may well have been contained in a small subset of SABR had it not been for fantasy baseball." Having your own team meant you did your own winning and losing, so you took a harder look at players and value. A good fantasy player would exploit the difference between the perception of the player—spun by the accepted experts—and the reality of his production. "You would then hear people say, 'Well, he's a good fantasy player, but not on a real team,'" says Olbermann, "Well, what the hell does that mean?" Challenging orthodox thinking became the norm and spurred a new line of thought. "When it's your money, or your own reputation on the line, and you discover you've been sorely misled," says Olbermann, "you start to wonder, 'How long has this been true?'"

Way back in 1984, the term "sabermetrics" hit the *Sporting News*—possibly for the first time—in a piece by longtime *Atlanta Journal-Constitution* columnist Furman Bisher. Bisher treated James, Thorn, and sabermetric pioneer Pete Palmer with respect, but also complained that linear weights "sounds as unappealing as rutabaga and homework." Bisher, like many sportswriters over the past 30 years, yearned for that old standby, the "simpler time," saying baseball was "a game played by countryfolk, at the county fair, on holidays, and Saturday afternoon." This is still the stock-in-trade of the resistant sportswriter, wondering why everything has gotten so doggarn complicated. Bisher, though, was born in North Carolina in 1918. He, likely, *did* see baseball in a simpler time. He probably did see "hayseeds driving in to challenge the city slickers," and was 65 years old when these formulas were gaining traction. So it's understandable that Bisher and others his age were reluctant to upend their training. Speaking from experience, not cliché, Bisher deserves a pass. Sabermetrics had to be alien to him after 34 years of sportswriting.

This column, however, became the prototype for the sabermetric hit piece; harkening back to the "simple game" in a "simple time." Not every sportswriter of the '90s was locking up the feed store to take the tractor to the ballyard. Most of these columnists railing at sabermetrics were city slickers who had plenty of that book learnin'.

There's this from 1990: "This is the new romance in baseball, an attempt to explain the entire game on paper, and it's about as romantic as a date at the Department of Motor Vehicles."

And from 2005: "Go ahead, disappear into a basement somewhere and play around with numbers. Be sure to remember HEEP, SKANK and VLZSKS, while you're at it. We'll be out in the sun, discussing a little thing we like to call 'runs batted in.'"

Getting sun seems to be vitally important to these rugged and tanned sportswriting outdoorsmen. Here's a potshot of recent vintage: "Oh, and let's not forget that sun-starved stat geeks insist wins are irrelevant." Or this from Mitch Albom's seminal SABR-hatefest in 2012, lauding Miguel Cabrera's MVP win over Mike Trout: "I mean, did you do the math? I didn't. I like to actually see the sun once in a while."

Are we really all that pale? I will say, though, if you're a national columnist—paid to be a sports observer—should you be proud of not taking your job seriously enough to do a little homework indoors, where the books and computers are? Along these lines, you'll notice some early stories on Bill James include a note on his height (he's 6'4"). This seemed to confuse the writers. Shouldn't he be smaller? Think about it: Who cares how tall Bill James is? The first time I met him, I didn't give it a thought. It had nothing to do with what makes him interesting. But it's a case of representativeness. Someone that smart is not supposed to be that large, I guess. Imagine the shock wave through the game had Bill James not only been tall, but tanned!

## Moneyball

In the midst of this resistance came an attack from outside the sporting press: Michael Lewis's *Moneyball*. Maybe the baseball revolution happens without *Moneyball*, but it certainly doesn't happen at the same speed. Lewis told me when Billy Beane saw the manuscript, he complained about being quoted cursing so often. Lewis, who had meticulously laid

out the A's method of operation, said he asked him, "Aren't you more concerned about losing your advantage?" He said Billy laughed out loud. "Do
you actually think anybody in baseball is going *read* this book?" Having
lived through such culture resistance, Beane thought *Moneyball* would
go the way of *Percentage Baseball*. "It was all public information anyway"
says Beane. "We never claimed to have invented anything. We were just
sort of taking the ideas of the Pete Palmers, the Earnshaw Cooks, the
Bill Jameses of the world, this was all info that was out there so anybody
could have used it."

Lewis, though, had both the ability to make complicated issues accessible to the public, and had a much more advanced sabermetric culture
to back him up.

Bill James's writing made sense to a baseball fan with an open mind
and intellectual curiosity. Michael Lewis's writing about Billy Beane
learning from Bill James made sense to everybody. Once it made sense to
everybody, there was no stopping it.

Twelve years after writing *Moneyball*, Lewis marvels at just how
quaint the A's operation actually was. "They weren't using R & D [re-
search and development], they were just grabbing what they could. They
were finding stuff that was public knowledge. They were reading Bill
James and *Baseball Prospectus*. They didn't discover FIP (Fielding independent pitching—see Glossary), they just read Voros McCracken, and
said, 'Holy shit, this is fantastic!' They built on it with what they also
knew, but they were just reading what was coming out."

The A's weren't forging into any new territory; they were beating the
system by merely *not rejecting* readily available information. "Even when
Sandy [Alderson, the GM who hired Beane] was here we were never
sheepish or shy about what we valued in a player," says Beane, "So the fact
that it was in Michael's book shouldn't have surprised anybody. As far as
letting out a secret, it really wasn't a secret."

Says Lewis, "They were totally dependent on Bill James and his dis-
ciples to figure out what they needed to do to gain and maintain an advantage."

I remember when the book came out in 2003. My wife asked me about it, and I said, brilliant as I am, "It's excellent, but we all know this stuff already." Sabermetrics, after all, was hiding in plain sight.

But of course the culture retaliated. The Knights of the Keyboard seized upon any slight factual discrepancy to discredit it. Lewis was savaged as someone who didn't understand baseball, since he "ignored" the contributions of some key A's players who were already on the team when Beane and assistant GM Paul DePodesta began filling out their roster. Beane was painted as an egomaniac for writing such a book about himself (I can't tell you the number of interviews where I had to point out to a ballplayer or ex-player that, in point of fact, Beane did not write the book).

The sportswriters and ex-players who savaged it missed the point entirely. *Moneyball* was about a team putting intellectual rigor into practice where it hadn't existed before. It was about, Lewis points out, a "paradigm shift," the concept introduced by Thomas Kuhn, author of *The Structure of Scientific Revolution*. Kuhn wrote that scientific advancement is not evolutionary, but rather is a "series of peaceful interludes punctuated by intellectually violent revolutions," and in those revolutions "one conceptual world view is replaced by another." Ex-players in the game or in the media had plenty of reasons to resist a "paradigm shift" led by Ivy Leaguers on computers. *Moneyball*, however, transcended the sporting culture and press. "Everybody outside of baseball was receptive to the book," said Lewis, "People inside baseball did everything they could to say the story was false."

At the time, I worked at ESPN with Joe Morgan—one of the most public critics of *Moneyball*. The Hall of Fame second baseman skewered the book while also claiming not to have read it. Joe was the analyst on ESPN's *Sunday Night Baseball*, and had a direct path to the national audience. He dismissed sabermetrics and *Moneyball* at every turn. We booked him on an ESPN radio show I was hosting in the year the book came out, and our producer said, "Oh boy, you guys are going to go at it." But I knew Joe. I had had enough off-air conversations and interviews with him at the Hall of Fame to know how his mind worked. As one of the greatest baseball players of all time, he was a deeply prideful man. He felt the game he had represented for so long was being insulted. There's a new way of doing things? We've had it all wrong all this time? Who the hell are you?

We start the interview. I asked him about leadoff hitters, the value of certain free agents, bullpen usage, and managerial strategy. At no point did I use the word "sabermetrics." And you know what? We had an excellent 10–15-minute conversation. Joe was insightful and on point. As long as the conversation wasn't framed as a "sabermetric debate," Morgan was nuanced and logical. It was the idea of a *Moneyball* concept that had him, like many ex-players then in the media, digging in his heels. For retired players, taught by men they respected, and validated in their thinking their entire lives, it was too late to be told that had been trained in an anachronistic system rooted in the previous century. That's understandable.

You know what's *not* understandable? For a paid observer/writer of the sport to feel the same way. A player is trained and emboldened by success. What excuse does a writer have not to take in new information, or at least honestly cover the shift in thinking that was happening in the industry he is paid to follow?

As Lewis wrote in the *Moneyball* postscript, "The game itself is a ruthless competition . . . But in the space just off the field of play, there really is no level of incompetence that won't be tolerated."

Lewis, clearly, is going to be waiting a while to win Sportswriter of the Year. He continues: "The Club includes not only those who manage it, but also, in a kind of Women's Auxiliary, many of the writers and commentators and writers who follow it, and purport to explain it. There are many ways to embarrass The Club, but being bad at your job isn't one of them."

The writers would fight on for years, hating on Lewis, Beane, DePodesta, and eventually even Brad Pitt, who played Beane in the movie. (It seemed to tick off sportswriters even more that Pitt played Beane. "Billy isn't that good looking! What the hell!")

Meanwhile, between the time the book was written and the movie went to cable TV, almost every other team in the major leagues would arm itself with its own "baseball ops" and analytics departments. Too many outside the herd, or the Club, had seen the movie. It was clear a new way of thinking had arrived. The counterculture, available on the Internet, already being read by the next generation, was validated. To stay stuck in the past would become a professional embarrassment. Sabermetric pioneer Dick Cramer, who disproved the validity of clutch hitting as a "metric" in the 1970s, told me the movie brought an unexpected reaction: "*Moneyball* the movie comes out, a different public perception starts to take shape. And the pressures run the other way. It's an entertainment business, you worry about what your customers think."

In one case, it was forced on a club from ownership. "It wasn't resisted by everyone," says Cardinals owner Bill DeWitt Jr., "but it had pretty widespread resistance throughout the industry." DeWitt's father had owned the St. Louis Browns, and learned from Branch Rickey himself. Imagine this moment when DeWitt, with an economics degree from Yale, is reading all about the better way to view baseball through statistics, but his *own* ball club, his *own* professional baseball men, aren't interested. "I used to tell our guys, this is just a tool to use to make the best possible decisions. But it's hard to convince people used to doing things one way, that there was a better way. It's human nature." Sabermetrics, maligned and dismissed for so long, was about to become a top-down directive. "I thought it was incumbent upon us to build a first-rate analytics department," says DeWitt.

First in the field with a hard-core sabermetric approach, the A's would look like a mom-and-pop operation within a decade.

# Google Boy

Even after *Moneyball* explained it to the masses, the media was still ever vigilant in keeping us safe from sabermetrics. The Dodgers, seeing the success of the A's, hired Billy Beane's top analyst and assistant GM Paul DePodesta in 2004.

At the time, the A's had come off a four-year run of 91, 102, 103, and 96 wins. Surely the Los Angeles press would welcome the vanguard of the new wave, right? Of course not! DePodesta was mocked and belittled *on the day he was hired*. He was called a "computer nerd" who "speaks in megabytes." The assistant GM for the most efficient team in the game was called "the webmaster for that funky website called the Oakland Athletics." The incredible A's run was also deemed a failure because of their inability to win in the postseason, with "spreadsheets being unable to judge heart."

This was written about a baseball executive who had a major hand in building a team averaging 98 wins a season on a bottom-five payroll. Throughout his tenure—which lasted all of 20 months—DePodesta was called "Google Boy" and "Doogie Howser," with the Los Angeles press warning the populace that "The nerds have officially taken over the world." These are professional writers, covering sports full time in the nation's second largest city. "I was aware of it," said DePodesta about the welcoming party from the press. "I think the most difficult part of it was that everything everyone had heard about me had come from a third party, they had learned who I was from the book [*Moneyball*]. It made the job more difficult, everyone had gotten an inaccurate perception."

Now 43, DePodesta is the VP of player development for the Mets. He never expected to become a sabermetric GM, saying he never even read Bill James as a kid. He did, though, get an economics degree from Harvard, so after serving an apprenticeship with the Indians, he saw baseball very differently than other front office staffers at the time. Working under Billy Beane, he said the A's situation was a "perfect storm": ownership who left the front office alone, with a charismatic and progressive GM who *insisted* they make decisions with no fear of failure.

The ironic part is that Beane and DePodesta weren't the coming of the computer age, they were just a bunch of rogue operatives in a remote outpost. DePodesta came out of a rare breeding ground with the Indians.

Under general manager John Hart and assistant GM Dan O'Dowd, the Indians pioneered the modern baseball ops department by hiring a bunch of smart young kids who hadn't played major league baseball. DePodesta came in as a scout, working in a front office with Mark Shapiro, Josh Byrnes, and Neal Huntington. DePodesta trained Chris Antonetti to succeed him when he was hired away by the A's, and their intern at the time was Ben Cherington. All five of those "kids" would become major league general managers, most with great success. This was like a smaller, baseball version of the "Cradle of Coaches" in football, when Miami, Ohio turned out a long list of Hall of Fame head coaches, from Red Blaik and Paul Brown to Woody Hayes and Bo Schembechler. It was in this environment where the smart young hotshots found the proper training ground. DePodesta was the first to break out, and once hired by the A's he found himself taking the master class. "Billy liked to use animal metaphors. He would say 'in our situation, if we didn't take chances, we would be extinct.' He was absolutely fearless. If something failed, he would just shrug his shoulders. He would view it not as a failure, but as additional knowledge."

Hired by the Dodgers in February of 2004, DePodesta was fired in October of 2005. Some of his moves worked, some didn't. (When I told DePodesta this he shot back, laughing, "The moves pretty much all worked. It was misunderstood. Our job is to predict the performance of human beings, and predicting the performance of human beings going into situations they've never encountered. You can only stack the odds in your favor.")

In the two seasons he was there, the Dodgers won 93 games, and then 71. That's quite a drop in year two, but how many GMs are fired after only one full off-season? DePodesta was the first of the saber-execs to be hired, post–Billy Beane. With the sportswriting sharks circling, there was no room for error. Nerds using Google were about to get the books knocked out of their hands by the jocks—with their lackey-journalist pals—once more for old times' sake.

On the day Ned Colletti was hired to replace DePodesta, it was written that the Dodgers had traded "prep school for old school." Maybe the working-class bias against Ivy League privilege is warranted, but do you really want to be proud of drumming the smart people out of the industry you work in? "It was largely because of the book," says DePodesta. "It was still fresh and controversial. A lot of people didn't like the success we [the A's] were having, and the book made people feel uncomfortable. If the book hadn't been done, I don't think any of that stuff would've been written." But why would the writers care? "I don't know," says DePodesta. "I'm not sure it made any sense. Probably because Lewis made them look bad."

It is likely true that *Moneyball* drew the backlash on DePodesta. The broader effect, however, was positive to those who came out of the "Cradle of GMs." "When I met Billy [Beane], he was making about 400 grand a year," said Lewis. "Now it's about five million and an ownership stake. Theo Epstein, if all this didn't happen, would be making a couple of hundred grand, and people would be saying, 'Hey, he's doing a good job.' Instead he's a rock star who gets paid millions and millions a year!"

As baseball has become a GM's game, the money and focus have gone to the man who puts together the roster. "Look at Paul DePodesta," Lewis added. "He was always worried he didn't look the part. He always wanted to fit in and look like he belonged in a baseball organization. Now, if he gets a similar job to the one he had? Now he has swagger! He can march around the clubhouse like he's the big swinging dick!" It's a valid point. In the Dodger's front office as of this writing are Andrew Friedman, who looks more like the Peter Brand character from the *Moneyball* movie than DePodesta does, another former A's assistant GM Farhan Zaidi, and Josh Byrnes from the Cradle of GMs in Cleveland. Friedman was regarded as the best of the New Age sabermetric GMs while with Tampa Bay, but no one is calling him a computer geek. Maybe it's the new level of acceptance of the intellectual approach. Or maybe it's that he makes $7 million a year.

Ten years after DePodesta was chased out of town, 17 of the 30 GMs came out of elite colleges (i.e., *US News* top 25). It's certainly not a necessity; Billy Beane, who topped out in high school, is still in the lead pack: "I've been saying for ten years, 'In ten years, I personally won't be able to apply for my own job.' Which is fine, you know? Bob Cousy was one of the greatest point guards of his era, but I don't think he'd start for the Celtics now."

What's most amazing to me is that in the 10 years after *Moneyball* a whole generation of fans came of age on sabermetrics, while the baseball industry did the same. You had teams filled with smart young people in their baseball operations departments, while you had younger fans growing up with the ability to do their own research on their computers.

Yet right smack in the middle—holding out, gumming up the works—was the old mainstream media types who still held the big jobs. I worked right in the middle of it—on the 6 p.m. ESPN *SportsCenter* and ESPN Radio, and then on MLB Network, and then also on NBC Sports Radio. It was possible to have the same conversations about player value with a fan at Citi Field, on Twitter, or with a major league club executive. But when you went to the national media, you had a fight on your hands. The media, supposedly a conduit between Major League Baseball and the fans, was the last group to get on board.

The Spink Award, the Hall of Fame's highest sportswriting honor, went to Murray Chass in 2003. He wrote the following for the *New York Times* in 2007:

> To me, VORP epitomized the new-age nonsense. For the longest time, I had no idea what VORP meant and didn't care enough to go to any great lengths to find out. I asked some colleagues whose work I respect, and they didn't know what it meant either.
>
> Finally, not long ago, I came across VORP spelled out. It stands for value over replacement player. How thrilling. How absurd. Value over replacement player. Don't ask what it means. I don't know.
>
> I suppose that if stats mongers want to sit at their computers and play with these things all day long, that's their prerogative. But their attempt to introduce these new-age statistics into the game threatens

to undermine most fans' enjoyment of baseball and the human factor therein.

People play baseball. Numbers don't.

It's amazing to me that Chass, who always displayed a superior grasp of complex labor issues during his tenure at the *New York Times* was so obstinate about getting what amounts to a better batting average. Chass is regularly skewered by the baseball intelligentsia, but anyone joining the party now should know Chass covered the baseball strike and lockouts with fervor. He was a dogged reporter with an eye for detail.

If you're adept at covering baseball's economic issues, why wouldn't you want to know what it took to buy and assemble talent just above what is known as "replacement level"? Replacement level, as a concept, is what any team can gather at the minimum salary. You and I, if we suddenly acquired a new major league franchise, could build a relatively inexpensive minor league system that would feed the major league club. Given the labor rules—you have six years of control over a player once he hits the major leagues—it is not cost prohibitive to build exclusively from your farm system. What gets pricey is building above and beyond this level. This is basically replacement level. A team of players straight out of Triple-A, promoted to the majors, would make the major league minimum, roughly $500,000 per player. That team would not be very good, but it would win some games. Triple-A players would lose often, but they would not be humiliated. The level of play to the majors is closer than you think. They would not, though, be making the playoffs. You will need to augment that Triple-A roster with additional talent. What you need to know next is how much will it take to get that talent?

This is *value* over the replacement player (VORP, see Glossary). This is where you need to know whether you should spend the extra millions for good but not great players such as Martin Prado or Chase Headley, or go with your Triple-A third baseman. Or, to put it another way, how many wins above replacement (WAR) he may be worth.

If you've ever sat in the stands or watched a game on TV and said, "Hey, we need more pitching," you are interested in this stuff. If you ever wondered, "How come the other club has all these good players, and our players stink," *you should be interested in WAR and VORP.* Initially it does seem complicated, and maybe you tune it out. If you're a fan, that's okay. If you're a professional baseball analyst, writer, or columnist it is not okay.

# MVP, OMG

Mitch Albom is a former National Sportswriter of the Year and a best-selling author. Here he is in 2012, in a column labeled "Cabrera MVP a Win for Fans, Defeat for Stat Geeks":

> Statistics geeks insisted [Miguel] Cabrera was less worthy than An-
> gels rookie centerfielder Mike Trout. Not because Trout's traditional
> baseball numbers were better. They weren't. Cabrera had more home
> runs (44), more runs batted in (139) and a better batting average (.330)
> than Trout and everyone else in the American League. It gave him the
> sport's first Triple Crown in 45 years.

This is true. The Sportswriter of the Year missed 25 years of advances in the industry, but he is dealing here in facts. This will soon change, though:

> But Trout excelled in the kind of numbers that weren't even considered
> a few years ago, mostly because A) They were impossible to measure,
> and B) Nobody gave a hoot.

Nobody, I guess, except almost every team in the major leagues. The most advanced clubs using analytics—the Rays, A's, and Red Sox—made a combined 12 postseason berths in the previous 10 years.

Today, every stat matters. There is no end to the appetite for categories—from OBP to OPS to WAR. I mean, OMG! The number of triples hit while wearing a certain-colored underwear is probably being measured as we speak.

This is straight out of the narrow-minded sportswriting playbook. Check out the similarity of that statement to what was written about Branch Rickey in 1950, when he hired statistician Allan Roth:

> Roth is the figure filbert brought in by Branch Rickey to record every possible statistic on Dodger players almost down to the total drops of perspiration per nine inning game.
>
> —Steve Snider, United Press, December 28, 1950

Sportswriters through the century have purposely confused statistical relevance with statistical minutiae for a laugh. There is a lot of stat flotsam out there. It's the job of the professional sports observer/analyst to know the difference, and offer what is actually meaningful for the reader. It is easier, though, to mock, make up a fake stat, and go have dinner. Albom continues, in the grand tradition:

> Besides, if you live in Detroit, you didn't need a slide rule. This was an easy choice. People here watched Cabrera, 29, tower above the game in 2012. Day after day, game after game, he was a Herculean force. Valuable? What other word was there? How many late-inning heroics? How many clutch hits? And he only missed one game all year.

For starters, there are plenty of words other than "valuable" to describe Cabrera's production—you're a writer, why don't you come up with a few? As for "how many late-inning heroics" and "clutch hits," why don't *you* tell us? And then tell us how it compares to Trout? That's what this is all about. Albom then adds:

Why not also consider such intangibles as locker-room presence? Teammates love playing around—and around with—Miggy. He helps the room.

This is what Bill James, a long time ago, called—excuse the language—the bullshit dump. When you're out of facts, you dump all your extraneous thoughts into a huge landfill of muck that is beyond analysis. Not that a ballplayer can't be a good teammate, but perhaps Trout also "helps the room" as well?

What about the debilitating power of a three-run homer? How many opposing teams slumped after Cabrera muscled one out? How about team confidence?

These are definitely questions. Questions Mitch can't answer. I would say it's rare for a three-run home run carry over to the next day. At that point the team will need some fresh new runs to win the game. As for the guys actually answering the answerable questions, he has this:

Which, by the way, speaks to a larger issue about baseball. It is simply being saturated with situational statistics. What other sport keeps coming up with new categories to watch the same game? A box score now reads like an annual report. And this WAR statistic—which measures the number of wins a player gives his team versus a replacement player of minor league/bench talent (honestly, who comes up with this stuff?)—is another way of declaring, "Nerds win!"

To answer Albom's many questions: 1. All major sports with large revenue at stake are coming up with new categories. We live in a time of sophisticated analysis. 2. The criticism of a box score being too confusing goes back to the 1800s. There have always been people who won't evolve or lack the ability to think at an abstract level. 3. The WAR stat was devised by those with an economic slant on a game filled with measurable production. I was explaining WAR to economist (and Cardinals fan) Michael McKee, and within one minute he told me, "That makes perfect sense. The value of something is defined as what it would cost to replace it."

I realize this is an advanced concept, but a National Sportswriter of the Year should either appreciate that smart people are doing work that is beyond his level of education or at least not make fun of what he cannot comprehend.

It's no use spending too much time on this, except for the purposes of illustrating what happens when people make the leap from not understanding something to slamming it because they don't understand it.

This of course, will happen to the sabermetric generation as well. A whole new way of examining the game is on the way; either with Statcast, or something else. Rob Neyer is one of the most influential sabermetric writers and a brilliant thinker. He wondered, "In a few years, maybe the data from wearables will be all the rage. And maybe I won't care. Will I write a column saying 'Wearables Are a Pain!'? I hope I'll just say I'm not interested. Rejection is a whole other level of arrogance and fear."

I have a feeling the sabermetric class will be different. Pete Palmer, the mathematical brains behind *The Hidden Game of Baseball*, was seventy-seven years old when I sat down with him at the SABR Analytics Conference in 2015. After I paid my respects, and thanked him for his pioneering work, he shot this out: "Can *you* tell me why we don't see more sacrifice flies?"

Palmer pointed out that the success rate for scoring a run on sac flies is currently above 90 percent, which is way too high. He said the break-even rate is in the 30 percent range if you are sending the runner after a fly ball is caught for the second out. Third base coaches send runners only when it's obvious they will score. Getting a runner thrown out at the plate looks bad for both the third base coach and runner. But taking more risks will lead to more runs, even with more runners being thrown out.

The mathematician who revolutionized the game is still asking questions. Not wonky calculus, just wondering if a coach who doesn't take a chance has any idea what the actual chances are. The sabermetricians were never about the numbers, whether it be on-base, VORP, or WAR. They were about asking questions no one else—either covering or managing the game—seemed to be asking.

Bill James, Earnshaw Cook, Pete Palmer, John Thorn, Dick Cramer, and Michael Lewis couldn't hit a curveball. If that's how you judge the merits of their ideas, I can't help you.

A few months after we spoke, Paul DePodesta left the Mets. He is now the chief strategy officer for the Cleveland Browns, answering directly to ownership. That he was hired at such a high executive level by an NFL team after nearly two decades in baseball speaks to the reach of the sabermetric movement.

In the Browns' news release, the club said DePodesta would "provide the organization the comprehensive resources needed to make optimal decisions."

I asked DePodesta, sabermetric pioneer and casualty, why he thought people resisted perfectly good information. He referred me to another pioneer. In his introduction to *Common Sense*, the 1776 pamphlet that advocated the American Revolution, Thomas Paine wrote, in part: "a long habit of not thinking a thing WRONG, gives it a superficial appearance of being RIGHT, and raises at first a formidable outcry in defense of custom."

It is true. We had the same baseball language for decades, and had developed a long habit of not thinking any of it was wrong. Trained to respect the authority of the experts, why would we think they were all so wrong and for so long? As for the "formidable outcry," Paine's next line is prophetic of revolutionary thought, large and small: "But the tumult soon subsides. Time makes more converts than reason."

# 4

# The Epiphany

"The world as we have created it is a process of our thinking. It cannot be changed without changing our thinking."

—Albert Einstein

I'm in a major league clubhouse in the late '90s. I'm still pretty new to ESPN, and I hadn't been in a major league locker room in a while. In my previous job as a television sports anchor, I'd been spending more time at high school football games than Shea Stadium. Given that it had been a few years, this made changes in major league clubhouse all the more noticeable. And something *had* changed.

So there I am saying hello to major league ballplayers. And all I can think of is that these guys are . . . jacked up. I mean, these dudes are massive. Not just the slugging first baseman, but the second baseman who, previous to adding 20 pounds of lean muscle mass, was my size. Shaking their hands you could feel the power. These guys were muscular, vascular with rounded shoulders and fully formed rear deltoids. I know what professional athletes look like, and I know they are almost always bigger and taller than you think. I had also spent a good part of the '80s and '90s in boxing gyms in the New York area. I had trained alongside Mike

Tyson in Catskill, and seen world champion fighters on a regular basis. The baseball clubhouse of the late '90s didn't remind me of any of that. What it *did* remind me of was the bodybuilding gyms on Long Island. And in some of those gyms, it was known that there was another level. A chemical level.

And yet, nobody was talking about steroids. Back at ESPN I spoke to some of the baseball people. I said, "Hey, when did these guys get *huge*?"

During the Summer of Love, 1998, the McGwire-Sosa home run race captivated the country. It was front-page news, leading the national news broadcasts, and taking over magazine covers. I hosted ESPN Radio's *Sunday Morning Magazine*, and author Mitch Albom (I'm not picking on Mitch; it just happened to be him) was doing a guest spot. I asked him if he had any qualms about the home run race. He said, "What's not to like?" At that moment, I was in a tough spot. *Nobody* was talking steroids. The McGwire/androstenedione controversy hadn't happened yet. I was live on the radio, and faced with either bagging out or confronting the issue. I said, "Well either the balls are juiced, or the players are." Albom just laughed. He said, "Do you have a theory for the Grassy Knoll, too?"

I grew up a working-class schnook in Levittown, Long Island. By the time I was 20, I was going to New York Tech, working at Sears in Hicksville, and most nights going to the gym with my friends from the Sears Security Squad. Yes, in 1983 I was a 20-year-old store detective, catching shoplifters, often chasing them down in the parking lot. It beat my previous job, which was at Bethpage Burger King. I was studying journalism, clueless, with zero connections.

This was the heyday of Arnold Schwarzenegger. Guys were weight-lifting and bodybuilding. In baseball, however, the experts at the time said it would make you "too tight," unable to throw or hit the ball. Major league ballplayers, in the early '80s, were still being told to stay away from weights. Now, I'm a nobody, playing in Long Island softball leagues on weekends, and even I know better than this. Today resistance training is used by almost all major league players. Thirty years after being told

point-blank to stay away, players are told they should be training for baseball by lifting weights in some form or another.

In the 1980s, the stance of the American College of Sports Medicine was that steroids didn't work. Its official position was, "There is no
conclusive scientific evidence that extremely large doses of anabolic an-
drogenic steroids either aid or hinder athletic performance." Incredibly,
this was its position even after the strapping East German women's swim
team dominated the 1976 Olympics. Even after the movie *Pumping Iron*
made Schwarzenegger a star in 1977. Even after Ben Johnson tested
positive for stanozolol at the Olympics in 1988. I lived through this time,
and trust me, it's hard work being that stupid.

In my college sociology class, I wrote my term paper on how the
medical community's official stance on steroids was akin to their state-
ments in *Reefer Madness*, and would backfire. In the 1930s, authorities
didn't want kids smoking marijuana, so they made *Reefer Madness*, a
movie that showed how smoking weed led to insanity and murder. It
would, within a few years, be regarded as laughable, just like baseball
experts telling players not to lift weights, and the medical community
saying steroids didn't build muscle.

Think of how differently the "steroid era" could have turned out had
it been honestly confronted. Had a policy been implemented with the
knowledge that athletes had a lot to gain by using steroids, but that it
needed to be regulated to avoid abuse and organ damage.

Even in my limited experience at the time, I learned that the people
in charge are not only not always right, but can be consistently and laugh-
ably wrong.

Watching the Baseball Age of Enlightenment unfold in front of me,
I've had a rare front-row view of the revolution. I have seen brilliant
people uncover things hidden in plain sight and a way of thinking that
would affect not only how I saw baseball, but everything in this world.

Most of the brilliant people I have come across need a translator to
the masses. Those equipped with a high level of brain function frequently

lack the patience or ability to relate readily to others. I saw the best explanation, believe it or not, on the website "Cracked." It said essentially, "Do you know how you feel when you're speaking to someone of limited intelligence? To have to explain yourself several times and they still don't get what you're saying? That's how a really smart person feels when he's speaking to you."

When it came to baseball, the smart people started writing just as I was getting out of college, and I could not figure out why no one was listening. Stunningly, I am still having the same baseball conversations 20 years later. My advantage in understanding the analytical breakthroughs came from my advanced training in a valuable field of study: Nonsense Recognition. Or to use Mitch Albom's take on me, I see Grassy Knolls everywhere.

I grew up in Levittown, the nation's first prefab suburb. Growing up, I always felt a certain lack of identity. Not only were all the houses the same, one neighborhood blended seamlessly into the next. The homogeneous suburban sprawl extending out of Queens just kept chewing up land eastward through Long Island. It really didn't matter if you lived in Levittown, East Meadow, or Bethpage, each town was a just a matter of where the line happened to be drawn on a map. There were no town centers, no town identity, just an endless hodgepodge of neighborhoods, parkways, and strip malls.

Not that I was complaining. My father, a decorated NYPD detective, moved my mother, my sister Susie, and me out of New York City to a place where you could breathe clean air and find plenty of fields to play ball. It was the post–World War II American Dream, but for me it was an intellectual void: suffocating, lacking in imagination and creativity. It was not a community welcoming a free flow of ideas. Manhattan was seemingly in a death spiral and some felt that our little piece of suburbia did not have to join it. This anti-intellectual faction did not encourage debate, nor wish to hear from academia. This strain of conservatism was soon made known to the rest of the country.

When I was in junior high, our school board found several books in our high school library they would later describe as "anti-American, anti-Christian, anti-Semitic, and just plain filthy." These included Kurt Vonnegut's *Slaughterhouse Five* and Bernard Malamud's *The Fixer*.

One night, while the whole thing was under review, some of the board members went to the high school library, and acting against the wishes of the superintendent of schools, pulled the books off the shelves. Hey, look, we're banning books! It would be challenged by a remarkable group of students, led by a senior named Steven Pico. This would become a landmark Supreme Court case: *Board of Education, Island Trees Union Free School District v. Pico*. We're famous!

In a major First Amendment victory, the board of ed would be rebuked. In a close vote, the court ruled "Local school boards may not remove books from school library shelves simply because they dislike the ideas contained in those books and seek by their removal to 'prescribe what shall be orthodox in politics, nationalism, religion, or other matters of public opinion.'" It's of interest that "orthodox thinking" was not only a way of life in my hometown, but also a goal of public policy.

The case started in 1976, and was heard by the Supreme Court in 1982. My high school would be involved in a highly publicized First Amendment case during my entire high school career. Do you know how many times we discussed this case—involving our very own school—in my six years at the junior high and high school? Zero.

In this environment, being one of the smart kids not only wasn't valued, it was openly mocked. There was an intellectual cluster in my little part of working-class Long Island, but make no mistake, we were badly outnumbered.

I'll have you know that I was voted "Most Intelligent Student" by my fellow classmates at J. Fred Sparke Elementary School. Having peaked intellectually at age eleven, I became a decidedly mediocre student through high school. I had allowed the culture around me to dictate my future. Not everyone in my school gave up because of anti-intellectualism. My mediocrity was on me. I vowed I would never allow it to happen again.

It was good training for the future. The ignorant, I learned, were not only numerous, they were belligerent and dangerous. Ignoring them did not make the situation better—they needed to be attacked head-on.

# The Revolution

I loved baseball as a kid. I played it, read about it, and I fell in love with the history of it. My father and grandfather would take me to Yankee Stadium—the first Yankee Stadium—and I would devour the *Yankee Yearbook* page by page. Sitting in the Stadium, I felt connected to something, something significant. We lived closer to Shea Stadium, and while the Mets in those days were the better team, the Yankees were rooted in something deeper and grander. The Mets may have had Seaver and Koosman at the time, but the Yankees would always have Ruth, Gehrig, DiMaggio, and Mantle. Yankee Stadium was a place of history and permanence, where the gods roamed.

Knowing how much baseball history I was reading, my father took us on family trips to Cooperstown. I was a baseball history buff, and knew everybody's numbers. I would compare Cobb and Speaker, Musial and Williams. Was Joe Morgan the best player in the National League? Was Johnny Bench better than Yogi Berra? These were normal baseball questions. I was certainly a student of the game, a lot more hard-core than most of my friends, but I wasn't a stat geek, playing Strat-O-Matic. I was just always wondering who the best players were. I loved baseball, not the numbers.

Back then, you had to wait for the Sunday newspaper to see the stats. I would check the batting leaders like everyone else. I remember being at the kitchen table and excitedly telling my dad that Roy White was among the league leaders in runs scored, and that Chris Chambliss was in the RBI leaders. No one had to write a column on it, the stats could tell you what was going on. I had subscriptions to *Sports Illustrated*, *Sport Magazine*, and *Baseball Digest* (this made me feel like a *real* fan). Each year I bought the Street and Smith's *Annual*, and when I found out that a regular citizen was allowed to buy the *Red Book* and *Green Book*—the full stats roundup used by the sportswriters themselves!—I felt like I was in the inner circle.

I was *not* a rebellious baseball fan. If the baseball writers voted Thurman Munson the MVP, I figured it must be the right call. Like everyone else, I wanted Phil Rizzuto in the Hall of Fame, but I knew it was because I loved listening to him as a broadcaster. The guys voting were the experts. Growing up where I did, it was ingrained; the people in charge were the people in charge for a reason. Listen to your teachers, listen to your boss. Keep your mouth shut. Who the hell are you? Keep your head down, do what you were told, and you might make something of yourself. Questioning authority was not among the options.

# The Education

This Levittown training would not only forge me into a reflexive contrarian; it would lead me to my life's vocation. I may not have known what I wanted to do when I grew up, but I most definitely knew what I did *not* want to do.

In the early '80s, I was working in a department store and was part of a group of 20-somethings armed with college degrees and pursuing careers in the Sears men's shop. In our world, nobody had an uncle, friend, or old prep school classmate who could connect us to some corporate gig. We weren't impoverished, but we were on our own, with no guarantees. I worked with a group of young guys waiting to go "on the job." The "job" was policeman. I had heard Long Island cops made about 55 grand a year—which may or may not have been true—but to the 1985 version of me, this sounded like CEO money. So while I wanted to be a TV reporter, I was realistic about my chances. I took the police tests in New York City, Nassau County, and Suffolk County. I was called by all three, and went for the big bucks in Nassau. I took the physical and the psychological exam, and awaited the call for the police academy.

I made a deal with myself. If I could keep getting professional TV and radio jobs—part-time, freelance, *anything*—I would stay with the dream. If it dried up, I would not spend any time jobless, living off my father. I would become a cop.

One of the freelance jobs I got was with Mutual Radio in New York. For each story I turned in I would make a full 25 bucks. Given the commute into the city, I lost money on the deal.

What strengthened my resolve was the Long Island Rail Road. If you want to be depressed, load yourself into one of those cars some summer morning. I had taken the train into the city before, but playing dress-up and doing the actual morning commute is different. It's jam-packed, boiling hot, and you're pressed body to body with several hundred other people. Somehow I had thought our dads had a pretty sweet deal getting to go into the city every day. Now I looked around and saw the misery. Men in nice suits with sweat rolling down their faces and soaking through their white shirts. I remember looking into their faces; they looked blank. Something had been sucked out of them: life, energy, hope. I spent only a few weeks going into the city, and I still didn't know what exactly I wanted to do with my life. I did, however, know what I *wasn't* going to do, and that was to join the lemmings on the LIRR. I would dig ditches, work in a deli, or be a cop, but I was not joining the rats in the rat race.

Within a year, I went from Sears security to news reporter, and then sports anchor. I had survived. So had Long Island, given that Nassau County was about to arm me against its citizens. A short 12 years later, I would land at ESPN.

I wish I could say I had an epiphany, a moment when suddenly everything became clear, and the old ways faded. More often than not, though, a shift in thinking comes from an accumulation of knowledge and events. Oakland A's general manager Billy Beane said he actually did

have a revelation. "My Eureka moment was in 1993, at the '93 World Series." Then the assistant GM of the A's, Beane's watching the '93 Phillies,
and all that cumulative knowledge is staring back at him. "I'm looking at
Lenny Dykstra, John Kruk, Darren Dalton, and I'm looking at the walks,
the on-base, and I'm seeing what [early sabermetrician Eric] Walker and
[Bill] James are saying being played out," says Beane.

The '93 Phillies were the second worst team in batter strikeouts, and
had the second fewest stolen bases. They were just fifth in the NL in
home runs, with no single player hitting as many as 25. What they did
was walk, and what that did was score runs. They had three players with
over 110 walks. Four guys topped a .390 on-base. They outscored the
second best team in the league by 69 runs. To Beane the lesson was clear.
"The narrative was that they were this scrappy swashbuckling team—that
was why they won. But you could see literally why they won, it was right
there on paper." The Phillies walked, therefore they won.

In the pre-Internet age, a sportscaster relied on his own books, the
Associated Press wire, or a trip to the library for background and information. Describe this to a kid today and it must sound like we're on
horseback, shooting arrows at buffalo. Back then, having a sports almanac
and a *Baseball Encyclopedia* on your desk made you a super-genius. Then
in 1993, while shopping for a good updated *Baseball Encyclopedia*, I instead stumbled on the keys to the kingdom.

It was an encyclopedia, filled with records and facts. *Total Baseball*,
though, was much more. Published first in 1989, it was written and com-
piled by historian John Thorn, and mathematician/sabermetric pioneer
Pete Palmer. There was a chapter reprinting the ideas of *The Hidden Game
of Baseball*, Thorn and Palmer's 1984 sabermetric manifesto, blasting the
old-school accounting. *Total Baseball* was filled with essays about players,
ballparks, and scandals. It was simply one of the greatest baseball books
ever put together.

It was also a revolutionary look at the game. The top line of the
player's baseball record had home runs and RBIs, but then it continued

to a bunch of numbers I had not considered. There, behold, was the first "slash line." In order, were "AVG, OBP, SLG"; batting average, on-base percentage, and slugging percentage. The new language had been laid out.

The next category was PRO+. This was to be known eventually as OPS+. These guys added the on-base to the slugging, and then adjusted it to the run-scoring environment of the time. You could now make instant comparisons between Stan Musial and Mickey Mantle, or Tris Speaker and Kirby Puckett. For each season, beyond the traditional columns on runs, hits, and doubles, there was "Runs Created," "Adjusted Production," and a precursor to WAR: "Total Baseball Ranking." These guys looked at a very different game. It was mind-blowing.

Shortly after, I started to read Bill James. Like most hard-core baseball fans, my first exposure to Bill James is the baseball version of dropping acid. I've never dropped acid—I missed that boat completely—but here is a straight, no-meds version of what Tom Wolfe wrote about in *The Electric Kool-Aid Acid Test*; my doors of perception were being blown open, man. Reading James's unrelenting questioning gave me a vivid illustration of scientific inquiry. Like most everyone else, I had somehow glazed over all of that in Chemistry and Biology. Apply it to baseball? *Now* it all made sense. And nothing would ever be the same. Other baseball writing, by comparison, would seem like a gossip column.

There was no Eureka moment for me, just a continual education, an evolution that continues to this day. At the time, I wondered, "This stuff is out there, and it's irrefutable. . . . Where is everybody?"

Reading James and *Total Baseball* gave me the foundation of the new language. If you wanted to know what a hitter was doing, you wanted to know two numbers before anything else; his on-base percentage and his slugging percentage. Then, as now, if you are to know *anything* about a player's hitting, you start there.

I started using the on-base and slugging terms when I did highlights for ESPN's *Baseball Tonight* in 1999. A coordinating producer told me, "Why do you use that, when nobody knows what they mean?" I told him slugging percentage went back to the early 1900s, and had been on the back of baseball cards in the 1930s. If a baseball fan didn't know it, it was time for them to learn it. He replied by nicknaming me "Sluggo."

Whether it was doing *Baseball Tonight*, or *MLB Tonight* for MLB Network 14 years later, speaking the new math made me "one of *those* guys," someone who wasn't going along with the accepted language. I had been reading *Total Baseball* and Bill James for almost a decade, so why should I dumb it down? I had been in TV sports for 15 years. If a weatherman becomes a meteorologist and gains insight into weather systems through data, should he continue to put little smiley faces on "Mr. Sun" as he always has, or should he pour his energy into giving an accurate forecast? I was speaking every day about the measuring systems of baseball, so I refused to ignore the advances in the industry.

*Baseball Tonight* had pioneered the use of newspaper columnists on TV, putting Peter Gammons on the desk. When I was on *Baseball Tonight*, we had top-notch baseball minds, like Gammons, Tim Kurkjian, Jayson Stark, and Buck Showalter. We also, though, had Rob Neyer on ESPN. com, who wrote from a decidedly sabermetric point of view. This is before FanGraphs, and in the early days of Baseball Prospectus. I tried to get Rob on the air, and was dismissed with a wave of the hand. Why should we put on Rob Neyer when we can put on an ex–major leaguer, or a *real* baseball writer? I would be able to get Rob onto the *ESPNews* segments regularly three years later, but I always envisioned a baseball desk with a player, writers, and sabermetric analyst. That's what we are doing now on *MLB Now*—it's just 15 years later, and we're still the *only* ones doing it.

While some of the *Baseball Tonight* guys did resist sabermetrics, a few of them practically forced me into the next level of baseball understanding. Gus Ramsey and Mike Epstein were producing *Baseball Tonight* in 2001. They kept telling me there was a computer baseball game I *had* to play. I told them I wasn't interested. One night, they badgered me again, saying "You can spend the whole night drafting a team. *We* will write your whole show." I figured they had been drinking, but okay, I'll do it. This was my first venture into WhatIfSports.

On WhatIfSports, you can draft any major league player you want, in any single season: 1968 Bob Gibson; 1927 Babe Ruth; 1948 Stan Musial. It's just that you have a budget of $80 million, and those legendary seasons are going to cost you. Of course it took me all of five minutes to realize *this is the greatest thing in the history of earth*. Gus and Eppy smiled, and shook their heads. I know, I know, I'm an idiot. Okay, back to the draft.

I filled my teams with guys I liked: Graig Nettles at third, Bobby Murcer in center field, and some old-timers like Mickey Cochrane. I put together a nice little team. I thanked the guys, and entered it into the league. I then asked Gus, "Does it matter who you pick? Do some teams win more than others?" Gus told me, "Oh, it matters *a lot*."

I had put together my team as if the pricing system was set up perfectly. This was not the case. Some things, like home runs and RBIs, were overvalued, while on-base percentage was undervalued. It was like real baseball!

There were three simulated games a day, and my bunch of nice-guy '70s Yankees started losing like a bunch of late '60s Yankees. This was awful. This league was filled with the *Baseball Tonight* crew, including the researchers and guys from the Elias Sports Bureau. I had to readjust my thinking.

I started combing through the reams of data offered up at each and every position. Every player since 1885 is eligible. It was a new world of possibilities; what if you loaded up on two 500-inning pitchers from the 1880s and had them start every game? What if you went with an incredible bullpen? What if you went with high on-base percentage and no power? All dead-ball? All home runs? I went over the pricing system night after night. After I redid my first team to make it respectable, I went to join a new ESPN league, this time with a Frankenstein-like super-team. I was working with Max Kellerman, my partner on ESPN's Friday Night Fights, and we would go over our analysis again and again. This was a test for the Jamesian baseball mind. We worked on creating a monster.

These were the lessons: On-base percentage is king. The guys who did the pricing knew on-base was important, but they fell way short in charging for it. Not only that, but they priced the batting average within the on-base too much, meaning walks were undervalued. Typical! Stolen bases were next. We found out what they did for the players who played before caught stealing was tallied; they basically put a zero in the algorithm. Meaning all those dead-ball guys would steal like mad, and almost *never get caught.*

The art form would be in finding just the right combination of absurd on-base hitters with enough power, and adequate fielding so your collection of dead-ball guys wouldn't sink your team with errors. You also learned things that would later be confirmed by lineup optimization; you needed the best possible on-base to lead off, and it should come from walks, where you wouldn't waste power. The number two batter should be a beast, basically your best hitter. That lineup needs to be front loaded. The cleanup hitter can have a slightly lower on-base, but he should be your best power hitter. Most of these findings would later be confirmed by *The Book: Playing the Percentages in Baseball*, a brilliant work of analysis published in 2006. When you have two or three teams playing three simulated games a day, you learn it firsthand—if you're paying close attention.

You learned in pitching that strikeouts and walks were the categories that would most affect performance, base runners allowed (WHIP) (see Glossary) was more important than ERA, and wins, of course, were to be ignored. When it came to relievers, a league average pitcher could be your closer, as long as you had two savage setup man for high-leverage spots. The key wasn't to be great, but to be *just good enough.* That's the key to winning: Be above-average everywhere. No holes, no weak spots.

It was a sensation through ESPN, with Bill Simmons, the sports guy, in several of our leagues. In a 2006 *ESPN The Magazine* column, the Sports Guy wrote about the greatness of playing WhatIf in a piece titled "I See Dead People": "This is the ultimate gift from the procrastination gods. Most people check their e-mails; I check WhatIf. My buddy

Gus and I waste 30-minute phone calls on WhatIf stories. We launch in-house leagues at ESPN every few months, most of them won by trash-talking Brian Kenny, the Steinbrenner of Bristol. When I started on Jimmy Kimmel's show, I quickly converted two co-workers (Hench and Sal); now the day doesn't start until we've babbled on about the previous night's games."

I don't know if I was the Steinbrenner of Bristol as much as I was the Billy Beane of WhatIf. I was winning championships, but every so often the WhatIf engineers would change their prices, always cutting into the advantages we'd found. You could still win, but you had to work harder to exploit smaller-market inefficiencies. I remember speaking to Billy Beane around 2002, and somehow I got to explaining WhatIf. I told him it was once easy to stay ahead of the competition, but that everyone was now hip to us. "That's what's happening to me!" he exclaimed. "All the loop-holes are closing!"

In baseball and in WhatIfSports.com, there was a brief period of a knowledge gap. Sabermetrics provided a window of opportunity for the A's—before financiers who understood the numbers game bought the Red Sox and Rays.

The study of baseball is a constant evolution. For a time, knowing on-base and slugging made me a radical member of the mainstream media. I didn't think that would last 15 years. My leaving ESPN for MLB Network brought me to a different level of immersion. I was though, for most of the ex-player/analysts, the first sabermetrician they had seen in person. It was for a time quite a culture clash. Later, many writers would infiltrate the *MLB Tonight* set, but for the first two seasons, it was just me, and the ballplayers. Most of the time, the players would stare at me as if I had been dropped in from space. They had never heard the stuff I was talking about. The worlds had remained separated. On the occasions I kept my ears open, I too was able to learn. During the 2011 post-season I told Mitch Williams—The Wild Thing—that Jim Leyland was making a mistake, he should be batting Victor Martinez third instead of fifth. Martinez was the Tigers' second best hitter during the regular season. I confidently (or smugly) told the Wild Thing that Martinez was "a .400/.500 hitter." Mitch said simply, "He ain't today." Martinez may have been an excellent hitter for the full season, but he had looked lost at the plate through the series. I was looking solely at the theory of lineup construction, but Mitch saw that Leyland was looking for the best lineup *that day*. I said, "Mitch, you're right."

The schism between new schoolers and old schoolers is starting to close. Each year we have an off-season rankings show called "Top 10 Right Now," where we rank the top 10 players at each position. The first two seasons I hosted the show, we had major disagreements with our ex-ballplayer/analysts. Our researchers put together a formula using various metrics and we called it "The Shredder," as if we had some secret machine. My rankings usually aligned with the Shredder, while the ex-players would let loose with a steady stream of "I'm gonna shred the Shredder," "You'd better send the Shredder back to the shop." We had "controversial" results, like setup men at the top of the Relief Pitching Top 10. Carlos Beltran made the outfield Top 10, but Albert Pujols didn't at first base. Ben Zobrist was way up, Brandon Phillips way down. Every show, there was a new analyst, and a new assault on the Shredder.

Then in 2015, the battle just ended. One analyst after another—Sean Casey, Cliff Floyd, Darryl Hamilton, Bill Ripken, John Smoltz, Dan Plesac—would come in with a list that was often closer to the Shredder's than mine. Reputation was no longer enough, quantifiable production was in. All analysts were now looking things up, giving hard evidence for their rankings.

So if I appear stunned every time I hear "Brian Kenny is all about the numbers," understand where I'm coming from. Yes, I love sabermetrics but baseball to me is my prized 1971 Topps Baseball Cards, the classic set with the black borders. I would use those cards to put out a team—in the shape of the baseball diamond—on my bed every night when I was a kid. Johnny Bench would be behind the plate, Hank Aaron in right, Pete Rose in left. This was before you could just buy the whole set, so I didn't have Willie Mays or Roberto Clemente. It was still a pretty good team. Sudden Sam McDowell had a cool pose, so he got to pitch. When I got a Thurman Munson—in an awesome action shot—he split time with Bench.

One time, in a late-night WhatIf drafting session, Max Kellerman and I were putting together a team we hoped would conquer another ESPN grouping. Max wanted yet another solid but boring Eddie Murray season. I told him I was tired of Eddie Murray. "What you don't under-stand," said Max, "is that I don't even think of it as Eddie Murray. It's Eddie Murray's *numbers.*" He then asked, "When you see your team there on the computer screen, do you see little men running around on a field?" I was stunned. Doesn't everybody? I saw Jackie Robinson darting to sec-ond, Pee Wee Reese cleaning up at short, and Tim Raines running wild. It was a Hall of Fame team sprung to life, and they were playing *for me.*

It can be the cards on the bed of my childhood home, the sound of a Yankee game on the radio in the backyard, hitting grounders to my own sons, or a season played on a computer sim engine. Life is better with a ballgame going.

Baseball is played both out on the field, *and* in our minds. I've found it to be beautiful both ways.

# 5

# The Godfather

"Genius gives birth, talent delivers."

—Jack Kerouac

The Godfather wanted a cup of coffee, so we were on the move. We went down the two flights of stairs from the Red Sox offices at Fenway Park, through the old wooden doors, and out into the daylight of Yawkey Way. Ten thirty in the morning—game time still three hours away—the streets were already jammed with fans.

I wondered, are we going to be able to get through this crowd? What would people do when they saw the most influential thinker in the modern history of baseball walking in their midst? Red Sox fans are among the most knowledgeable in the country. They made former GM Theo Epstein into a matinee idol, as famous as any player.

I whirled around: Nothing. No autographs, no cell-phone photos, not even a nod. The fans were oblivious to the man who brought on baseball's Age of Enlightenment. The man whose work—directly and indirectly—ended the city's eighty-six years of baseball agony. Bill James—the Godfather of Sabermetrics—walked through the streets of Boston, unnoticed.

So much has been written about James, much of it extremely positive.

Over the last few years, though, minimizing James's impact has become fairly popular in baseball writing. I suppose a backlash was inevitable. So let's be clear on this: When it comes to the analytics revolution in sports, *Bill James cannot possibly receive enough credit.*

One book after another these days, even those that do a credible job of examining analytics, will take pains to tell you that "Branch Rickey had a statistician," or "statistical study in baseball did not start with Bill James," or that "several clubs in the '80s hired sabermetricians." And it's all true. Except that Branch Rickey's attempt to educate Major League Baseball fell on deaf ears, and most of those sabermetricians hired in the '80s and '90s were mocked, derided, and run out of town.

Old-school orthodox thinking, in fact, may have survived another century had the Kansas City A's been any good. As a kid in rural Kansas, young Bill was a big A's fan: "Charlie Finley would fire his announcer every year, so every season it was always a different set of people. They would always come in and tell you how good this team was going to be, and by the end of the year they've lost a hundred games. To a kid, this is very puzzling."

I would have guessed Bill James came from a family of engineers. How else do you develop that kind of intellect? Who else would grow up to question authority with such understanding, curiosity, and venom? But Bill James was the youngest of seven children, with a father who was a farmer, and a mother who died when Bill was four. In a single-parent home, they were isolated and impoverished. Rob Neyer worked as James's researcher for four years. He too has difficulty figuring out how this mind sprang up in the middle of Kansas. "There's no explanation for it. It's a genetic accident," says Neyer. Granted an incisive intellect, James developed his relentlessly savage critical thinking because of his anger at his circumstances. "I got it from an emotional distance from the world," said James. "It's a cliché of writers that we have miserable childhoods and it's true. You're writing through a miserable childhood and that's the way you see the world."

Emotional distance is a vital component. Economics requires a dispassionate approach. In baseball, you might like a certain player, or be drawn to his game for a variety of reasons. Perhaps he has great speed, or takes a big swing. But what does this all actually mean? Sabermetricians asked the question, "Does any of that translate into his performance?" We can appreciate the aesthetic, but when it comes to winning, who cares what a ballplayer looks like?

As SABR pioneer Pete Palmer said, "Back in those days there always seemed be a lot of talk about a player's attributes, but not enough about the performance it brought about." In other words, sportswriters were drawn to the stories of players. Grit, determination, the "Will to Win" to use the Hawk Harrelson anti-SABR nonmeasurement. All of these things are required of a top athlete, but what the hell does it all mean when it's only the top sliver of the top athletes competing against each other? If you are more determined and resolute than the next guy, that's terrific. But how does it translate onto the field? This was a subject about which James was adamant—separating emotion from production.

Reading James in the '70s and '80s was a revelation. It wasn't the math, it *was the questions*. After you read the *Baseball Abstract*, or the staggeringly interesting *Historical Baseball Abstract*, most baseball writing seemed like utter nonsense by comparison. He was an outsider, a champion of the underrated, eviscerating the overrated. It was a blunt, opinionated critique, coming from someone who wasn't looking to spare anyone's feelings.

A few blocks from Fenway Park, we talked in a local restaurant. When Bill James is concentrating on a baseball question, the rest of the world not only recedes, it ceases to exist. Waitresses and busboys come and go, music is blaring, but Bill James speaks in full paragraphs with fully fleshed-out concepts. I had often wondered what *he* thought would happen once he started to gain an audience. "I was surprised at how quickly we broke through, reached the audience and established that the audience was in fact larger than I thought. I was then surprised by how quickly the schisms developed between that new audience and the old audience."

"Schism" is a good way of putting it. When I read the *Historical Abstract*, it was as if a fog was lifting in my mind. Things became not only clear, but it showed that my perspective, while rigorous, was shallow. I needed to back up, and question *everything*. His methods of comparison; the constant questioning and unflinching logic were mind-blowing. It was so *obvious* his process was light-years ahead of everything else done to that point. Which, given the depth of baseball literature, is saying something. My only question from the first time I read him to this very day has been: Where is everyone else? Why doesn't everyone see this? "It was an a priori rejection of it," said James. "Something went wrong in their fifth grade math class, they didn't understand the story problem, and they rejected it. They hit a wall, and we were on the other side of that wall."

The battle lines were being drawn. Some saw the light immediately. "Bill James changed my life," says Peter Gammons. "He changed the way I watched games." Gammons, then with the *Boston Globe*, would see players with good reputations, who appeared to be effective ballplayers. "I started to study things, and think, 'Yeah, they're good, but what does that mean?'"

But while James was building a devoted following, most people around the game refused to learn a new way of thinking. I would spend more than two decades trying to explain something James had made so very clear, only to see grown men get visibly uncomfortable, and then angry. With so much baseball knowledge already crammed into their heads, a new way of thinking seemed not only unnecessary, but a rejection of everything they had learned before. "It was totally impossible. They had already turned it off," said James.

On the day we met, the Red Sox were in last place and James was uptight about that afternoon's game with the Orioles. "We're like a fighter on the ropes," said James. "One more shot and we may get knocked out." If you thought Bill James, Red Sox executive, would be sitting back, bemused at the small-sample reactions of the mortals, you would be wrong. He was taking a negative-50 run differential very personally.

I asked the big question: Why do people have such trouble accepting good information? Bill had obviously given this a lot of thought: "Because people horribly overestimate the extent to which they understand the world. The world is billions of times more complicated than any of us understand, and because we are desperate to understand the world, we buy into these explanations that give us the illusion of understanding."

As Bill speaks, his eyes dash and dart. He's not bored, or lacking in concentration, it just appears as if he has an overload of electrical impulses firing in his head. There is often a look of frustration on his face in explaining something that, to him, already makes perfect sense. Rob Neyer saw this often. "I've come across a lot of smart people since I've worked with Bill, but there's no one else like him," says Neyer. "His brain is just working at a different level. To the point where it's frustrating for him. He thinks of things, not just in baseball, but in everything, things he sees randomly, in business or society, and his brain makes these leaps to these questions, that wouldn't even occur to most of us." This may explain the schism that continues to this day. "It's difficult to grapple with the *answer* to a question," says Neyer, "when you wouldn't have even considered the question itself."

It is said success has many fathers, while failure is an orphan. With sabermetrics having been fully integrated and now forcibly embraced in the major league game, you would think there would be resentment among those few founding fathers for the man who has garnered the most attention. This, however, is not the case. To a man, Pete Palmer, John Thorn, Dick Cramer, and Baseball Info Solutions founder John Dewan—all hugely influential figures in the movement—have nothing but respect for James, many freely referring to him as a "genius."

Jack Kerouac contributed a column in 1962 for *Writer's Digest* called "Are Writers Born or Made?" In it, he writes that genius "doesn't mean screwiness or eccentricity or excessive 'talent.' It is derived from the Latin word *gignere* (to beget) and a genius is simply a person who originates something never known before."

James's essays would answer questions no one was even thinking to ask. In the 1982 *Baseball Abstract*, for example, he attacked those who had begun to cynically say "baseball is not a sport, it's a business." This was a popular thing to say as revenue skyrocketed in baseball, and free agency changed the rules of roster building. It was the type of thing that made you appear worldly. Bill wrote that this was nonsense, that baseball was of course a sport, no matter how much money came in. He pointed out that tuna fishing is also a lucrative industry, but we don't think of tuna as a business, because no matter what, *tuna is food*. You can *say* "tuna is not a food, it's a business," but it's still just food.

James would *continually* come up with questions that had either not been asked, or more likely had been answered lazily. He brought an intellectual rigor to his writing. You would read his tangential thoughts, think, "Damn, I hadn't thought of that," followed by "Why is this guy writing about sports, isn't there something more vital he could be doing?" James long ago stopped apologizing for applying this genius to baseball, explaining this is what he really liked, and this is what he was going to do.

Many geniuses share this passion for baseball. Kerouac himself used to run his own fantasy baseball league, naming the teams, drawing up team booklets, and playing his own simulated games. He players had made-up names, with stats and backstories. He would have different ways of deciding the games, and write post-game wrap-ups. Pre-Internet, this took enormous amounts of time and energy. He played out this league, complete with 80-game seasons, for years, and years, into his adulthood, even after he wrote the classic book of yearning to break free, *On the Road*.

I shared this information with James. He smiled broadly. "Yeah, isn't that weird?" I said perhaps it's a case of someone looking for a sense of control, Kerouac having lost a brother when he was young. "It is! Baseball is an orderly universe, and that appeals to people who see disorder in the universe," James responded.

James and Kerouac are both creative geniuses. Dick Cramer was a chemist, Pete Palmer a mathematician. All these intellectuals are obsessed with baseball. Why? "Because baseball is a world that gives you a chance to understand," said James. "The world at large is so complicated you know almost immediately you can't figure it out. But baseball will send you all these little signals that suggest you have a chance to figure this out. Baseball is a very, very orderly universe. Baseball players stop here or here or here (motioning to bases), whereas in basketball they just run around at random. The players [in baseball] take turns, this guy bats then this guy bats then this guy bats whereas in basketball anybody can shoot. The very orderly nature of it creates a very orderly universe. That appeals to people who are seeking order, which is to say, thinkers."

James's writing also began before the Internet made information readily accessible to the masses. Once anything and everything could be looked up, it would become obvious that most baseball analysts were just talking to hear themselves tell stories. Sortable statistics, when used correctly, would tell you what's what far more accurately than the sportswriter who was getting his information from the players and entrenched "experts." Sabermetrics wasn't cold and impersonal, it was *the truth*. Websites like Baseball Prospectus and Fire Joe Morgan sprang up based on sabermetric thinking, skewering stupidity, James-style. Mainstream media would remain obtuse, but the *Game of the Week* was no longer the only outlet for baseball. The old-school dam could no longer hold back the flood.

Over several years, James came up with one revolutionary theory after another. They include the following:

1. Getting on base is the most important thing in offense.
2. Speed for a leadoff man is nonessential. Getting on base is of primary importance.
3. Walks are the most ignored offensive category.
4. Minor league performance predicts future major league performance as accurately as past major league performance.
5. A low-strikeout pitcher will not thrive long-term.
6. No player is "worth 15–20 wins."
7. Run differential is a better predictor of team performance than current won-loss record.

8.  A team filled with "average players" is not average, it's a power-house.

9.  There is a defensive spectrum. A player can move from a tough position to an easier position, but rarely the other way around.

It's hard to describe the resistance to all these things we now take for granted. But teams regularly had a speedster at the top of the lineup, looking speedy, and making outs. The 1961 Yankees, James pointed out, had Bobby Richardson lead off for a team that set a new major league record for home runs. Did anyone wonder why he played all 162 games and scored only 80 runs? Bill certainly did. Richardson had a .295 on-base percentage. This was something Bill was bored with, and tired of writing about, by about 1980. Thirty-three years later, Shin-Soo Choo, a player who had *never made an All-Star team*, got a $130 million contract. Seems a little steep to me too, but at least front offices were recognizing what was important: Choo had a career .382 on-base percentage. The media, of course, was stunned. They usually are.

James made questioning orthodox thinking a regular process. "Bill didn't teach me how to think about baseball," says Rob Neyer. "He taught me how to think about everything."

# Death to the Curse

I remember speaking with Red Sox co-owner Tom Werner just after the 2003 season. The Red Sox own NESN, the New England Sports Network, and they were making me an offer to be the studio host for Red Sox coverage. Already at ESPN, I was passing on the offer, or at least waiting for it to double (hey, I have kids). Werner was still feeling the sting of the loss to the Yankees in the ALCS. I told him not to get caught up in that, that the age of pagan curses was over, and the triumph of science was about to begin. Their ownership group (Werner, John Henry, and Larry Lucchino) had brought in James and Theo Epstein. They were the first team to back sabermetrics with money, and were making one shrewd move after another. Werner sounded unconvinced. I remember telling him, "You're not going to just win a championship, you're going to win *multiple* championships." He laughed and said, "Wow, I hope so." He may not have fully known what he had unleashed, but to a trained sabermetric observer on the outside, it was clear. The Red Sox "curse" was mismanagement and bad luck. Now they had brought in sabermetric thinking *just* before the rest of baseball caught on. It was the last off-season of easy pickings, and they cleaned up.

The Sox hired Bill James in November of 2002, and immediately set out on a sabermetric spending spree. Invisible to the mainstream media, it was the talk of the sabermetric community. I would get phone calls from my friend Max Kellerman—my ESPN boxing partner and fellow hard-core Yankee fan: "Did you see who they just got? Another good move. They have Pedro and Manny, and now they're smart. This is awful."

I remember being in two Fantasy Leagues one year. One was an expert league, and the draft was brutal. All my favorites—my undervalued sleepers—were jumping off the board *way* too early. I stayed true to my draft strategy, and I was fine, but I got no breaks. A few days later, I had my other draft. This was with a bunch of co-workers, many of whom were also very good at fantasy baseball, but also with two or three guys who just weren't at the same strategic level. One guy was drafting only Cardinals. Another was drafting with his kid and making some inexplicable moves for the fun of it. All it took was two or three rubes, and it was *bargains galore*. Good players were left on the board too long, and there was talent stockpile building. I started *cleaning up*. There was way too much talent falling my way. I couldn't believe the team I was able to put together. This was essentially the Red Sox in 2003. The window was closing, teams were getting on the sabermetric bus, but Theo and Bill had one free pass, and slid on through.

Between mid-December 2003 and mid-February 2004, Boston added David Ortiz, Kevin Millar, Todd Walker, Bill Mueller, Mike Timlin, and Bronson Arroyo. This was just the Sox picking up the scraps. The

Twins had given up on Ortiz, and Millar had given up and was going to Japan. Yes, Boston had Manny Ramirez and Pedro Martinez, two supreme talents, but here's what production the Red Sox got from a few of their starters in 2002, and then from the shopping spree for 2003:

| 2002 Red Sox | OPS+ |
| --- | --- |
| Shea Hillenbrand | 105 |
| Carlos Baerga | 82 |
| Rey Sanchez | 75 |
| Tony Clark | 47 |

| 2003 Red Sox | OPS+ |
| --- | --- |
| David Ortiz | 144 |
| Bill Mueller | 140 |
| Kevin Millar | 110 |
| Todd Walker | 95 |

That's a serious upgrade at four positions. All for a combined $9 million in salary for the year. The media was busy lauding the "chemistry" of these guys a year later, when they won a World Series championship. They had forgotten the massive upgrade Bill James engineered in about the time most executives take to move furniture into their office.

The early 2000s were an interesting time. The A's were hard-core sabermetric, and the Yankees were the kings of on-base percentage. But the A's were poor and "couldn't win in the playoffs." Yankee dominance was easily explained away by money. Front offices were still not fully immersed in the new way of economic thinking—*Bill James Thinking*—and now the Red Sox had the Godfather himself. The next off-season they got Curt Schilling and Keith Foulke—the arms race was on, and the Sox went big-game hunting—but those first weeks of the new regime were classic Bill James.

With no holes in their lineup, the Red Sox won at least 95 games six of the next seven years, plus two world championships.

The Red Sox triumphed, by the way, with a fully operational Yankee Death Star operating in their division. Yankee playoff failure in those years obscures one of the more dominant runs in baseball history. The Yankees may not have won titles, but they were *averaging* 97 wins a season between the time Epstein and James were hired in Boston, and the next Yankee title in 2009. The sabermetric Red Sox had to duel with a neighboring baseball superpower, and yet they still thrived. Of course, once the Red Sox had won, there was still plenty of resistance to sabermetrics. The media strained *not* to hand much credit to James. John Thorn observed, "Red Sox failures (bullpen by committee) were attributed to him, while successes (2004 World Series title) ascribed to others."

For those who weren't there, here are the phases of sabermetric acceptance:

1. "It's the stupidest thing we've ever heard" (1960–1989).
2. "It doesn't work" (1990–1998).
3. "Okay, it makes low-spending teams better, but you can't *win* with it" (1999–2003).
4. "Okay, you can win with it, but only if you already have Pedro and Manny" (2004–2011).
5. "We've always been an organization that values information" (2012–2014).
6. "We're hard-core into analytics!" (2015–   ).

Billy Beane was the first GM (other than Branch Rickey of course), to use Jamesian thinking full-bore in his baseball job. I say "Jamesian thinking" because it is much more than "using numbers," it is using data *and* a rigorous, logical thought process. Beane didn't come up with this on his own, he was led there by his then boss, Sandy Alderson. Alderson wasn't a major league player, he was an ex-marine and Harvard Law grad who had an open mind and valued logistical information. How did Alderson learn these things? He read Bill James. How did he then train Billy Beane? He told him to read Bill James.

So yes, Bill James did not bring about the revolution on his own. It took many different people. But most all of these talented people who brought about the new way of thinking in baseball did so by reading Bill James.

So let's step back: The leading baseball intellectual is brought into the industry after decades on the outside. The team he joins is shrouded in melancholy loser-dom. Within two years of his hiring, the team wins its first championship in the age of electricity. Two years later, they win another World Series. Six years later, they win another. So, how many "Bill James's Thought Process Leads Red Sox to Unimaginable Success" stories do you remember reading in those years? I don't care if James was a crazy eccentric who was ignored by everyone, wouldn't you figure a few writers would be pointing out that James's being hired and the Red Sox' winning were at least quite a coincidence? Writer Jim Baker (a former James assistant) said, "In the wake of the Red Sox winning it all, there was precious little mention of Bill James and his role in their success. Either the media didn't understand the extent to which he contributed, or they did and couldn't bear the thought of it."

# The Magic Door

Later in the day, James and I met back up in the press box. We headed downstairs and took a shortcut through the Red Sox offices. Passing the conference rooms and cubicles. Bill moved closer to a door, turned to me, and said, "This is my favorite part." He opened the door, and suddenly we were propelled into a different world. In a split second, you are in Fenway Park. The door separates the offices from the field boxes on the third base line. It's like going through a magic door, leaving a typical drab office and jumping into the tumult of a Major League Ballpark. Your head spins. "How did that happen? Where the hell am I?" It's because you're not only instantly transported into a ballpark, you're shot into *Fenway Park*, which is like being blasted back in time. It's like one of those old Buster Keaton silent films where he opens a closet door and there's a locomotive chug-ging toward him. Keaton would slam the door and that world would just go away. Bill says "It's like *The Lion, the Witch, and the Wardrobe*, a door that takes you to a magical place." I almost expected to see Jimmie Foxx step up to the plate in a woolen uniform.

In our seats—Bill finds empty seats and sits down—my son and I get the rare privilege of watching a game with the master. It takes a few minutes before a ball is even put into play. We're both aware of the dy-namic of the "three true outcomes." Home runs, strikeouts, and walks make up almost one third of all offensive results these days. Only a week earlier, John Thorn had told me, "Baseball is nothing like it was meant to be, which was a game of fine fielding and clever baserunning." Instead we now have one drawn-out pitcher-batter strike zone duel after another. It's where the game is won, but when you're watching a game, you realize how much more *fun* the game would be if the freaking ball was just in play.

I ask Bill what he thinks of Thorn's suggestion of moving the mound back, as baseball officials did several times in the 1860s. "You can accom-plish the same thing by doing stuff that no one would even notice. You can regulate bat design. Moving hitters off the plate a little bit. Change the resiliency of the baseball, there's a million things you can do. You look at a bat now as opposed to a bat from the '50s, '60s, it's a lot differ-ent." Bill continued, barely taking a breath or his eyes off the game: "The way the bats are designed now encourages people to try to whip the bats as quickly as possible. Whereas if you have a heavier bat, with a thicker handle, the percentage move is to make solid contact. So you can sharply reduce strikeouts by three things: regulate pitching changes, regulate the shape of the bats, and move the batters off the plate by about an inch, so you can't realistically pull an outside pitch. You back the batter off the plate an inch, no one is going to see it from here. But it would make a difference." This is ballpark small talk with Bill James at Fenway.

I wonder how involved he gets with the day-to-day. Bill says it var-ies year to year. "Sometimes I worked well with Theo, and for a while

I didn't. I'm a consultant, I do what consultants do, look at what we're doing and try to promote a little more distance." Distance—the ability to see the forest and not the trees—had gone from a metaphor in a Bill James essay to the method of operation for James himself: "I'm in Kansas most of the time. I mean I very rarely miss a game on TV unless my wife has plans or something. I will often have a different perspective on it than everyone else, because everybody else's perspective tends to be shaped by one another."

While we're speaking, Red Sox rookie pitcher Eduardo Rodriguez is running into trouble. He had five strikeouts through three shutout innings, but just gave up a two-run home run to make it 3–1 Orioles. My son Peter, who made the trip with me, says "Okay, Brian Kenny, you putting your money where your mouth is and pulling him out? Right here in the fourth inning?" I hesitate. My basic theory is of course a full bullpen attack, and a quick hook for everyone. In real time, it still takes discipline to actually pull the trigger when it's so early.

"Gotta make the call now," says Pete, and he is right, it will all happen fast. Delmon Young singles. Chris Davis singles. I ask, "What do you think, Bill?" It's still only 3–1, but the bases are loaded. Bill says he thinks Rodriguez still has good stuff. I snap back, "Good stuff? He's giving up frozen ropes all over the place." If this was a Kung Fu movie, this is where the Master slaps the shit out of me for my insolence. Bill just smiles. I tell him, "I think if I'm running things, I suspend any manager who allows a starter to give up a five-spot in a single inning. You have to get him out of there." Rodriguez stays in. Within seconds, J. J. Hardy doubles, drives in two, and there's the five-spot. Pete shoots back, "You were already too late. Two guys on, that damage was already happening." Damn, Pete's right again. But he's young, grew up listening to me screaming at the TV baseball broadcasters, and reading Bill James. Bill and I can smack him around for *his* insolence, but he'd still be just as correct. Rodriguez gives up another single, then a sacrifice fly to center. It's now 6–1 Orioles. Manager John Farrell takes the slow walk to the mound. One thing is certain: he's *way* too late. Bill is shaking his head. In the postgame write-ups, no one will question the slow hook on the Red Sox starter. But not everyone was sitting with Bill James, who taught us to question everything.

Later, after a Red Sox rally, it's 8–6 Orioles in the ninth. Jackie Bradley Jr. leads off with a single. Boston is in business. I look around—even though they fell behind 6–1, it doesn't look as though anyone left the park. Remarkable. I've been all around the country to major league games, and most fans these days give up and make the move to beat traffic. Not so in Boston. Now the tying run is at the plate, and there's nobody out. They're being rewarded for their faith. I'm rooting for the Sox to come back so Bill can feel a little better. O's reliever Zach Britton has other ideas, getting the next three outs in order: 8–6 Baltimore. Pete says, "That one inning. Six runs. There's your ballgame." Damn. I was caught up in the moment, and hadn't thought of that yet. You *do* need distance—forest for the trees. Pete took his Bill James lessons seriously.

While taking in a game with Bill James is a baseball master class, it would be surprising to most fans just how emotional and nostalgic he actually is. He is more likely to compare Eduardo Rodriguez to another lefty flamethrower of the '60s than he is to be citing Rodriguez's numbers or projecting performance.

He is a very different person now than the one who shook up the establishment. Age and accumulated wisdom have had their expected effect. Having been in a baseball front office for more than a decade has given him an understanding of what it takes both to reach decisions and live with them. He rarely speaks in absolutes. He answers many questions with "I don't know" or "I'm not sure." He hasn't backed off his beliefs; he just seems to know what looks like the answer in the moment might not be the answer he'll reach in the years ahead. There is a famous Einstein quote, "The more I learn, the more I realize how much I don't know." As James himself wrote on his website *BillJamesOnline*: "As a young man, I put cleverness above respect for others. As a mature person, I hope that I wouldn't do that . . ." Before adding, "anyway I wouldn't do it in writing about baseball. I might do it if I was writing about politics."

James's drive came from his natural proclivity for economic thinking, but also his own desperate circumstances. Back at the coffee shop before the game, I had asked him about his parents. He answered, "My father was a small-town school janitor, and I have no mother. She died not long after I was born. I was four." It's a jarring statement. Not "my mother died when I was four," but "I have no mother." Bill was raised by a single father and six older siblings. His father was forced off the farm with a broken back when Bill was a child. "He had the attitude toward child-rearing that was common in his generation. And, he was not in any way a sophisticated person. But I mean, he stayed there and did the best he could to bring us up. I know how hard that was and I respect him."

In this bleak existence grew an angry child, with an intellect all but buried. "I was not a likable kid. That's God's truth, I wasn't. It wasn't exactly that I was rebellious, I was just a rude kid." You would think there would have been teachers that could see through the veil to the brilliance, but this was not the case. "Some teachers were helpful," says James, "but for the most part, I knew that they really didn't think highly of me." But the early bruising had its effect. "It was very helpful," he explains, "because when I got to that point where I was writing books and the established baseball professionals thought I was full of shit, I was like 'that's okay, I've dealt with this all my life, I don't care.'"

Bill took long pauses between his sentences. His eyes reddened. Bill James, right there, only an hour before the Red Sox were to play the Orioles, began to cry. "I was very used to it. I've put up with that all my life, and that's the way it was." Speaking of his upbringing had Bill feeling reflective and emotional. He didn't care what the baseball writers or critics said about his work because he had dealt with criticism his whole life. But of course he *did* care what they said; he just refused to change because of it.

He would react strongly, and now—as a successful grown man—not be particularly proud of that reaction. He sure as hell understood it, though: "I should stress I've tried to learn not to be rude. I mean, I have my whole life tried not to be, I've tried to learn not to offend people but . . . we were . . . *at the bottom.*"

He stared straight ahead, and composed himself so he could continue speaking. Seconds passed. We sat in silence.

"It's a cliché of a lot of athletes that they come from the very bottom of society ..."

The next words came slowly, and one at a time: "Well ... so ... did ... I."

That anger, isolation, and search for order in a random, cruel universe forged a brain that would transform Major League Baseball. The rude kid at the bottom of Kansas society would continually see things that had gone unnoticed for nearly a century, things we might never have seen without him.

If you were to make a list of the most influential figures in the history of baseball, you would need only seven men to complete the first tier: Alexander Cartwright, Henry Chadwick, Babe Ruth, Branch Rickey, Jackie Robinson, Marvin Miller, and Bill James. The order, by the way, is merely chronological.

# 6

# The Tyranny of the
# Batting Average

"When we diminish things like a Triple Crown, a batting title or 20 wins, we offend those in the other camp, because in doing that we are trying to take their touchstones away from them. This is not necessary or productive. We can argue our points without doing that."

—Bill James, 2014

With all due respect to the sabermetric godfather, do you ride a horse to work? A horse could get you to the office and back. So why do you hop in a car every morning?

When's the last time you used a rotary phone? An old-fashioned telephone is still a marvel, an incredible creation. But after 20 years of cell phones, try dialing those 10 numbers, one by one, to make a single call. Every so often, you might be forced to. When you do, it's agony. Technology and understanding move forward, and make once useful things obsolete.

In batting average, a single is as good as a home run, and walks don't exist. Yet the very first stat cited in most baseball conversations for 120 years—was the batting average. When you asked what a player was "hitting," you got the answer back in batting average. When you said a player was a "batting champion," it meant he led his league in batting average. When we memorized the lifetime numbers of our favorite players, the first number would be batting average.

Oddly enough, this did *not* come from a misunderstanding of what was important to measure. The founding fathers of baseball weren't simpletons—batting average *was* once a useful indicator of offense. In the era of little power, a ton of errors, and a walk being a pitching mistake, the batting average was a decent gauge of hitting. This is the 1880s we're talking about: handlebar mustaches, and players swinging the equivalent of table legs at the plate. Says baseball historian John Thorn: "The game was one of advancing a base at a time. Single, steal, and sacrifice. With most offensive events yielding a single base, the batting average made sense."

Until 1876, a batter could ask the hurler to throw the ball to a spot he liked. Walks were initially tabulated as a statistic for the pitcher, but not the hitter. Walks were actually listed as errors in the 1880s.

By the time we hit 1900, however, the walk had turned into a weapon. The crafty John McGraw—the Bill Belichick of his day—was just as cagey a player as he would become as a manager. McGraw led the league in walks twice, setting a National League record in 1899 with 124. Roy Thomas of the Phillies averaged over 100 walks a year for nine years in the aughts. "Drawing" the base on balls was starting to be seen as a skill. "It was regarded as a successful strategy because you got baserunners," says Thorn. "These guys tended to be up in the leaders for runs scored, which was highly prized." So walking was seen as a run-producing skill, right?

"No one made the connection," says Thorn.

Walks weren't tabulated by the leagues until 1908. We *now* know, because sabermetricians have gone through the old box scores game by game. But the players back in the old days, when they were playing, did not know how many walks they had. The legacy of walks as cheap goods continued for decades. "Look at Neddie Yost, the Walking Man," says Thorn. "Everyone thought, well, he leads every year in this oddball stat, but it's not worth anything."

Sabermetric pioneer John Dewan, told me he used to look forward to each November when he could finally get the year-end walk totals. I'm thinking he meant the early '60s or something. I asked what year he meant: "1987."

Bill James puts it eloquently: "Throughout most of the history of baseball this [drawing a walk] is regarded as an unworthy effort to game the system, exploiting the rules for a purpose not intended." A walk wasn't *intended* to be an offensive weapon, but it most definitely *is* one. Exploiting the rules for the purpose of winning has become an art form. Yet the origins of the walk would help minimize publicizing it as such, which held off the on-base revolution until the late 1990s. His first eight years in the majors, Wade Boggs had a .443 on-base percentage. This is in the 1980s, when James, Thorn, and Palmer are writing about on-base percentage constantly. Yet what was Boggs known for? His five "batting titles"—the freaking batting average! Writes James of the walk, "It is thought of as sneaky, lazy, something that people do who don't have the athletic ability to play the game the right way. This is how players have generally thought about this throughout baseball history."

You would think—I did—that while some scrappy types were living by the base on balls in the old days, that the overall walk rate would be much lower way back then. It's not the case. The walk rate of 1913, for example, was greater than the walk rate of 2014. The walks per nine of 1893 exceed that of 2000, the height of the steroid era.

I don't want to mischaracterize it. Looking at the highest walk rates season by season, only four of the top 40 come from the Dead-Ball Era. But to say that drawing a walk in the early days was not an offensive weapon is just not true. It's more accurate to say it wasn't *considered* a weapon by the opinion makers.

Yet, with the lack of power, there was a greater correlation between batting average and offensive excellence. In the Dead-Ball Era, the player with the highest batting average was frequently the best hitter in the league.

## "Batting" Champion?

Let's see how often the man who won the batting average title was also the league's best hitter. To simplify, we go decade by decade, to see how many times the batting average champion also led the league in OPS. OPS—on base plus slugging percentages—is a much better indicator of hitting production.

**Batting Average Leader/Also OPS Leader**

| | |
|---|---|
| 1900s: | 14 of 18 |
| 1910s: | 13 of 20 |
| 1920s: | 8 of 20 |
| 1930s: | 7 of 20 |
| 1940s: | 10 of 20 |
| 1950s: | 6 of 20 |
| 1960s: | 4 of 20 |
| 1970s: | 4 of 20 |
| 1980s: | 2 of 20 |
| 1990s: | 3 of 20 |
| 2000s: | 4 of 20 |
| 2010s: | 2 of 10 |

The blip in the '40s belongs to Ted Williams and Stan Musial, two outrageous batting average players who also walked and hit for power. Otherwise, it's a steady decline in batting average relevance.

In the Dead-Ball Era, 27 of 38 batting champions were also the best hitters in their league. This was in a day when the home run champ was frequently finishing with nine or 10 homers, and when some parks had no outfield walls, merely ropes. So a home run wasn't always a power shot, just a double to the gap that got past the ropes and into the crowd. It was customary for the patrons to move out of the way of the fielder, but as it was also the custom for the fans to be drunk, one can imagine some difficulty in one's retrieval efforts. So the difference between a double and a home run was not as stark as it would be when players were able to launch a hard white baseball into the upper deck.

In the first two decades of the 20th century, the leader in batting average was the league's best hitter 71 percent of the time. In the first two decades of the 21st century, this was true only 20 percent of the time. About the time Babe Ruth put on pinstripes, the "batting champion" was actually just the "batting average champion."

Baseball, somehow, did not notice. You can't even blame Henry Chadwick, the inventor of the modern box score, and advocate of the batting average. Chadwick had introduced things like bases per game, and even a weighted slugging percentage, but with the game being played the way it was in the 1860s, he backed batting average.

With players choking up on a large bat, their hands separated by several inches, it was a time of slapping the ball around the field to a bunch of dudes with no mitts. Chadwick would mock the player going for the long ball, calling it "showy." He was small ball all the way, but he was just playing the percentages. In his day, there were 12 errors a game! There's a wisdom to just smacking the ball out there and taking your chances. John Thorn points out that the attempt for the home run was actually bad strategy. "Because if it wasn't a home run it tended to produce a flyball, which was relatively easy to catch, especially in the days when you could catch it off a bound. You could catch it fair or foul off a bound." Think of a baseball game where the ball is a bit deader, the players don't have gloves, and where catching it on a bounce is an out. That does indeed make it worth your while to smack the ball on the ground. In the 1870s, more than half the runs scored came from errors. A fly ball was a much better proposition for a fielder.

This might seem obvious, but remember this is when the concrete is just starting to dry in the making of the baseball foundation. This is where all this small-ball worship—which continues to this day—comes from.

## Competitive Babe-Vantage

If you think baseball was slow to recognize sabermetrics, consider this; the Live-Ball Era started a *full decade* before the home run era did.

The greatest hitter in the history of the game, as he began dominating the game, was routinely slammed by the "purists." John McGraw, Ty Cobb, and the influential Henry Chadwick thought Babe Ruth was ruining the game. "Chadwick advocated hitting the daisy cutters, the ball that went low to the ground," adds Thorn. "That's why Babe Ruth's swing, in which he emulated Joe Jackson's all-or-nothing swing, was such a revolution."

Bill James has a fascinating theory of how Ruth even came to be the Bambino. It happened only because he was a pitcher. No one much cared if he swung from the heels; his hitting was superfluous, and as a pitcher, sporadic. The baseball culture, therefore—coaches, media, players—didn't pressure him into conforming. As I point out often in this book, the herd has ways of making you conform. Ruth had the good fortune to break the single-season home run record while still a pitcher. By the time he was ready to convert to an outfielder, it was too late to stop him. He already had shown that swinging for the fences was a worthwhile risk.

Think of that lucky accident. Had Ruth not developed as such a good pitcher at St. Mary's Industrial School for Boys, would he have developed differently as a hitter? It seems likely. The Live-Ball Era may have begun in 1920, but the live ball was actually introduced in 1909. You might want to read that sentence again. The cork-centered ball was introduced in 1909, and fully adopted by both leagues in 1911. *Yet the Dead-Ball Era played on, as if nothing had changed.* The ball was lively, but small-ball habits held strong, even at the expense of winning.

We think of 1920 as the start of the Live-Ball Era because Ruth played his first season as a hitter, and he hit a jaw-dropping 54 home runs. The death of Ray Chapman—struck and killed by a pitch in August of that year—spurred the leagues to replace soiled baseballs throughout the game. This likely led to more home runs in later innings, but this started only late in 1920. Ruth was already on a home run binge. According to most of the evidence, that live ball was in play a full nine years before Ruth showed baseball a better way to win.

There are rewards for the those who successfully break from the herd. In this case, the American League wouldn't recover for years. A full seven seasons later, Ruth still out-homered every other club in his league, *by himself.* The upper-cutting power-hitting Ruth, later joined by Lou Gehrig, gave the Yankees a home-run-hitting competitive advantage until about 1932.

Had Henry Chadwick made it to the Ruth Era, baseball may have turned out very differently. He had already thought through slugging percentage and total bases per game. He was a thinker; he helped bring overhand pitching into the game, and established the distance from the mound to home plate. He even tried Winter Baseball—on skates—in the 1880s! The future Hall of Famer was fluid in his thinking, not stuck in the past in any way. But the incredible innovator died in 1908, and left this earth knowing the game only from a small-ball perspective. Baseball analysis calcified without him.

# The Hidden Game

The first offensive statistic to consider will be that venerable, uncannily durable fraud, the batting average. What's wrong with it? What's right with it? We've recited our objections for the record, but we know as well as anyone else that this monument just won't topple; the best that can be hoped is that in time fans and officials will recognize it as a bit of nostalgia.

—John Thorn and Pete Palmer, *The Hidden Game of Baseball*

In 1984, the language of "batting average," ".300 hitter," and "batting title" were still so entrenched that Thorn and Palmer didn't allow themselves the thought of actually convincing anyone it was bunk. I was on television twenty years later fighting the same fight, wondering why the first number I would always see when a batter stepped to the plate—when the little graphics went in front of a player—was the batting average.

Within the baseball industry, it's doubtful anyone in a front office today judges a player based on his batting average, except within the concept of the slash line. The slash line is the batting average/on-base percentage/slugging percentage. It is useful to know what the player's batting average is within the on-base percentage. Ichiro Suzuki and Jorge Posada might both have a .400 on-base, but one is getting there with a .350 batting average with 50 walks, the other with a .310 batting average and 90 walks. Very different players. With all other things things being equal, of course you want a higher batting average within the on-base. It's just that the batting average alone tells you just a small part of the story.

This statistical choice, made in the 1870s, outdated by 1920, had influenced decades of players. Think of all the emphasis on this one part of offense. Not caring nearly enough about walks or power. Why should they? A .300 average got you paid. It would be on your mind all the time. What if a .500 slugging percentage had the same cachet, the same power of language? We undoubtedly would have seen more power hitting. The tail wagged the dog for decades.

If batting average wasn't the standard indicator of excellence, would Rod Carew have been a different hitter? What about Tony Gwynn or Bill Madlock? If batting average was merely a component of the on-base percentage, would these artists of the '70s and '80s have had the fanatical devotion to spraying the ball around the park, seduced by the riches available to a "batting champion"? All three of those hitters were excellent offensive players, but ballplayers, like all humans, react to incentives. I think they would have been very different indeed.

Batting average will continue to recede in our baseball language until we barely know it is there. Running alongside it is another link to baseball's cow pasture past, ready to join it in the backroom, with the other antiques.

# Kill the Error

Take a good look at a baseball scoreboard. It's now about 300 feet long and brilliantly lit, with videos playing and hundreds of pieces of electronic information all over it. Yet the three main numbers are the same as the ones put on the first wooden scoreboards, changed by hand, in the 1800s: Runs, Hits, Errors.

Runs make sense; they determine the winner. Hits would be the next most important subgroup, since, as we've established, most hits were singles, and walks were mistakes on the part of the pitcher. When the decision was made to list the most important things in the box score or on the scoreboard, the game was not the crisply played sport we currently enjoy. Games were played on choppy fields, the ball was a tarred-up mess, and the fielders were barehanded.

There were, on average, about 12 errors a game.

As time passed, fielders got gloves, and fields became manicured. Here's what happened to the E:

## Errors per Game

| Year | Errors/Game, Both Teams |
|------|-------------------------|
| 1876 | 12 |
| 1886 | 7 |
| 1896 | 5.2 |
| 1910 | 3.6 |
| 1920 | 2.8 |
| 1930 | 2.8 |
| 1940 | 2.3 |
| 1950 | 1.9 |
| 1960 | 1.8 |
| 1970 | 1.7 |
| 1980 | 1.7 |
| 1990 | 1.5 |
| 2000 | 1.4 |
| 2010 | 1.2 |
| 2015 | 1.2 |

By 1950, errors were no longer a big factor in a major league game. One per team, per game is nothing. But by then they had become part of the baseball culture: Runs, Hits, Errors.

The best teams these days average one assessed error every other day. It's a very small part of the game. We have an emotional reaction to a botched play because it stands out so vividly. One of the benefits of working at MLB Network is that you watch an enormous amount of baseball. I watch five or six games at a time, bouncing back and forth, nearly every night. When you watch that much baseball you realize that, in the modern game, errors are not terribly significant.

It happens all night long: a ball in the hole, fielder knocks it down, no play. I'll be sitting there with two former major league players, and the question goes up:

ME:            "Is that an error?"
ANALYST #1: "You gotta make that play."
ANALYST #2: "That's a tough play."

Happens all the time. Occasionally there's an obvious botched play, but as we now know, these actually happen, on average, about once a game. You know what else happens? A ball rolls past a shortstop, or drops in between outfielders, where no error is charged. Happens all the time and we think nothing of it. When assessing defensive impact, errors by defenders are nothing compared to the range of the defensive player.

Check out American League shortstops in 1984. Alan Trammell of the Tigers made just 10 errors. Dick Schofield of the Angels made 12, Spike Owen of the Mariners 17, Robin Yount of the Brewers 18, while Cal Ripken Jr. of the Orioles had 26.

Trammell, playing just 114 games in the field, was second to Schofield in fielding percentage that season, and won the AL Gold Glove. (Fielding percentage comes from the percentage of errors you make within your putouts and assists.) Now check out the raw totals for plays made at shortstop that season:

| Player | Putouts | Assists | Double Plays |
| --- | --- | --- | --- |
| Ripken | 297 | 583 | 122 |
| Owen | 245 | 463 | 86 |
| Schofield | 218 | 420 | 95 |
| Trammell | 180 | 314 | 71 |
| Yount | 199 | 402 | 80 |

I know Ripken is playing more games, but holy cow. Just looking at the raw totals, he made 52 more putouts, 120 more assists, and 27 more double plays than the *next best shortstop* on this list. The amount of ground balls induced by the pitching staff certainly has to be taken into consideration, but please, Spike Owen is the next best on this list, and Cal Ripken made 172 *more plays* over one season. I'm not sweating the extra nine errors.

It's not fair to Trammell, given the shortened season, but he won the Gold Glove on the strength of 16 fewer errors than Ripken. Ripken was responsible for 386 more plays. It's certainly more drastic at shortstop, given the numbers of plays being made, but errors, once again, are insignificant as compared to the range of a fielder. For decades we judged fielding on errors. It was a misjudgment.

In the 2014 postseason, we had another outstanding illustration of the power of range. The Royals' outfield, manned by Alex Gordon, Lorenzo Cain, Nori Aoki, and occasionally Jarrod Dyson, created an outfield where the ball never seemed to hit the ground. Gordon's record of defensive runs saved had been a topic for years, but now, in the glare of the postseason, fans and media saw it played out in front of them. The Royals' defense was awesome to watch. It was clear it was a big part of their first postseason run in 29 years.

Not surprisingly, the Royals were ranked first in defensive runs saved, as tallied by Baseball Info Solutions. The best defensive team in baseball. The Royals also made 104 errors, ranking them the 21st best defensive team in baseball. Which metric do *you* think is more accurate? Were they the best defensive team in the majors, or the 21st best? Errors are memorable, but range is much more significant.

It comes down to putting away the old habits, and paying attention. I'll repeat this observation: *There is a disconnect between what we value when we watch the game, and what we value after it.* While we watch a game, we frequently see that the difference between what is called a hit and what is called an error is arbitrary. Only afterward does the significance of this discussion become absolute. Afterward, we revert to our habits.

# Error in Judgment

Game 3 of the 2013 NLCS, the St. Louis Cardinals are having a disastrous day in the field against the Dodgers. Locked in a scoreless duel between Adam Wainwright and Hyun-jin Ryu, Cards center fielder Jon Jay and right fielder Carlos Beltran watch a fly ball drop between them in the fourth, leading to the first run of the game. In the eighth, second baseman Kolten Wong ran down a ball in the outfield, then fired to second, allowing Carl Crawford to wheel around third base and score. The outfield also misplayed an A. J. Ellis hit into a triple.

The Dodgers would win the game 3–0. It was deemed a "Defensive Disaster" in the media, and would actually lead the Cardinals to trade for center field defensive whiz Peter Bourjos in the off-season to shore up the outfield defense. Baseball Info Solutions counted up nine "defensive misplays" in the game. We spoke of the Cardinals' defensive lapses on our *MLB Tonight* postgame show as the no-doubt, make-no-mistake key to the game. So, how many Errors, with a capital E, did the Cardinals make in this slop-fest?

Zero.

An error often isn't assessed if a fielder doesn't actually touch the ball. It often isn't assessed if the fielder can't quite reach it, either. It isn't charged when a fielder throws to the wrong base.

Counting up "errors" does not accurately measure defense. Charging an error seems like a necessity when a player boots the ball, but as we've seen, we know it doesn't actually happen very often.

You might have a problem giving a "hit" to a player who has reached on an error. It will feel strange, but two things to think about:

1.  Reaching on an error is often based on the skill of the hitter. The players who have routinely reached on errors the most have not been just speedsters, but hitters who make hard contact to the left side of the infield, *and* can also run. Cal Ripken Jr., Robin Yount, and Derek Jeter are among the recent leaders in reaching on an error (ROE).

In his first 10 years, Ripken averaged 10 ROE per season. In his 18
full seasons, Jeter averaged nearly 11. There might be some obvious fielding clunkers, but these athletic hard-hitting players are also
somewhat responsible for forcing fielders into tough situations.

2.  In a strange bit of baseball accounting, a hitter reaching on an error
    is charged with an out. This out, however, never actually occurs. A
    player is standing on first base, yet he is charged with an out in the
    box score, and is technically 0–1. This is not the sort of thing that
    keeps me up at night, but if you worry about some sort of baseball
    "symmetry"—that everything must equal out, and we can't possibly
    call a bad defensive play a "hit"—forget it. It doesn't make sense
    the way it is now. A man is on base, and an out was never recorded.
    That's not an 0–1.

Look, you can call it whatever you like. A reach on error can be kept
separately statistically and put onto a player's on-base percentage. I'd just
as soon call it a hit and give the batter credit for putting the ball in play.
If you're worrying about the "sanctity" of the batting average, please read
the first half of this chapter again. Soon enough, no one will care.

If you think ROE will render historical batting averages off-kilter,
you're too late:

| Batting Avg | .400+ | .365+ |
|---|---|---|
| 1890–1950: | 24 | 151 |
| 1951–2011: | 0 | 20 |

Did hitters decline over the second 60-year phase of organized baseball?
Of course not. Batting averages are already not "fair." Errors counting as
hits won't create a historical imbalance.

The funny thing is, only in extreme cases does any front office pay
attention to errors when making a defensive evaluation. Where it counts
the most, the E is already gone. Yet there it is, 120 years later, in lights, up
on the scoreboard. Runs, Hits, Errors. Just like the old days.

# 7

# Kill the Win

"It seems to place the whole game upon the shoulders of the pitcher and I don't believe it will ever become popular."
—The *Sporting News*, on the Pitching Win, July 7, 1888

Even in 1888, those who followed the game wondered why some were bothering to assess a "win" or "loss" to one of the players on the field.

Did you ever notice the pitcher's win-loss record usually comes with a qualification? As in, "He's 3–7, but he's actually pitched much better than that." Or, "He hasn't won in a month, but he's actually been very effective." You know what we *never* say? "He has an ERA of 5.00, but he's actually been one of the best pitchers on the team." Or "he's slugging .500 this season, but he's actually struggling." Nope, when you talk ERA, slugging, on-base, even batting average, the number speaks for itself. There can be added context, like one bad outing making for a misleading ERA, but listen up to the next ballgame or sportscast, and you will hear the win-loss record come with an explaining qualifier almost every time. And why is that? Because the stat often has very little to do with the pitcher's actual performance. So if we are always explaining and apologizing for it, why do we even bother with it?

The win, oddly enough, was actually an early attempt at sabermetrics, trying to isolate individual production from that of the entire team.

By 1870, baseball was moving to the rules we understand to this day. No longer would it be a game of hitter vs. fielders, with the pitcher being merely an instrument to deliver the ball. Pitchers began to throw harder to induce outs from the hitters, and with that there was a need for different pitchers for different games. The strength of each team would now vary from day to day.

Followers would notice that pitching was a skill, and certain pitchers were better than others. One club, for example, might seem to be particularly tough when the "The Old Colonel" or "Big Red" or whoever was pitching. Teams and aficionados of this fascinating new game now tried to figure out which pitchers were better. This information was fun for fans, and also beneficial to gamblers. And the old boys *loved* to gamble.

At the same time, since pitchers threw the entire game, it did seem like a battle between these two men. The winner was frequently the better pitcher, so unlike every player on the field, this dominant figure would now be assigned something called a "win," or a "loss." It was simpler than figuring out the average runs allowed per game.

It made *some* sense. That year the *Sporting News* sounded off, pitchers finished 96.4 percent of all games. Basically, unless you passed out or had an old Civil War wound flare up, that game was all yours.

There was a greater chance then that the W-L record could, perhaps, tell the story of a pitcher's performance. And yet, if you are thinking we must continue to recognize this stat because of tradition, allow me to take that notion off the table. Here again is what was being written in the *Sporting News*, in 1888:

"Certain it is that many an execrable pitcher game is won by heavy hitting at the right moment after the pitcher has done his best to lose it." Even in the days of one pitcher going all day, the idea of one man being assessed a "win" wasn't universally agreed upon.

In 1913, having introduced earned run average, American League president Ban Johnson omitted win-loss decisions from the official record. He felt wins were not a good indicator of player performance, and wins and losses were not kept, nor listed with the individual stats. Imagine that, no wins or losses. When I mention that wins and losses could go away and nothing would change, people laugh. They can't make the distinction between the team wins and losses that make up the standings and the fictitious "win" or "loss" assessed to a single player after the fact. The American League would continue along just fine without the W through 1919.

In 1920, the W was back, but already pitchers were finishing only 57 percent of their games. In the 1930s the "CG" would be down to 43 percent, and even in the decade of the pitcher—the 1960s—it would be down to 25 percent, one quarter of all games.

Yet the soundtrack stayed the same through the decades, from radio, to TV, to the Internet: "Smith is 15–10, having won five of his last six."

By 2013, with bullpen specialization, pitch counts, and team-imposed innings limits, pitchers would complete just 2 percent of all games. Not only that, but the average length of a start for a starting pitcher would shrink to just five and two thirds innings.

Yes, the average starter would go barely long enough to meet the minimum qualifications for a W, and yet it remains the leading starting pitcher statistic, the first metric quoted by the play-by-play man, and the first numbers put next the pitcher's name in the scorecard, newspaper, or online preview.

Think about it for just a minute. A statistic is cited because we believe it to have value. We believe it accurately measures performance. That there is some factual relationship to a player's season. But a W goes not to a pitcher who pitches best, but to the pitcher who goes long enough into a game, having left with a lead that his teammates did not relinquish.

Individual statistics exist to isolate performance in a team game. Otherwise we wouldn't keep them, a team's record would suffice. Yet a pitcher who gets a W is dependent not only on his teammates' offense, but on his team's offense that specific day he is pitching, and is dependent on that offense scoring early enough in the game that he can have a lead to hold on to in the first place.

The pitcher is also dependent on his teammates in the bullpen (usually several of them), his teammates' defense in the field, the opposing team's starting pitcher, the opposing team's bullpen pitchers, the opposing team's offense, the opposing team's offense that particular day, and the opposing team's offense scoring at a particular time in the game!

Yet, check out the normal way we are introduced to any game in a newspaper or now website page: Yankees (Sabathia 14–10) vs. Red Sox (Buchholz 8–11).

It's considered such a vital statistic it's on the marquee. The teams, the starting pitcher, and the pitcher's win-loss record.

We take it for granted, thinking it stands for something. It is, in fact, baseball's leading anachronism, a survivor from the nineteenth century that was out of date by the time the live ball was in play.

# The Day in the W

In 2013, Harold Reynolds and I were pitted against each other in a new-school/old-school format for *MLB Now*. We sometimes would count up the topics we had on the show, and often found we would agree on thirteen of fifteen things. When we didn't agree? Yep, that would get rough. It went back to our days at ESPN together, working on *Baseball Tonight*. We would take turns in meetings saying, "Are you going to say that on the air? Well, good luck to you." We would be laughing, but we would be mystified by what the other was thinking.

We were talking pitching on the show, and Harold took a stand: "I don't care what you say, there is one stat you'll never get rid of, and that's the win. That's because some pitchers know how to win, and others will figure out a way to come up short. Wins matter."

Harold was staying with his belief that some pitchers were mentally tougher, got themselves out of tough spots, and went deeper into games than others. I don't doubt that he lived through that many times on the field. You're in a battle, and a teammate would easily have admiration for the guy who is leading the charge, in this case, the pitcher. But Harold was in the thick of it, and like most players was too close to see things clearly. I hadn't planned on becoming a sabermetric zealot, but after years of studying baseball, I refused to parrot some nonsense to the masses when it made no sense.

    I was trying to think of a way to show Harold, and the rest of the world, just how inaccurate the win stat is as a measurement. I started paying attention to all the hard-luck cases out there, night after night. A guy goes eight shutout innings, bullpen blows lead, followed by an obligatory shot of him in the dugout looking like his dog just ran away.

    I was on Twitter at the time, so I started putting it out there every day, and called it "The Day in the W." Here's the key: I thought I would have one or two hard-luck stories a night.

    Instead I found between four and 12 per night. One starter after another, pitching great, but somehow lacking some sort of fortitude, could not close the deal. Here's an example:

July 29, 2013: The Day in the "W":
Cingrani, Capuano, Lincecum, Redmond, Cosart, Corbin, Chen, Santiago:
8 great starts, 53.1 IP, 1.53 ERA, 0 "Wins"

July 30: The Day in the "W":
Weaver, Garza, Danks, McAllister, Lohse, Samardzija, O'Sullivan, Leake:
8 excellent starts, 58 IP, 1.71 ERA, 0 Wins

Back-to-back nights, 16 starts with a combined sub-two ERA. No wins. When you begin following it every day, it becomes even more apparent. It's random. It's inaccurate. It has nothing to do with a pitcher's drive or character. In every single pitching category, these pitchers would be rewarded for an excellent start: In the W, it's as if the start did not exist. Try it sometime. I did it for a full summer, now it's your turn. You think you'll find a hard-luck start or two. It'll be five or six almost every night.

# Harvey

Matt Harvey provides another illustration in the uselessness of the W. Before he hurt his elbow in late August of 2013, he was the MLB leader in fielding independent pitching (FIP) (see Glossary), league leader in strikeout percentage, and swinging strike percentage. He had already started the All-Star Game, and was the talk of baseball. His season-ending injury was major news in baseball, and devastating news for the Mets. So let me ask you, do you remember his "record"? Of course you don't. It had very little correlation to his performance, so we just dismiss it. It was 9–5. So what good is it, if we have to dismiss it?

In one start in May, Harvey went nine shutout innings, allowing one man to reach base. Twelve strikeouts, no walks, one single. But the Mets were also shut out by Chris Sale of the White Sox, so Harvey left a scoreless game, and the Mets lost 1–0 in extra innings. In that game, Harvey was almost as dominant as a pitcher could possibly have been for one single contest. And at the end of the year, in the win-loss stat, it was as if that game had never happened.

This is an important point. In real time, we absorb and appreciate the great outing. But statistics are shorthand in many ways. At the end of the year, those who judge Matt Harvey for 2013 will say "he was 9–5." When he retires, we'll say something like, "Matt Harvey won 254 games." When this happens, voilà!: Nine shutout innings, 12 strikeouts, a one-hitter will vanish. It never happened.

Harvey had several of these games in 2013. In seven different starts, he threw 53 innings, giving up only six runs. That's an ERA of 1.02. An

ERA that would lead the league in any year—the greatest of all time if it could be done over a full season. Want to guess how many wins he got? That's right, *zero*! His great work, over seven games, seen in the prism of the W-L, *does not exist*.

Let me ask you this—do you care about a relief pitcher's win-loss record?

Do you care that Mariano Rivera, from 2001 to 2012, had an average "record" of 4–3? Or that Hoyt Wilhelm, in his 21 seasons, had an average record of 9–7?

Of course you don't. Rivera and Wilhelm are the top two relief pitchers in baseball history. The win-loss record doesn't apply to them.

*Why* doesn't it apply to them? Because the "record" is a poor reflection of their work, that's why. I'm sorry if I'm the one to break this to you, but the same goes for *all pitchers*.

## The Numbers

Let's take a very broad look at starting pitchers who have given good performances, and examine whether that was accurately reflected in their win-loss record.

Consider a pitcher who throws seven innings, giving up two runs. You'd take that every time. That's a 2.57 ERA. If you did that for the season, you would be among the league leaders. With a performance that would have you among the league leaders, you also should figure to get a win most times out, wouldn't you? Why yes, you would. Want to guess what percentage of pitchers throwing seven innings and giving up two runs have gotten a win?

**7 innings, 2 runs—1920–2014**

| Games | Wins | Percentage of Pitchers Getting Win |
|---|---|---|
| 10,981 | 4,095 | 37% |

Crazy, isn't it? Seven innings, giving up two runs. Sixty-three percent of the time, no W.

How about eight innings and two runs? This is now an ERA of 2.25. Incredibly, the percentage getting a win in this instance is even lower: 33.6 percent. Throwing precisely eight innings, and giving up precisely two runs, two thirds of the time a pitcher comes away without a win.

Now maybe this is due to a good number of pitchers throwing complete games while trailing, and on the road. In this case, when pitchers were throwing a lot of complete games, that would leave a lot of eight-inning losers. But the low percentage of wins is stunning.

While we're locked into these two solid starts—seven or eight innings, giving up two runs—let's look at what happens to pitchers in the current game, with shorter outings, and more relief work.

# 2012–2014

### Percentage of Pitchers Getting Win

| | |
|---|---|
| 7 IP, 2 runs allowed: | 43% |

Think that through. More than *half* the pitchers—57%—throwing seven innings and giving up just two runs, *did not* get a win.

How about eight innings and two runs?

| Total Games | Wins | Pitcher Win % |
|---|---|---|
| 199 | 104 | 52% |

Almost half of the pitchers with this excellent start—a 2.25 ERA—did not get a win.

I wanted to make sure we weren't missing pitchers who were throwing seven and third and seven and two thirds innings, so let's combine all pitchers over these three recent seasons going between seven and eight innings, allowing just two runs:

## 2012–2014
### 7–8 IP—2 runs allowed

| Total Games | Wins | Pitcher Win % |
|:---:|:---:|:---:|
| 1,021 | 478 | 46.8% |

Including all starts between seven and eight innings, where the starter leaves the mound to applause, having given up just two runs, *more than half* will not get a win.

At the end of the season, that seven- or eight-inning start will show up in every stat we speak about: ERA, FIP, Strikeout %, everything.

But when we speak of how many wins this pitcher had, more than half of these starts do not exist.

I don't think this is a concept most fans think about. The "win" total is part of the baseball language. Once on MLB Network with me, Ron Darling referred to a pitcher saying, "I think he'll win 15 this year." Realizing what he just said, and whom he said it to, he then said, "Oh, sorry," laughed, and began to try to put it in different terms.

I stopped him short, because I knew exactly what he meant. Saying "I think he'll win 15" is shorthand for "I think he's a good pitcher. Better than average. Not an ace, maybe not even your number two starter. But kind of a better-than-you-thought-he'd-be number three." We have all developed this language. Not just of the "20 game winner," but of what any variation of the win total, or win-loss record will be.

The problem is, the language has a very loose correlation to the performance.

What matters, in the final equation is this: How many innings did you pitch, how many runs did you allow? If you want to strip away defense, it's: How many guys did you strike out, how many did you walk? The win or loss is superfluous and has no bearing on anything.

# The Numbers

Let's go over the loose correlation between what's considered a "good" performance, and a pitcher's chance of getting a win:

### Likelihood Pitcher Will Get the W, 2012–2014

| Innings | ER | % Wins |
|---------|-----|--------|
| 7 | 0 | 74.4 |
| 7 | 1 | 56.8 |
| 7 | 2 | 43.3 |
| | | |
| 8 | 0 | 78.0 |
| 8 | 1 | 69.4 |
| 8 | 2 | 52.3 |
| | | |
| 9 | 0 | 97.5 |
| 9 | 1 | 88.4 |
| 9 | 2 | 84.6 |

You can pick at any of these numbers. Consider for a moment, eight innings, one run. A completely dominant performance, yet more than 30 percent of the time, it doesn't go into the win column.

We have this story that is fed to us that some pitchers "know how to win." It's simply not true. Pitchers can pitch deeper into games to give themselves *a better chance* of getting a win. They cannot, however, will their teammates to score more runs. A player might want to have better at-bats for his pal, but it doesn't work that way, and no correlation has ever been found.

This is what matters: how many innings you pitched, how many runs did you give up. That's it. That's all. A pitcher's job is to get outs.

# Shafted by the W

You can't show me a pitcher with 200 innings and a 2.00 ERA who had a bad season, or one with a 5.00 ERA who had a good one. There are bad defenses, and there are variations with the batted ball, but there are limits.

ERA may also be flawed—too team dependent, too dependent on random bounces between fielders—but it's a decent indication of what a pitcher has done. FIP shows what a pitcher is most responsible for and is a better indicator of future performance. But if you're arguing against either one of them, you are splitting hairs compared to the massive disconnect to performance that occurs with W-L.

If you're still holding out, here are some great seasons with a skewed view from the win column.

## Cy Young: 1905 (18–19)

Oh, the delicious irony. The Win King himself threw 320 innings of a 1.82 ERA, and still finished 18–19. If only there was a Cy Young Award back then for the sportswriters to deny him.

## Lefty Grove: 1926 (13–13)

Greatest Pitcher Ever lacked Will to Win en route to first of nine ERA titles. Had a 2.51 ERA in 258 innings. Completed 20 of 33 games, throwing out the "gotta go deep to win" excuse. The 1926 A's also won 83 games that year, so it's not just that his team stunk. It just happens.

## Warren Spahn: 1952 (14–19)

Even the Live-Ball Era wins leader is not immune to the eccentricities of the W. Had a 2.98 ERA five shutouts, and led the NL in strikeouts. Eddie Mathews was 20, Hank Aaron hadn't arrived, so a great season turns into a "19 game loser."

### Orel Hershiser: 1989 (15–15)

A year after winning the Cy Young with his 59-consecutive-scoreless-inning streak in 1988, Hershiser had just about the same year in 1989. I know you don't think that, because he was 23–8 in '88, and just 15–15 in '89. But check it out:

| Year | IP | ERA | ERA+ | FIP |
|------|------|------|------|------|
| 1988 | 267 | 2.26 | 149 | 3.18 |
| 1989 | 256.2 | 2.31 | 149 | 2.77 |

I know you're thinking Hershiser simply didn't allow himself to lose in '88, and he did throw eight shutouts. But he threw four in '89. The difference between 23–8 and 15–15 is happenstance.

### Nolan Ryan: 1987 (8–16)

211 IP, a 2.76 ERA. Led NL in ERA+ (see Glossary), FIP, and strikeouts, with 270. It takes a lot of choking to get an 8–16 record out of that. Nolan, I'm kidding!

### Roger Clemens: 1996 (10–13)

His last season in Boston. Actually was the AL strikeout leader, throwing 242 IP. Was 5th in ERA+, 2nd in FIP, 5th in pitching WAR. It's hard to envision the old W-L facilitating his exit from Boston, but in those days a 10–13 helped create the perception he was in irreversible decline.

### Clayton Kershaw 2009, 2010: (8–8, 13–10)

This is early Kershaw, before he was recognized as the best pitcher in the game. In his first two full seasons, he had the eighth best ERA+ in baseball, and was second only to Felix Hernandez in opponents' OPS. Yet his 8–8 and 13–10 helped keep him under the radar. I know, you knew he was great the moment you saw him, sure you did. He had 30 and 32 starts those years, and got zero Cy Young Award votes.

Kershaw also deserves a special commendation in the #KillTheWin fight. At the 2012 All-Star game, he came over to our MLB Network set, and immediately Harold Reynolds and Dan Plesac asked him if he thought wins should be "killed." The guys chuckled, anticipating the predictable ballplayer-trained "Will to Win" pabulum. Kershaw, though, said he thought there were many more important categories and thought the W-L was frequently misleading. Harold and Dan groaned, lamenting a missed opportunity to crush me.

I seized on it, asking, "Can we then count on you for the Kill the Win program?" Kershaw answered diplomatically, "How about we just *de-emphasize* the win?"

I'll take it, Clayton.

## Blinded Me with Ws

Knowing all this, doesn't factoring in a pitcher's win-loss record in a Cy Young Award analysis seem silly? No one seriously studying the game should even bother to consider it. And yet, here are some recent examples where it was the leading reason for the media to crown the best pitcher in each league:

### 2005 American League

| Player | ERA | IP |
|---|---|---|
| Johan Santana | 2.87 | 231.2 |
| Bartolo Colon | 3.48 | 222.2 |

Santana pitched nine more innings, giving up 16 fewer runs, and Colon was pitching in a pitcher's park. Santana was also much more dominant in things he was largely responsible for: striking out 81 more batters. The baseball writers, it should be noted, are not asked to give their Cy Young votes off the top of their head. They can check records, even write things down.

Santana has every advantage in terms of run prevention: fewer hits, fewer base runners, and more strikeouts. If anyone covering baseball professionally that year had bothered to check, Santana also had eight starts where he allowed just 15 combined runs but did not get a single W. That's eight starts—60 innings—of a 2.25 ERA (good enough to lead the AL by a wide margin), where he receives zero credit in the "Win" column.

So you want to tell me why Colon got 17 first-place votes, and Santana got 3?:

|         | W-L  |
|---------|------|
| Colon   | 21–8 |
| Santana | 16–7 |

Doesn't that 21–8 look pretty? That's what the voters thought. Colon won the award for pitcher of the year.

## 1990 American League

|         | ERA  | IP    |
|---------|------|-------|
| Clemens | 1.93 | 228.1 |
| Welch   | 2.95 | 238.1 |

Bob Welch did pitch 10 more innings than Roger Clemens. You want those 10 innings? They come with 31 more runs allowed. Or, if you prefer, two five-inning starts where he gives up 15 runs in the first one, 16 runs in the next. No thanks, I'm good!

Welch also pitched in the spacious, pitcher-friendly Oakland Coliseum, while Clemens pitched in hitter-friendly Fenway Park. I won't bore you with the park effect numbers, but in the AL that year, Oakland had the best park to pitch in, and Boston had the toughest. If you could flip their parks with these numbers, you'd still have a tough time convincing me Welch was better. Clemens was *easily* the better pitcher that year—the AL leader in ERA, ERA+, FIP, and Pitching WAR.

Then of course, there's this:

|  | W-L |
|---|---|
| Clemens | 21–6 |
| Welch | 27–6 |

Guess who won the Cy Young that year. 21–6 has a nice look to it, but the 27 wins bypassed the part of the sportswriter's brain where logic is synthesized, hit them right in the brain stem, and forced them to vote for Welch. The A's righty got 15 first-place votes, Clemens just 8.

## 2010 American League

The rise of sabermetrics, coupled with the fans' ability to look things up for themselves, forced voters to raise their game. In 2010, Felix Hernandez won the AL Cy Young despite a 13–12 "record." It felt like a watershed moment, a breakthrough on the grip of the "W." Hernandez, though, led the league in ERA and innings, and was second in strikeouts by one. It really shouldn't have been complicated.

### 2010 Cy Young American League

| Player | 1st Place | IP | ERA | W–L |
|---|---|---|---|---|
| 1. Felix Hernandez | 21 | 249.2 | 2.27 | 13–12 |
| 2. David Price | 4 | 208.2 | 2.72 | 19–6 |
| 3. CC Sabathia | 3 | 237.2 | 3.18 | 21–7 |

Pretty easy pick. Yet this was a seen as a monumental victory for sabermetrics. How about a victory for paying attention?

# The Made-Up Stat

The irony of holding tight to a pitcher's win-loss record is that the win is nonexistent. It never actually happens on the field of play.

Think about it. Most stats in sports are a direct reflection of a physical act. A double actually happens; a man hits the ball, and ends up on second. A strikeout also occurs; three strikes, have a seat. The W is an abstraction conferred after the fact. It's totally made up.

It's not only made up, it can change on a whim. In the early 1910s, if the official scorer thought the pitcher who left with a lead had pitched poorly, he could reserve the right to award the "win" to another pitcher

These phony-baloney rules are still on the books, but for relievers only. In 2013, Mariano Rivera finished off the 9th inning for the Yankees against the Orioles. He came in with a one-run lead and held it. That is normally what is referred to as a "save." The official scorer, however, deemed David Robertson, the man in line for the "win," unworthy of such an honor. He pitched one inning, and gave up three runs. He was also the last Yankee pitcher on the mound when his team took the lead for good. He was, in point of accepted fact, what is known as "the pitcher of record." The scorer, though, is within his rights to choose the relief pitcher he views as "most effective." It's in the rules. He switched Rivera's "save" into a "win."

This sent people into a brief tizzy. How can you do that? Rivera isn't looking to "win," he's looking to "save"! He's the all-time saves leader!

The scorer did us all a favor. Did anything of any importance change as a result of his ruling? Of course not. Robertson was charged with a bunch of runs, Rivera was not. A day after it happened, it was forgotten.

That leads to this realization: If the pitching win and loss just went away, nothing would change. Not the standings. Not the playoffs. The W has nothing to do with which team wins and The L has nothing to do with who loses. You'd still have ERA, runs allowed per 9, FIP, xFIP (see Glossary), SIERA (see Glossary), and RA/9 WAR (see Glossary) (figures innings into the equation, which is extremely important). We now have Statcast, which is giving us spin rate, perceived velocity, and much more. It's getting more and more granular. We can now judge "stuff" the way only a good scout used to be able to do. But even with the advent of the pitching skill stat—FIP (strikeouts, walks, home runs)—and the advances of Statcast, it still comes down to this: How many innings did you pitch and how many runs did you give up?

# #KillTheWin

Anyone who thought the W was on its way out, though, was sorely mistaken. As I continued to hammer these points home on TV, radio, and Twitter, some ahead of the game analytically, on their websites, would claim we all know the W was arbitrary so I should pipe down. The "war had been won." But it isn't over yet.

In the midst of the #KillTheWin run in that summer of 2013 came the All-Star Game. The Midsummer Classic is a traditional benchmark of analysis. Who are the best players? Who deserves to represent their league?

The American League starter was Max Scherzer. If you listened only to the media, you would quickly conclude that Scherzer was the best pitcher in baseball. The Tigers' righty was having a breakout season, as his strikeout rate was indicating for years. He was also 12th in the AL in ERA. Now, if media members were paying attention to Scherzer's FIP, or opponents' OPS, they would have sound evidence for Scherzer's deserving the starting spot. This, however, was not the case.

The reason Scherzer was starting was because he was 13–0. With the best run support of any pitcher in the game, he had a W-L record that editors saw as a headline. Once that narrative is imprinted, it's not easily dissolved. Asked at the All-Star Game press conference, his manager, Jim Leyland, one of the most respected managers of his generation, cited his win-loss record.

With one pitcher's spot left to fill on his AL pitching staff, Leyland named Orioles righty Chris Tillman. On a staff that had room for nine starters, Tillman was 29th in the league in ERA, 35th in fielding independent pitching. Nowhere near the top starters in the league. Hiroki Kuroda of the Yankees did not make the team. Kuroda was 3rd in the AL in ERA, and 19th in FIP. If you want to go deeper, Kuroda was sixth in opponent's OPS, Tillman was 44th. Batter for batter, it just isn't close. Go ahead and match them up:

|         | ERA  | IP    | R  |
|---------|------|-------|----|
| Kuroda  | 2.65 | 118.2 | 36 |
| Tillman | 3.95 | 111.2 | 50 |

Kuroda had allowed 14 fewer runs, pitching seven more innings. Park effects were about even, and Kuroda also had faced the tougher offenses. Context must be taken into consideration, but nope, Kuroda was just flat-out better. But, oh, then there's this:

|         | W-L  |
|---------|------|
| Kuroda  | 8–6  |
| Tillman | 11–2 |

Asked at the news conference why Tillman made the All-Star team, Leyland answered, "You win 11 games by the All-Star Game, that pretty much says it all."

I study baseball every day and I never have any idea of a pitcher's win-loss record unless someone points it out to me. I don't use it for Cy Young analysis, game prep, or even for light reading. In the preseason it doesn't predict anything, during the season it doesn't reveal anything, and after the season it doesn't explain anything. It's useless.

Yet here I am watching managers name their All-Star teams because of it. Every headline and game summary of a Max Scherzer start led with it. Every play-by-play man in the majors begins his introduction of the day's starting pitcher with it. Somehow it lingers.

I am amazed by how many good writers and broadcasters, when confronted by the silliness of the W-L, then try to come up with a way of replacing it. Quality starts, a win-loss record based on team record for a pitcher's starts, or a "deserved win-loss." Let me give you some advice: Let it go. It's a waste of time. The W-L is still there. In the standings. It doesn't work anywhere else. Use that baseball brain space for things that matter.

Ben Reiter of *Sports Illustrated* was on *MLB Now* with me, and during a break he said, "You know what's funny? When I'm looking at pitchers, I *never* look at the win-loss record anymore. I mean, *why?*" Welcome to the club. In twenty years, it'll be an afterthought.

# 8

# Kill the Save Too

"Roles are bullshit. Your job is to throw strikes when I put your ass out on the mound."

—Dick Radatz, pitching coach,
two-time American League saves leader

Bullpen usage is, of course, insane, and the save statistic is barely worth writing about, except once again to wonder why otherwise smart and competitive people do things so stupidly.

Today's relief aces are treated like rare exotic flowers, to be taken out only in certain conditions. They work the ninth inning only, preferably with nobody on base, and they top out at 70 innings for the season.

I hesitate even to write at length about the save. Most fans know it's nonsense. Yet it not only shapes the way we think about closers; it has transformed the way the pitching staff is utilized.

Notice I didn't just say "the way the bullpen is utilized," but the pitching staff as a whole. Take a step back. You've established one pitcher as the best on your staff—batter for batter. You then:

1. Artificially restrict his innings.
2. Keep him from the most important parts of the game.

Does this make sense?

The save began as an admirable attempt to quantify the value of relief pitching; Jerome Holtzman of the *Chicago Tribune* came up with the save statistic in 1960. He did so after Roy Face received accolades for an 18–1 win-loss record for the 1959 Pirates. Holtzman was a sportswriter after my own heart, battling the inaccuracy of the dreaded W. He figured there had to be a better way of measuring relievers than the haphazard nature of getting a win or a loss. Little did he know his efforts would make stat geeks of all managers and pitchers for decades. A made-up stat transformed the industry.

# The Caged Beast

In the 2004 National League Playoffs, the Dodgers faced the Cardinals in the Division Series. Here's a look at LA's starting pitching:

|  | ERA | IP | SO | BB |
|---|---|---|---|---|
| Jeff Weaver | 4.01 | 220 | 153 | 67 |
| Odalis Perez | 3.25 | 196.1 | 128 | 44 |
| Kazuhisa Ishii | 4.71 | 172 | 99 | 98 |
| Jose Lima | 4.07 | 170.1 | 93 | 34 |
| Hideo Nomo | 8.25 | 84 | 54 | 42 |

Only one starter has an ERA in the 3s. If you were hired as the manager the morning of Game 1, you could tell immediately after looking at the stats that you would want to limit the innings of your starters if you had a good bullpen. Did the 2004 Dodgers have a good bullpen?

|                    | IP    | ERA  | SO  | BB |
|--------------------|-------|------|-----|----|
| Eric Gagne         | 82.1  | 2.19 | 114 | 22 |
| Guillermo Mota     | 63    | 2.14 | 52  | 27 |
| Giovanni Carrara   | 53.2  | 2.18 | 48  | 20 |
| Dudaren Sanchez    | 80    | 3.38 | 44  | 27 |
| Yhency Brazoban    | 32.2  | 2.48 | 27  | 15 |

That's five effective relievers. Three are having sensational years, and one—Gagne—is a big-time strikeout pitcher. Gagne was fourth in the NL in strikeout rate that season, having broken the all-time strikeout rate record the year before.

If this is all you knew, if you had no restraints on how you could use that guy, you'd make sure he got a lot of work, right? Being that he's one of your best weapons, you would know that unleashing this beast on the opposition is one of your priorities.

Gagne was used twice in the series. Both times came in the eighth inning, with his team trailing—8–3 and then 6–2. The Dodgers lost three games to one, and Gagne had no bearing on the outcome.

Does this make sense? No, it does not.

And his manager was skewered, right?

I covered this series myself at the park for ESPN. To my knowledge, there was no criticism anywhere of Gagne's usage.

I remember watching the games, and not being outraged either. But I started to think about how not using your best inning-for-inning pitcher in big spots became accepted.

It was as if the Dodgers had Gagne in a cage beyond the outfield wall—kind of like Mighty Joe Young—where he's rattling the bars and frothing at the mouth. People gawk and scream, while the Cardinals quake in fear. However, everyone knows as long as the Cardinals can keep the lead, that dude has to stay in his cage. If you're St. Louis, it's a beautiful setup.

This series is just one example of how the game is always on the line.

The Cardinals had at least six runs in each of their three wins—getting them by the fourth, fifth, and seventh innings. Ballgame. Over. Dodgers manager Jim Tracy, using accepted bullpen dogma, saved his best pitcher for a big moment later in the game. But those big moments had already come and gone. You need to use your weapons.

## Lost Lesson in Winning

The history of bullpen usage is a stunning example of baseball's inertial reasoning. It made sense that it took a few years for teams to go to the bullpen. The game, as we mentioned, began with the pitcher serving up pitches for a batsman to smash.

In 1904, starters finished 88 percent of their games. By 1920, the percentage of complete games had gone down to 57 percent, with starters going an average of seven and one thirds of an inning. It was time for teams to start investing some resources into the bullpen. But they did not. The pen was for the guys who couldn't cut it, or were on their way out of the game.

In 1924 though, the Washington Senators had a stacked rotation—Walter Johnson led the number one staff in the league—so they got creative with a young guy named Firpo Marberry. A hard-throwing rookie, he started 14 games, but also relieved in 36. He pitched 93.1 innings as a starter, and 102 as a reliever. Pitching in 50 games, he finished with a 3.09 ERA, helping the Senators to a 92-win season and the AL pennant.

In the World Series, Manager Bucky Harris used his new weapon. Marberry worked the ninth in Game 2, started Game 3, pitched the eighth and ninth in Game 4, and then in Game 7 pitched the sixth, seventh, and eighth, yielding to Walter Johnson in the ninth.

The Senators beat John McGraw's Giants in the 12th inning of Game 7 and won the World Series.

The Senators had given the rest of the league a template to winning baseball. It responded by ignoring it. Marberry stayed in the pen for a few years, then moved to the rotation.

Between 1920 and 1930, complete games went down from 57 percent to 44 percent. The live ball had changed the game, but teams did not recognize the full impact. Clubs now had all the more reason to bolster their bullpens and commit to a relief ace. But that didn't happen. Even with the Senators' success, credit went to the Big Train and the rest of the starting staff. No other club felt compelled to jump on board and create their own Firpo Marberry.

## The Fireman Emerges

Let's check in on what we now take for granted: the Modern Save-Driven Closer. Here are some of the best relievers in the game from 1987 to the present—Mariano Rivera, Trevor Hoffman, Dennis Eckersley, among others, in their best seasons:

|  |  | Avg IP | ERA |
| --- | --- | --- | --- |
| Mariano Rivera | 1997–2011 | 69 | 2.01 |
| Trevor Hoffman | 1994–2007 | 61 | 2.61 |
| Billy Wagner | 1997–2008 | 64 | 2.40 |
| Joe Nathan | 2003–2013 | 67 | 2.24 |
| Dennis Eckersley | 1987–1997 | 68 | 2.87 |
| Troy Percival | 1995–2004 | 59 | 2.99 |
| Robb Nen | 1994–2002 | 73 | 2.66 |
| Jonathan Papelbon | 2006–2014 | 66 | 2.35 |

Seven of the best relievers of a generation and not one averaged 75 innings a season. Not only that, but all just happen to land within 14 innings of each other in average usage. These stats speak to the homogenized usage pattern.

So let's check out some numbers from a bygone era. Cities were decaying, drugs were rampant, but the top relief pitchers were productive, working early, and often. It was the late 1970s and a club's best reliever was called a fireman:

|  |  | Avg IP | ERA |
|---|---|---|---|
| Clay Carroll | 1968–1977 | 106 | 2.77 |
| Sparky Lyle | 1968–1979 | 94 | 2.61 |
| Rollie Fingers | 1969–1981 | 117 | 2.85 |
| Wayne Granger | 1969–1973 | 96 | 3.03 |
| Tug McGraw | 1969–1980 | 97 | 2.87 |
| Dave Giusti | 1970–1975 | 93 | 2.80 |
| Mike Marshall | 1970–1976 | 118 | 2.98 |
| John Hiller | 1973–1978 | 114 | 2.45 |
| Al Hrabosky | 1973–1979 | 80 | 3.00 |
| Goose Gossage | 1977–1985 | 93 | 2.10 |
| Dan Quisenberry | 1980–1986 | 116 | 2.48 |

These relievers, for 10 to 15 years, threw around 100 innings a year. It was a low-run-scoring era, but this was not Cy Young going to the pasture to toss a mudball at an ex-Confederate. This was modern baseball.

The '70s and '80s were the closest we have come to optimal usage of the relief ace. This would all change with the success of Dennis Eckersley and Bruce Sutter in the '80s. Not only did minimizing their innings fit perfectly into maximizing the "save" stat, it also simplified things for managers. Instead of having to make a difficult judgment call at any point in the game, a skipper could just wait until the ninth inning and let the save stat make the call for him. Best of all, he would never have to face any criticism for doing so.

# Swatting a Fly with a Buick

You can save your best relief pitcher for the ninth inning when you have a three-run lead. As the heading says, the Buick will get that particular job done, but aren't there bigger jobs for your car?

You see it all season; team has a four-run lead in the ninth, closer is sitting down. Lead is cut to three and the closer gets up. This happens almost completely because of the save. It shows how stats can influence a manager's thinking. It's the wrong stat, and the wrong situation.

In the outstanding book *The Book: Playing the Percentages in Baseball*, the line between "need your closer/don't need your closer" is actually identified.

Tom Tango, Mitchel Lichtman, and Andrew Dolphin point out in *The Book* that a league average pitcher, with a clean slate and a three-run lead, is just fine for the ninth inning. On average, they found, the difference between Mariano Rivera—the best reliever in the game—and a league average pitcher is *one blown save per season*.

For a two-run lead? Different story. They found the chances of blowing the lead doubled. That makes two more blown saves per season. A one-run lead, even with nobody on and nobody out, is, though, a high leverage moment. The chances of a league average reliever blowing a save is three times as likely as compared to going to a relief ace. This is definitely when you want your relief ace out on the mound.

# The Relief Ace

So we ask: Before the save stat sucked the logic out of our brains, did anyone ever stumble upon optimal relief ace usage?

In 1950, Jim Konstanty won the National League MVP Award. I initially took a closer look at his season to blast the sportswriters for another misplaced narrative-driven vote, but came away with a very different view.

The 1950 Whiz Kid Phillies won 91 games to capture the pennant, outlasting the Dodgers. They over-performed somewhat, with their run differential indicating their record should have been 87–67. Led by a 23-year-old Robin Roberts (304 innings, 3.02 ERA) they had the number one pitching staff in the league.

Konstanty came out of the bullpen, pitching 152 innings with a 2.66 ERA. The ERA might not seem impressive, but this was a high-run-scoring year—Konstanty had the best ERA in the league among those with at least 150 innings. Konstanty appeared in a league-high 74 games. In a 154-game season, this is almost *half* of the Phillies games.

When you think of applying a relief ace to high-leverage situations, and use this weapon in half your games, you are creating an extremely valuable player. Since he comes out of the pen, you get to choose when you want him in—a crucial spot, when there is a game to win—and when you don't want his excellent run prevention wasted.

The Phillies did go overboard. On September 15, the Phils put him in a tie game in the ninth, and kept him until it ended in the 18th. A complete game, plus one inning. Already at 124 innings, he probably could have done without that extra 10 innings. He got blown up three times in the final week of the season, sending his ERA from 2.19 to 2.66.

He pitched that 10-inning outing, a nine-inning outing, and six times he worked both ends of a doubleheader. Clearly the Phillies liked using Jim Konstanty—and abused him.

So let's use Konstanty in a more reasonable way; take away the marathon relief appearances and the doubleheaders. That's 13 more innings than we'd want in the extra inning games, and nine in the second end of a twin bill.

Now the 152-inning epic is already down to 130 innings. It's still a heavy load, but it is down to a more normal 1970s fireman season. He also worked 23 times on back-to-back days. Let's cut that in half. At two innings a pop, let's call it 23 innings. Now we're down to 107 innings.

Since World War II, 107 innings or more has been done 51 times, by a pitcher relieving at least 80 percent of his games. It can be done.

We don't even have to leave the 1950 Phillies to see the value of Konstanty's season. When I first looked at his season, the 74 games stood out. Appearances, games finished, innings, and ERA begin to tell us how valuable a pitcher throwing these many innings can be. We now, though, have more sophisticated ways.

# High Leverage

Robin Roberts threw a monstrous 304.1 innings that year. Almost exactly double Konstanty's 152. He started 39 games, finishing 21 of them. An old-school season that we don't see anymore. Here are the two side by side:

|           | IP    | ERA  | WAR |
|-----------|-------|------|-----|
| Roberts   | 304.1 | 3.02 | 7.3 |
| Konstanty | 152   | 2.66 | 4.7 |

Roberts, who led the NL in WAR, has a huge edge on Konstanty in that category. It's easy to say Roberts was more valuable. At 300 innings, you would hope so.

Now imagine a reliever comes on with men on first and second, and turns the situation from two on, no outs, to two on, one out. That reduces the chances of scoring a run immensely. Obviously a pitcher gets more credit for these kinds of outs. The idea is to get your best pitchers into these spots. Konstanty was put into these positions all the time, but Roberts is dealing with so much volume, he still has a better RE24 (see Glossary).

And yet, there is another way of looking at value: How did the pitcher affect his team's chances of winning? This will be dependent on the score, and will be skewed by using a pitcher in tight games. It will also be affected by the volume of work—the number of innings will increase the win probability added. Look at 1950 in a different way:

**1950 NL—Win Probability Added Leaders**

|  | WPA |
|---|---|
| 1. Konstanty | 5.5 |
| 2. Roberts | 5.4 |
| 3. Jansen | 3.9 |

In terms of affecting a team's chances of winning, *now* Jim Konstanty is the best pitcher in the National League. Being in high-leverage situations and being able to affect the chances of winning varies from player to player. It's not a "fair" way of ranking pitchers, but it does reflect what has happened, and who affected winning the most. Looking at it this way, yes, the sportswriters have a quantifiable reason to think what they did; Konstanty seemed to be the man most responsible for the Phillies winning all those games. Indeed they were correct.

More important than telling us who was more valuable, this statistic tells us about how a team can manipulate results with the proper application of excellent pitching. In another season, even if both had the same ERA and innings pitched, it is likely that Roberts's 300 innings would have a greater effect on his team's winning. What is interesting is that it's *possible* for a reliever to have a greater impact than even an excellent starter with many more innings pitched.

Studying the statistics tells us something about what works. A moderate workload, properly applied, can be just as valuable as an excellent season with twice as many innings.

## The Promotion

Let's ask the question: Does using your closer the way baseball does now—from around 1988 to the 2010s—best lead to winning games?

There may be a few ways to answer it. First, how many of the top 20 seasons in relief—going by bWAR (see Glossary)—do you think came from the modern closer-centric bullpen?

The answer is: None.

Going to win probability brings a similar finding. Fourteen of the top 20 seasons—measuring pitcher impact on winning from the bullpen—come from pitchers with at least 100 innings. Let's see how many "modern closers"—post-1988—make the top 20:

### All-Time Single Season Leaders
Win Probability—Relief Pitchers

|  | Year | WPA | IP | ERA |
|---|---|---|---|---|
| 1. Willie Hernandez | 1984 | 8.65 | 140.1 | 1.92 |
| 2. John Hiller | 1973 | 8.39 | 125.1 | 1.44 |
| 3. Doug Corbett | 1980 | 7.81 | 136.1 | 1.98 |
| 4. Stu Miller | 1965 | 7.23 | 119.1 | 1.89 |
| 5. Dan Quisenberry | 1980 | 7.01 | 128.1 | 3.09 |
| 6. Goose Gossage | 1975 | 6.98 | 141.2 | 1.84 |
| 7. Troy Percival | 1996 | 6.58 | 74 | 2.31 |
| 8. Eric Gagne | 2003 | 6.56 | 82.1 | 1.2 |
| 9. Tug McGraw | 1972 | 6.52 | 106 | 1.7 |
| 10. Aurelio Lopez | 1979 | 6.49 | 127 | 2.41 |
| 11. Keith Foulke | 2000 | 6.40 | 88 | 2.97 |
| 12. Trevor Hoffman | 1998 | 6.26 | 73 | 1.48 |
| 13. Dick Radatz | 1963 | 6.23 | 132.1 | 1.97 |
| 14. Jose Mesa | 1995 | 6.14 | 64 | 1.12 |
| 15. Ray Narleski | 1955 | 6.11 | 111.2 | 3.71 |
| 16. J. J. Putz | 2007 | 5.95 | 71.2 | 1.38 |
| 17. Billy Wagner | 1999 | 5.89 | 74.2 | 1.57 |
| 18. Goose Gossage | 1977 | 5.87 | 133 | 1.62 |
| 19. Mark Davis | 1989 | 5.79 | 92.2 | 1.85 |
| 20. Joe Nathan | 2004 | 5.77 | 72.1 | 1.62 |

Only two "post-1988" closers make the top 10. Percival and Gagne, despite a surge in talent, and more innings than ever before coming from the bullpen. Only eight make the top 20, and that includes a rare 88-inning closer workload by Keith Foulke in 2000.

So if a manager today thinks saving his best relief pitcher for "save situations" à la the "modern closer" brings about the best chance to win ballgames, he is sadly mistaken. Mariano Rivera, the greatest closer of all time, had his highest WPA as a closer in 2004, good for only 53rd all-time. This isn't his fault; he just didn't have enough high-leverage moments to gather up a high win probability. Rivera, as it turns out, was criminally underutilized.

It's clear: The relievers of the '60s, '70s, and '80s had a bigger impact on the chances of winning.

Any manager who is saving his closer/relief ace/fireman/stud for the ninth inning is thinking the following: *I'm saving him to seal this win, when the game is most on the line.*

And this is simply not the case. The game is *frequently* on the line in the ninth; I'm not saying it isn't. But the act of saving your best pitcher—inning for inning—for a situation that may not come (a one-run lead in the ninth) is not worth the exchange. This is clearly borne out by the WPA top 20.

Throughout the history of baseball, it seems the best usage of the relief ace came in the 1970s. Not only is the 1970s fireman giving you more overall volume (run expectancy and WAR—see Glossary), the fireman is doing more to add to the overall win probability.

The workload may have been too much. It is difficult to say top arms were, or weren't, burned out. Pitchers then did miss time and parts of seasons after the heavy workloads. But plenty of relievers nowadays miss time after throwing 65 innings as well.

Let's take this small step back to the 1970s. I would tell a GM today the following: Your closer is now your fireman. Have a little ceremony in spring training if you think it helps. Get a fireman's helmet and use it to knight him if you think it will help lock this idea into everyone's mind.

If he rebels by saying "I get paid for saves," remind him who is paying him. Remind him that a fireman throwing 95 innings gets paid more than a diva-closer throwing only 65 innings. Pay him accordingly.

Now you have the freedom to unlock the cage of the bullpen, and free your best pitching monster *whenever you see fit.* This will be very bad news for everyone you play.

# 9

# Bullpenning

"The ability to learn faster than competitors may be the only sustainable, competitive advantage."

—Arie de Geus, Royal Dutch Shell

Imagine you run a local semipro baseball team in your hometown, and I'm bringing in a traveling club for an exhibition game. We've never seen each other before. All we know is that we have players about the same age and level of talent.

Your starting pitcher throws a good game, giving up only a few runs over the first six innings. My team starts with a pitcher who is throwing all-out, full-throttle, leaving after two innings before he ever bats. My club then changes pitchers almost every inning, with each pitcher throwing all-out, like a reliever. We never let a rally go unchallenged, always throwing out a fresh arm, and matching up with platoon advantages in the late innings. You use the standard three or four pitchers, I use six or seven. Seem unfair?

Of course it is.

So I have a question: Why don't we do that?

# Worlds Collide

It's the first ever World Baseball Classic in 2004. I was calling games for ESPN at the regional tournament in San Juan, Puerto Rico. In this grouping, only two teams would emerge from a pool of powerhouses: Venezuela (Johan Santana, Miguel Cabrera), the Dominican Republic (Albert Pujols, David Ortiz, Jose Reyes), and Puerto Rico (Carlos Beltran, Bernie Williams), along with outmanned teams from the Netherlands, Panama, Italy, and Australia. Also in this bracket, straight out of the Cold War, was Cuba.

I remember being on the field when the clubs came out for a workout the day before games began. We were all interested in getting a look at the Cuban team. The team of mystery arrived. I said to my producer, "Do they not have steroids in Cuba?"

They looked athletic, but it was like going back in time. Like watching the 1986 World Series, when players were lean and skinny. In 2004, a world fueled by hormones and resistance training, these dudes looked way too light to play with big leaguers. Yes, they had immense success internationally, but that was against amateur teams. We were all fascinated by this proud but seemingly outgunned team. We thought they had no shot.

Cuba opened up against Panama. Cuba's starting pitcher was Pedro Lazo. *He* wasn't a lightweight; 6'4", 245 pounds, everything a starting ace is supposed to look like. Lazo was 33 years old, a two-time Olympic gold medalist, and a part of four World Cup championship teams.

Second inning, Lazo gave up a single and 2 walks. Cuba's manager, Higinio Velez, came to the mound, seemingly to slow things down and calm his pitcher. Instead, Velez signaled to the bullpen. Lazo was out. The winningest pitcher in Cuban league history had given up one run. On the telecast, I was incredulous. He's done? It's 1–0 in the second inning! I had never seen anything like it.

It soon became clear. The Cubans were not bound by tradition, un-written rules, or keeping players in their roles. The Cubans were there to win innings, win games, and win tournaments. They did not wait to see if their starter would settle down. No one had earned the right to stay out there. They would throw one pitcher after another at you, all dependent on the situation. Cuba, who we thought to be completely outgunned by nations laden with U.S. major leaguers, would be one of the two teams to emerge from pool play in San Juan. They would then go on to beat the Dominican Republic in the WBC semifinals, and lose to Japan in the one-game WBC championship game. Quite the debut on the world stage.

Cuba didn't do a full bullpen attack; they just weren't locked into a certain model where a starter had to get rocked to get taken out. Nor did they have a closer who waited for the ninth inning. It was something I didn't forget. I went back to my shows at ESPN and talked about the strategic impact of the WBC. Wouldn't major league teams try to copy this formula? I should have known better.

## Origins of the Starter

Start by asking: "Why do all major league teams pitch the way they do?" And the answer is: Because that's the way we always have done it. Which is an even worse reason than you think.

If we were devising the game of baseball right now, there is no way we'd send out day after day one guy to throw for as long as he could, until he quantifiably began to fail. An optimal pitching staff would be made up of roughly the same number of pitchers, but with the workload divvied up very differently.

Let's start with the obvious; just as sprinters can run faster than distance runners, it's easier to pitch in relief. Even operating out of a superior talent pool, starting pitchers have, overall, a higher ERA than relievers.

**2003–2014**

| Starter ERA | Reliever ERA |
|:---:|:---:|
| 4.28 | 3.92 |

Relief pitchers started churning out lower ERAs around 1955, about the time relief pitchers became more regular weapons around each league. This is not a trend that will be reversing. You might be thinking, "They have lower ERAs only because they throw for shorter periods."

Well, that's precisely the point.

Yet still to this day, one man strides to the mound and pitches for as long as he can until fatigued. The only difference is how long. Cy Young or Clayton Kershaw, we're still pitching like it's the 19th century.

# Specialization

The move toward using more pitchers for fewer innings each, or bullpenning, is happening in baseball, but it's occurring reluctantly, almost grudgingly. But the trend is unmistakable: more pitchers, throwing fewer innings.

In 1933, each team used about 11 pitchers a season. By 2014, we were up to 23 pitchers a season. The pull of bullpenning is powerful. It is happening, it's just coming step by step, instead of one club having the guts and ingenuity to make an institutional decision and thereby gain a massive competitive advantage by doing it systematically.

When I was sitting in Fenway Park with Bill James, I asked him when his Red Sox would start bullpenning. He laughed, and asked me if it made for a better game. I said it was just tradition that made us *think* we liked the concept of the starting pitcher, pointing out if we were sitting together at an American Legion game, teams using six pitchers a game wouldn't bother us at all. Bill shot back, "Well, no one shows up at American Legion games."

I'd been down this road before with Bill. He knows bullpenning is more efficient, a better way to win baseball games, but he just doesn't like it. It violates his baseball sensibilities. Yes, the baseball sabermetrician/ anarchist is also a nostalgist: He likes baseball the way it's been played all these years. He's entitled to this feeling, but I don't agree with it. Or maybe I'm just throwing my own bomb into the baseball mix. I press on, asking, "Think anyone will do it, eventually?" Bill conceded the point. "Yes, because it's logical. I think it's the end point on a continuum we've been moving along for 100 years. We're going to get there unless something stops us and baseball just doesn't do that."

John Thorn concurs: "Specialization is an irresistible force within our species as well as within the game. The idea that we're going to go backward on this—you can't do it with evolution, you can't do it with the game of baseball either. In the long view it is irresistible."

This "crackpot" strategy I've been pushing for a decade—greeted with laughter for years—is, according to the leading baseball intellectuals, an inevitability.

## The End of the Starter

The only reason we still have starters is because once upon a time one pitcher was all you used for the whole day. In 1910, 62 percent of all starters finished their own games. In 2014 it was down to 2 percent.

As recently as 1988, there were 622 complete games in one season. In 2014, it was down to 114. In 1971 and '72, Fergie Jenkins and Steve Carlton were the MLB leaders in complete games. Each had 30. By 2015, four complete games was enough to lead the majors. It's barely worth tracking.

An average start was still up over seven innings as recently as the 1940s. In 2014, the average start is down to five and two thirds innings. Just over half the game.

This is a significant difference. Relief pitching is almost literally half the game. And yet we still have the same pitching structure: The starter comes out to applause—like a Broadway actor playing the protagonist—and throws for as long as possible—until he shows tangible evidence he cannot continue. There are now pitch counts, and anything over 100 pitches makes managers nervous, but basically a pitcher goes until he begins to give up too many runs. What sense does this make? Let's ask some questions, and answer them.

**Why do we have starters?**
Because there used to be just one pitcher on each side per game.

**Why was that?**
Because they used to throw a pitch just for the batter to hit.

**Why do the best relief pitchers not enter the game until later, rather than in high-leverage situations earlier in the game?**
Two reasons: First, bullpens in the old days weren't deep enough to have several effective options. Once the best guy was used up, there was usually a big drop-off. And second, because of the mistaken belief that the game is on the line late, but not early. The knowledge of win probability metrics now makes this kind of thinking obsolete. A 4–1 lead with the bases loaded in the fifth? Run the numbers! You think there will be a bigger threat? You're still making a calculated decision, but at least now you can make it with a greater knowledge of the odds.

**With the 25-man roster, will teams have enough pitchers?**
Yes, it can be worked out so pitchers get adequate rest, but innovative teams don't use a 25-man roster. Drawing on their minor league teams, the Yankees used 29 pitchers in 2015. "We talked all winter about where we could be in a situation where we're really taking a guy every 10 days" says Yankee GM Brian Cashman. "Call a guy up, max him out, send him back out and get a new guy up. It's just kind of a revolving door." Every team in the AL East used at least 21 pitchers in 2015. The Dodgers, hit by injuries, used more than 30. Smart teams use their AAA and

AA teams to augment their pitching staff, get bullpen innings, and keep their best pitchers for high-leverage moments.

**Why do the best pitchers in today's game throw either 200 (starter), or 65 (closer) innings?**
No reason whatsoever. If starters are the track equivalent of milers, and closers are sprinters, then baseball is training for only these two types of races. While we're using the track analogy, doesn't it stand to reason we might have some pitchers who are the equivalent of 200, or 400 meter runners?

We have "starters" because of 19th-century tradition. We have "closers" because of 1980s tradition. Neither is an optimal strategy.

# The Rockies

When Dan O'Dowd joined us at MLB Network, he had just left the Rockies after 15 years of being the club's general manager. From what I had seen, the Rockies were one of the last of the sabermetric holdouts. They had just enough success—a pennant in 2007, a wildcard berth in 2009—to justify their obstinance. They also had a ready-made excuse—one that may be altogether plausible: Playing at high altitude, with constant high-scoring games puts too much strain on a pitching staff to make winning sustainable. So what O'Dowd said to me in an *MLB Tonight* meeting snapped my head back.

We were previewing the 2015 Rockies, and not a lot was expected from the team. O'Dowd was clearly frustrated, having just left his post after four straight losing seasons. What he said next encapsulated the baseball culture war of the last generation: "What I most regret is that I failed to inspire people to embrace the idea of looking at things differently."

I looked up from my iPad. "I'm sorry, what?"

O'Dowd continued. "We had to recognize that our world was different. We were the only ones playing in our world. But change is emotionally difficult to accept in this game."

I had always wondered about Colorado. I had openly applauded their attempt to change pitching tactics in 2012. With the worst ERA in baseball that June, the Rockies radically switched to a four-man rotation, with a 75-pitch limit for their starters. I believe, though, I was one of the few applauding. The sabermetric writers at FanGraphs and Baseball Prospectus were also intrigued. The mainstream media blasted them:

> This is what the Rockies' season has come to: The rotation is so bad that the manager would rather see middle relievers soak up important innings than having the opening-day starter perform the task.
>
> In a season defined by surprises and disappointment, Jim Tracy provided both Tuesday, explaining that Jeremy Guthrie was going to the bullpen and that the team was moving forward with four starters on a 75-pitch count.
>
> Seriously.
>
> The dateline isn't Williamsport. This isn't Little League.
>
> Troy Renck, *Denver Post*, June 19, 2012.

I vehemently disagreed with that critique on MLB Network almost every night. I didn't think it was a perfect solution, but at least they were trying *something*.

The Rockies' starters had a 6.31 ERA, they had lost 11 of 12, sliding to last place in their division. Would the media have preferred they continued to sink doing the same thing night after night?

The answer, of course, is yes. Failing conventionally is accepted. A GM has to answer for a losing season, but there are all sorts of buffers: injuries, the manager, and underperforming players. O'Dowd would eventually have to answer for putting together the roster of a losing team, but by showing ingenuity he was placing himself in the crosshairs much sooner than he would have otherwise.

Coming midseason, the change was understandably jarring for the players. Manager Jim Tracy played the good soldier, but clearly this idea wasn't his. His pitching coach, Bob Apodaca, quit days later. O'Dowd said agents hated it, because pitchers wouldn't get wins! All the while, O'Dowd said, "I was getting blown up in the national and local media."

> When I first heard the Colorado Rockies' plan for their pitching staff going forward, I thought it was a joke. It turns out I was right. It's a joke all right. A joke played on the Rockies' faithful.
> —Scott Nulph, *Wyoming Tribune Eagle,* June 28, 2012

Now we see how a perfectly reasonable idea dies a lonely death.

Only a complete turnaround from the pitching staff could have saved this idea, and the talent just wasn't there to do it. Their team ERA was slightly lower, and their winning percentage slightly higher after they started bullpenning. They had pledged to bring back the pitch limits system the following season. Upon hearing this, *USA Today* wrote that the Rockies "were throwing in the towel on 2013." It's a tough crowd. O'Dowd's grand experiment was basically finished by the end of the year.

I often wondered which club would make the breakthrough. Rich clubs would have no incentive. They already have an advantage in buying talent. And if you're successful, why challenge the very structure of the game you're winning?

No, it would have to come from a team that was desperate enough to try something radical. But it couldn't come from a team that had terrible pitching, because the idea would fail. Denver had all the incentives to go for bullpenning, but even a mild change—changing the pitching goal from 100 to 75 pitches—caused a shockwave that made it too much trouble to continue. Bullpenning will happen, but it will have to come from a GM with the autonomy and equity to see it through.

O'Dowd didn't have the talent, or the backing, to buck the traditional cultural norms. "It's hard to get anyone to look through a nontraditional prism," he said. "Change is just too emotionally difficult to produce in this game."

# Do the Math

There are 162 games in a season, nine innings a game. That's 1,458 innings a season. We've just established that each team uses, on average, 23 pitchers a season. That's 63 innings a pitcher. Let's back it off to just the main pitchers you'd prefer using—we'd certainly rather not dig too deep into our Triple-A pool. In 2013, Orioles manager Buck Showalter—the state-of-the-art tactician—used 13 pitchers for realistic innings.

Thirteen pitchers used equally is still just 112 innings a man. Let's say we use our top two pitchers for 200–220 innings each (again, I'm not advocating any ideology for its own sake; if you have two studs, you're getting some extra work out of them). That leaves the 11 other pitchers to divvy up 1,058 innings. Now we're down to 11 pitchers at 96 innings per pitcher.

Let's also figure we might have two relievers who are optimal at the traditional 75 innings of high-leverage work. That leaves nine pitchers for about 900-plus innings. We're still at a manageable 100 innings a man for the bullpenners.

Here's how a full bullpen attack could work with just the standard 13 pitchers:

| | |
|---|---|
| Ace: | 220 |
| #2 Starter: | 200 |
| Fragile Reliever: | 75 |
| Fragile Reliever: | 75 |
| 9 pitchers: | 100 |

It's doesn't have to be all that complicated. Clearly some former starters will be just fine throwing 130 innings, while a few max-effort types could be held to 80–90. Not that anyone noticed, but the 2014 Orioles had seven relief pitchers throw between 50 and 76 innings, and had 14 different pitchers finish games. That's the basic flying squad of relievers we're talking about.

You don't know about it, because Buck Showalter is careful not to be too public about being so smart. He'd rather you just think he has a "quick hook." The M.O. is not to eat innings, but to *prevent runs*. We have nine pitchers slated for basically 100 innings each of relief work. Can this be done, you ask? Why yes, dear reader, they have already done it.

# The Game Is Always on the Line

Let me ask you something: Would you bring your closer in the fourth inning? I know, now sabermetrics have gone too far! Except it's not Bill James telling you to do that, it's the major league manager of the 1970s.

The "ninth inning closer" model has bolstered the myth that the game is on the line only in that final inning. It certainly is more obviously on the line at that point, but the fact is, most games are decided before then. Somehow, teams managed to forget this at some point in the late '80s.

In the A's three-year championship run in the early '70s, Rollie Fingers was often brought out for the fifth and sixth innings. In the '74 World Series, Fingers and Mike Marshall matched up in a heavyweight reliever showdown, both coming in early (the fifth and sixth) and working multiple innings. In a five-game series, Fingers pitched nine and one third innings, giving up two runs, while Marshall worked nine, allowing just one run. Fingers and Marshall are clearly two of the best ever, but think of the effect of that usage. Between 2011 and 2014, no closer/relief ace/fireman pitched more than 8 innings in *any* playoff series. Even in the vaunted Royals bullpen of 2014, the most innings in the World Series for *any* reliever was 6.2 for Kelvin Herrera, and that's in a seven-game series over nine days. The A's and Dodgers got at least nine innings out of their studs—in a five-game series over just six days.

Now we get to Billy the Kid. By 1977, the hyper-competitive Billy Martin was managing the Yankees. Facing the Royals in the American League Championship Series and trying to get back to the World Series as a manager to get his first championship, he refused to follow a path of conventional losing:

- Game 3: Yankees down 3–1 in the sixth, Martin brought in Sparky Lyle with two on and two outs. Lyle finished the game.
- Game 4: Yankees up 5–4, George Brett at bat with two on and two outs. Martin went back to Lyle. It was the fourth inning. Lyle got Brett, and finished the game. Yes, from the fourth inning.

After the game, Martin would issue a proclamation destined to be ignored for decades: "Why save your closer for some other moment when that could be the do-or-die moment that decides a do-or-die game?"

- Game 5: Yankees down 3–2 in the eighth, Martin brings back Lyle when the Royals get first and second with two outs. Lyle gets the out, Yanks get three in the top of the ninth, Lyle gets final three outs in the ninth to seal the pennant.

Lyle came on in the fourth, the sixth, and the eighth, twice with his team trailing. Martin was giving his team the best chance to win by bringing in the man who had the best chance to get him outs. That's a guy who, if pitching today, would be called a closer. He would stay safely in the bullpen, encased in glass, until his team had a lead with three outs to go. In that 1977 series, Lyle might never have had a ninth inning lead to protect.

Billy Martin was weaned on '40s baseball, schooled by the often brilliant Casey Stengel. Martin always saw the value of getting a lead, especially in big games—it put pressure on the other team, and Martin loved putting pressure on the opposition. In this case, his Yankees were down 2 games to 1. A Brett base hit—*even in the fourth inning*—would leave him down one with 15 outs until the end of his season. He didn't see why he should lose a lead to George Brett when he had Sparky Lyle sitting in his bullpen. Lyle had the best ERA in the American League that year. A 2.17 ERA for a full 137 innings. In retrospect, Martin going with the best pitcher in the league to face the Royals' best hitter seems obvious, doesn't it?

It is almost inconceivable now that a club would bring in their best reliever in the fourth inning of a game, even in the playoffs. Thirty years after using their weapons fully and creatively, major league managers would lose regularly with their best weapons loaded, and unused.

## Holstering the Weapon

In 2013, both the Braves and the Reds would watch their seasons end with their top relievers safely watching 400 feet away from the mound. This is particularly baffling in that these clubs had not just two of the top pitchers in the game, they had the top two strikeout-percentage pitchers of all time:

### Greatest SO % Single Season

| | |
|---|---|
| 1. 2012 Craig Kimbrel | 50.2% |
| 2. 2012 Aroldis Chapman | 44.2% |

Think about that. There are times in any game where what you need is not just an out, but a strikeout. Here are the two best *ever*. But in the decisive Game 4 of the NL Division Series against the Dodgers, Braves manager Fredi Gonzalez followed the time-honored-but-surely-mistaken practice of saving his relief ace for the ninth inning. The good—but not great—David Carpenter gave up a 3–2 lead in the 8th. Three Atlanta outs later, their season ended, with baseball's strikeout king standing in the pen, looking very threatening.

The Reds' loss was worse. It was a one-game playoff, where you can plan an all-out attack strategy. Skipper Dusty Baker used seven pitchers against the Pirates that day. Not one of them was Aroldis Chapman. Baker cleared out his bullpen, and still avoided using the best lefty reliever in the sport. In a game where his season ended.

## Expanding the Pool

I asked Dan O'Dowd, if he could have implemented a plan without any resistance, what would he have done in Colorado. "I'd have a 13-man staff: two closers, two long relievers, and nine multi-inning pitchers." Simple enough. He then added, "It would also allow me to access pitchers who aren't star quality."

This is a pivotal point. There are a number of reasons why a pitcher would fail as a long-inning traditional starter. You need a variety of pitches, command, knowledge of pitch sequencing, and "stuff" good enough to get through the dreaded third time in the lineup, when hitters have started to better track your pitches. So how big is that talent pool of pitchers who don't quite have all these skills, but have enough to pitch fewer innings? It would, you would think, be pretty large. Lately, we've seen the following pitchers make this type of leap from starting to the bullpen:

### Notable Relievers' Career Splits

|                 | Starter ERA | Reliever ERA |
| --------------- | ----------- | ------------ |
| Wade Davis      | 4.57        | 1.43         |
| Andrew Miller   | 5.70        | 3.02         |
| Zach Britton    | 4.86        | 1.72         |
| Luke Hochevar   | 5.44        | 2.69         |
| Brian Matusz    | 5.51        | 3.16         |
| Glen Perkins    | 5.06        | 2.95         |
| Zach McAllister | 4.52        | 2.54         |

Here are pitchers who didn't just improve when going to the bullpen, they went from "dismal failure" to "incredible success." Maybe it's a guy with a more limited arsenal. Maybe he lacks concentration. Whatever it is, there are bound to be a lot more of them than there are successful seven-inning pitchers. When you access this talent pool, you open yourself up to having mediocre starters move to a more limited role where they can excel.

## The All-Star Model

The All-Star Game has become an excellent example of bullpenning. All-Star Game managers, trying to limit pitcher usage, have stumbled upon an extremely effective way of preventing runs. Over the last decade the All-Star Game has become a primer on an all-out bullpen attack.

Here's how many innings the AL pitching staff threw in 2013:

| | |
|---|---|
| Scherzer | 1 |
| Sale | 2 |
| Hernandez | 1 |
| Moore | 1 |
| Balfour | 1 |
| Holland | $\frac{1}{3}$ |
| Cecil | $\frac{1}{3}$ |
| Delabar | $\frac{1}{3}$ |
| Rivera | 1 |
| Nathan | 1 |

Extreme? Yes? That's 10 pitchers. Effective? Oh yes, they combined for a three-hit shutout. It is an All-Star team, but remember, they are also facing another team loaded with All-Star hitters. Yet after the game, hitters will tell you how they had "no chance" facing a pitcher going full throttle, and then a brand-new pitcher doing the same in the next at bat. It brings up another benefit of bullpenning: the less you see a pitcher, the harder he is to track. Here's batter OPS (on-base plus slugging) by at bat, against starting pitchers, followed by OPS the first time against a reliever:

### 2014 Batters' OPS by Times Facing Opponent

| | |
|---|---|
| 1st time through order: | .677 |
| 2nd time: | .708 |
| 3rd time: | .755 |
| 1st time vs. reliever: | .682 |

On the whole, a batter has more success with each plate appearance against a starting pitcher. That success rate then drops when facing a fresh arm out of the bullpen for the first time. Armed with this information, why would you not switch pitchers—and looks—as often as possible? Or at the very least, switch pitchers after the other train has gone through the order the second time? If getting outs is your goal, there is no reason not to do this.

# The Opener

Let's say your club is not quite ready for the Full Bullpen Attack. You could gain a big advantage by making just one simple switch.

Start with this; we are continually told the toughest outs to get are the last three. This is not the case. The toughest outs to get are the *first* three.

More runs are scored in the first inning than any other. Here's a look since the start of the DH era:

### Runs Scored Per Inning, 1973–2015 (The DH era)

| | |
|---|---|
| 1st | 0.56 |
| 2nd | 0.45 |

| | |
|-----|------|
| 3rd | 0.51 |
| 4th | 0.52 |
| 5th | 0.52 |
| 6th | 0.53 |
| 7th | 0.50 |
| 8th | 0.48 |
| 9th* | 0.41 |

*Home team often doesn't bat in 9th.

The significant scoring advantage in the first inning would seem to be because this is the one time a team can arrange its lineup for maximum effect. Another reason might be because the starter knows he has a long day ahead of him and is pacing himself.

It also could be that many of those runs are coming from pitchers who "don't have it" that day and take a beating in that first inning. This may skew the runs per inning, but the fact remains that the first inning sees the most runs. So what if we used a pitcher just to get out of that inning?

An "opener," a pitcher who pitches just the first inning or two, solves two problems: He attacks the highest scoring inning, and he doesn't bat.

These are two powerful reasons already.

As of 2014, teams were averaging four relievers per game. Using one of your setup guys in the first or the seventh shouldn't matter. A pitcher working the seventh is someone you think is pretty good. A guy with a sub-3 ERA. Your relief ace should not be the opener. As much as the first inning is the top of the order, it's still a clean slate—nobody on, nobody out. A proper allocation seems to be the use of your third best reliever, a seventh-inning pitcher who normally works two innings. In the National League game, a 9 hitter isn't usually batting in the first two innings, so he's free to pitch the opening two, then step aside.

The man who would have been your starter can still be ready to go innings 3 through 6, 7, or 8. If you've got Kershaw working and you must win, go ahead and use him for the next seven innings. If you believe your ace is your best guy, let him close it out. He can do that in about 100 pitches, thanks to the opener. The point is, you work to your pitchers' strengths, and for most pitchers, shorter is better. Here's the basic structure:

Opener: 1st, 2nd innings
Starter: 3rd, 4th, 5th innings
Matchup Relievers: 6th, 7th, 8th
Relief Ace: 6th, 7th, 8th
Finisher: 9th

That's five or six pitchers. Once again, the average per team these days is four. It's not as drastic a change as it might initially appear. With the way the modern staff is used now, there are enough pitchers to bullpen. I have run this scenario through a sample 10-day plan. No pitcher is throwing multiple innings back to back, and no pitcher has to go three straight days. Everyone lands within a reasonable inning total at which we would expect them to succeed.

One last thought for those who think this is so radical. Giants' manager Bruce Bochy—who's just trying to win, and not shake up anybody—went to his bullpen in the *second inning* in both Game 6 *and* Game 7 of the 2014 World Series. The scores at the time were 1–0 Royals, and 2–2. The bases were loaded in that 1–0 Royals lead, but Bochy showed the way; the game is always on the line, and you need to act.

# New Rules!

Let's go over some new ideas as we begin to view the future of baseball:

1.  There are no starters, only pitchers. It made sense to have a starter in the 1800s, where only one pitcher was used per day.

2.  Sprinters are faster than milers. Pitchers are more effective in shorter spurts. Use them that way.

3.  Put each pitcher in a place to succeed. Tony La Russa tried three pitchers for three innings each while with the A's, which at the time was mind-blowing enough. Best, though, to tailor the distribution to your personnel. There are sprinters, 400-meter specialists, and milers. There are pitchers with one pitch, a wide repertoire, and anywhere in between. Some pitchers come armed with big-time fastballs and ultra-high intensity, while others rely on craft and can throw all day. Some have big platoon splits—better against same-handed batters—others are the reverse. The only rule is that you try to put each individual into the best position to succeed.

4.  If you insist on a starter, he doesn't have to start. There is a belief that the most difficult inning to pitch is the ninth. Perhaps psychologically, but it stands to reason the most difficult inning to pitch is the one where the offense is the most successful. That inning is the first inning, the only one where a team is assured of setting its lineup for the best result. Use a good reliever/sprinter type to work the first inning. You are just moving this pitcher's workload from the seventh to the first inning.

5.  If you insist on a closer, he doesn't have to close. By closer you mean "best relief pitcher." Use this man when the game is on the line. This can be simple, or this can be complicated. Let's say you're up 3–1 in the sixth, and your opponent loads the bases. Do you really need the WPA to tell you the game is likely to be decided right here? The win probability can be checked throughout the game by your analytics staff. They're starting to put this stuff on the outfield scoreboard—it's time for managers to know it too.

6.  There are no rules restricting bullpen moves so take advantage. When a move is too effective in a sport, it is outlawed. An offensive lineman can't grab a defender with his hands, a cage fighter can't kick to the groin, a basketball player isn't allowed to guard the basket, swatting away shots. Why? Because all of these things are

*too effective.* A baseball team that makes a multitude of moves, with pitchers throwing in shorter spurts is exploiting a competitive advantage. Once this becomes clear, there is a possibility rules will be put in place to stop it. There have already been columns calling for banning the defensive shift and limiting pitching changes. Until then, it's time to attack with the full staff.

7.    Use your weapons! One argument against bullpenning would be using up your pinch hitters. True, but this is a *good* thing. Possibly the biggest gain to be had offensively, by any NL team, is to replace your offensive sinkhole of pitchers hitting with trained hitters. The average OPS (a crude number, but good enough for this exercise) for a pitcher is .306. The average hitter in the National League (where pitchers hit) has an OPS of .694. If you pinch-hit for your pitcher every time, you would then gain .388 in OPS with every at bat. The gain of .388 points is the equivalent of adding an All-Star hitter to your lineup. An All-Star, by the way, costs about 12–15 million a year on the open market. Pinch-hitting *every* time is probably not possible. But holding your pitcher at bats down as much as possible is a tremendous gain for your offense, at no extra cost.

## The Future Advantage

If professional baseball were starting now, there's no way we would use the current model. We would "bullpen" most days. It will take a certain amount of reconditioning, no doubt, but the benefits of doing this would be enormous.

No more "starters," no more "relievers," no more "wins." Another once useful habit from the nineteenth century will be broken, giving the first to get there a huge advantage.

# 10

# When Bad Contracts Happen to Good People

"You never get what you deserve. You get what you negotiate."

—Don King

I have a theory. I believe a team, even a big-money contender, would benefit by adhering to the following principle:

Never sign a big-money free agent.

I mean never.

More specifically, never sign a player old enough to be a free agent to a long-term deal. You will still want to. You will think the free agent you covet will be the one who is different. The one who will age well. Your guy will definitely be the guy who defies the odds. Sure he will.

I've studied all the $100 million contracts in baseball history. It's a nice round number, and even though it ain't what it used to be (beach-front property has shot way up, as you know), $100 million is still a legitimate milepost of a big-money baseball deal.

On the day these deals are signed, everyone lines up at the news conference to praise the organization for shooting the locks off their wallets, and choosing to "do what it takes to win." It's tough to look at the signing of a legitimate star player as a bad thing. But you're not just signing that healthy young player smiling in front of the local media. You're signing a future version of that player who will rust before your eyes.

There are no easy answers, but there are patterns and cautionary tales. Here they are, the first 30 $100 million free agent contracts. I'm throwing in Daisuke Matsuzaka, Yu Darvish, and Masahiro Tanaka, even though they came via the Japanese posting process. WAR/Year represents the average WAR per year over the life of the contract. In the column on the right I render my verdict on the deal: good, bad, or inconclusive.

### $100 Million Free Agent Contracts

|  | Span | Years | Money (Millions) | Ages | Average WAR/Year | Verdict |
|---|---|---|---|---|---|---|
| Kevin Brown | 1999–05 | 7 | $105 | 34–40 | 3.3 | Good |
| Mike Hampton | 2001–08 | 8 | $121 | 28–35 | 0.5 | Bad |
| Manny Ramirez | 2001–08 | 8 | $160 | 29–36 | 4.6 | Good |
| Alex Rodriguez | 2001–10 | 10 | $252 | 25–34 | 7.1 | Good |
| Jason Giambi | 2002–08 | 7 | $120 | 31–37 | 3.1 | Good |
| Carlos Beltran | 2005–11 | 7 | $119 | 28–34 | 4.6 | Good |
| Daisuke Matsuzaka | 2007–12 | 6 | $103 | 26–31 | 1.5 | Bad |
| Carlos Lee | 2007–12 | 6 | $100 | 31–36 | 1.4 | Bad |
| Barry Zito | 2007–13 | 7 | $126 | 29–35 | 0.4 | Bad |
| Alfonso Soriano | 2007–14 | 8 | $136 | 31–38 | 1 | Bad |
| Alex Rodriguez | 2008–17 | 10 | $275 | 32–41 | 3.6 | Bad |
| CC Sabathia | 2009–15 | 7 | $161 | 28–34 | 6.1* | Good |
| Mark Teixeira | 2009–16 | 8 | $180 | 29–36 | 3.0 | Bad |
| Matt Holliday | 2010–16 | 7 | $120 | 30–36 | 3.4 | Good |
| Cliff Lee | 2011–15 | 5 | $120 | 32–36 | 4.2 | Good |
| Carl Crawford | 2011–17 | 7 | $142 | 29–35 | 1.2 | Bad |
| Jayson Werth | 2011–17 | 7 | $126 | 32–38 | 2.5 | INC |
| CC Sabathia | 2012–16 | 5 | $122 | 31–35 | 1.1 | Bad |
| Jose Reyes | 2012–17 | 6 | $106 | 30–35 | 2.2 | INC |

| | Span | Years | Money (Millions) | Ages | Average WAR/Year | Verdict |
|---|---|---|---|---|---|---|
| Prince Fielder | 2012–20 | 9 | $214 | 28–36 | 2.1 | Bad |
| Yu Darvish | 2012–17 | 6 | $112 | 25–30 | 2.0 | INC |
| Albert Pujols | 2012–21 | 10 | $254 | 32–41 | 3.3 | Bad |
| Zack Greinke | 2013–18 | 6 | $147 | 29–34 | 5.8* | Good |
| Josh Hamilton | 2013–17 | 5 | $125 | 32–36 | 1.1 | Bad |
| Masahiro Tanaka | 2014–20 | 7 | $155 | 25–31 | 3.1 | INC |
| Jacoby Ellsbury | 2014–20 | 7 | $153 | 30–36 | 2.6 | INC |
| Shin-Soo Choo | 2014–20 | 7 | $130 | 31–37 | 1.8 | INC |
| Robinson Cano | 2014–23 | 10 | $240 | 31–40 | 4.9 | INC |
| Jon Lester | 2015–20 | 6 | $155 | 31–36 | 3.1 | INC |
| Max Scherzer | 2015–21 | 7 | $210 | 30–36 | 7.1 | INC |

*WAR/Year before opting out of contract

There were seven more in the 2016 off-season. It's obviously too early to make a call on any of these.

There are wild discrepancies between perception and reality in many of these deals. Many players remembered as busts actually produced very well over the length of the contract. The key point is that most of these deals were seen as good deals for the clubs at the time of signing. When you're spending $100 million, the expectation is huge success. What we have learned from these deals is instructive for all teams. Let's go through the most revealing:

# Kevin Brown

Signed going into his age 34 season, he is remembered as a bust, but Brown was better than you think. Overvalued for the same reason as Jack Morris and Mike Hampton; he was damn good for two different teams in two years, when both teams had success. In searching for reasons that teams win, remember a sportswriter maxim: It's much more fun to lump the credit to a superstar, to "chemistry," or to some sort of alignment of the planets and pixie dust than to say "seven guys played a lot better that year."

After two sensational years with the Marlins and Padres—leading both to pennants—Brown did this with the Dodgers:

|      | IP    | ERA   |
|------|-------|-------|
| 1999 | 252.1 | 3.00  |
| 2000 | 230   | 2.58* |
| 2001 | 115.2 | 2.65  |

*led NL

That's nearly 600 innings of a 2.77 ERA in one of the highest run-scoring periods in baseball history. Yes, he got hurt in 2001 but these were excellent seasons.

Then this happened:

|      | IP   | ERA  |
|------|------|------|
| 2002 | 63.2 | 4.81 |
| 2003 | 211  | 2.39 |

Still injured, 2002 is a complete loss. But 200-plus innings of a 2.39? Why is this guy remembered as a bust?

From 1999 to 2003—the five years with the Dodgers—do you know how many pitchers had a better ERA+ than Kevin Brown? Two. Pedro Martinez and Randy Johnson. With his injury, he didn't pile up the expected innings, but even a cumulative stat like WAR has Brown eighth best in that period.

No, the deal is considered a bust because his team didn't win while *he* was excellent.

# Alex Rodriguez

At the time, one of the most famous numbers in sports: $252 million. Seen as everything wrong with sports, this deal put a bull's-eye on A-Rod that he would never shake.

"According to sports economists and marketing experts, the off-the-chart A-Rod deal pushes Major League Baseball a giant step closer toward impending disaster."

Yet, this is the greatest free agent signing ever. I mean it's also *so* good it's unlikely anyone will ever be a better baseball player signing as a free agent.

I know what you're thinking: "Hey, didn't they run A-Rod out of town on a rail?" Why, yes, they did.

In 2003, the Rangers were sick and tired of Alex Rodriguez, and they showed him the door with seven years left on his deal (ages 28–34).

What the Rangers failed to understand is what they were actually sick and tired of. They thought they were sick of Alex Rodriguez. They were not. They *were* sick of losing. And they were tired of taking crap for having the highest paid player in the game.

But A-Rod? They needed to isolate the player from everything around him. It's not tough. Let's run through the first three years of the Alex Rodriguez deal, his three years in Texas:

|      | G   | OB/SLG     | WAR |
|------|-----|------------|-----|
| 2001 | 162 | .399/.622  | 8.3 |
| 2002 | 162 | .392/.623  | 8.8 |
| 2003 | 161 | .395/.600  | 8.4 |

I have to admit, when I looked this up, I began laughing out loud. *This is the guy they had to trade?*

Let's be clear: The Rangers didn't say, "We think this guy is juicing, and we don't believe in this artificial performance." No, no, no. They traded him because he was branded a loser, and not worth the money. He wasn't a "winning ballplayer." If we were advising the Rangers back then, we would tell them to stop talking to A-Rod, and just sit back and watch him play. Oh yeah, and play every day. Because he missed one game in three years.

Since 1961, these are three of the top 10 shortstop seasons in WAR. Each season is not only staggeringly good, they are remarkably consistent. Here's where he ranked among the American League leaders those three years in Texas:

WAR: 3rd, 1st, 1st
Total bases: 1st, 1st, 2nd
Home runs: 1st, 1st, 1st
Double plays as SS: 2nd, 1st, 1st

Yep, this guy *has got to go.*

The Rangers in those years had all sorts of offensive talent: Juan Gonzalez, Michael Young, an aging Rafael Palmeiro, and a young Mark Teixeira. Pretty good group. Yet they went 73–89, 72–90, and 71–91. Hitting overall was not an issue.

Their team ERA in those years? 5.71, 5.15, and 5.67. I think we've located the problem. Solution? Blame A-Rod!

A-Rod of course went to the Yankees, moved to third base to accommodate the incumbent *winning* shortstop (Jeter), and over the next five years, had an average WAR of 7.5. That was the second highest WAR in baseball for those years, trailing only Albert Pujols.

Over the 10 years of this contract, Rodriguez was a 7-win player, averaging 7.1 WAR. So Rangers owner Tom Hicks, super-agent Scott Boras, and A-Rod were all correct: $252 million was *not* too much to spend on a ballplayer. Not one going into his age 25 season, anyway.

The second A-Rod deal? That's another story. A-Rod opted out with three years left on the original deal, and renegotiated a new 10-year, $275 million deal. Year one of that deal would start a new seven-year extension starting in his age-35 season. Just reading that you know how awful it is.

But the $252 mil? Money well spent.

# Jason Giambi

In many ways the cautionary tale for free agent spending. Giambi is everything you will think you want but don't: a big slugging first baseman who was great in his 20s but is now going into his 30s.

And yet this signing is unfairly remembered as a bust. While the Bombers appeared to get a less-juiced, post-BALCO Giambi, here's what he did in the Bronx:

### Giambi as a Yankee, 2002–2008

| OB | Slugging | OPS+ | Avg WAR |
|---|---|---|---|
| .404 | .521 | 143 | 3.1 |

He played half seasons in 2004 and 2008, but was otherwise quite productive. It was, however, a shell of his super-juiced godlike performance the previous three years:

### Giambi with Oakland, 1999–2001

| OBP | SLG | OPS+ | Avg WAR |
|---|---|---|---|
| .462 | .634 | 186 | 7.6 |

Damn.

Only Barry Bonds had a higher OPS+ in those three years. Giambi was better than Manny Ramirez, Sammy Sosa, and Mark McGwire. Giant hormone-fueled supermen roamed the earth in those days, and Giambi was just about the most fearsome.

But was the Giambino a Bronx Bust? No, he was not. He had the 11th best OPS+ in baseball over those seven years.

No, he is remembered as a bust because of his team's failure in the postseason. I say postseason because, while the club won an average 97 games a year in that period, the lack of a World Series title made the Giambi/Mussina years seem disappointing.

This was not Giambi's fault, not even in the postseason. He played in 32 games in the playoffs, putting up a studly .409/.510 in 127 plate appearances. In one of the most famous games in baseball playoff history, he hit two solo home runs off Pedro Martinez in what turned out to be the Grady Little/Aaron Boone game. Again, Giambi and Mussina (three shutout innings, got out of a bases loaded jam left by Roger Clemens) are lost to "clutch" history because their clutchness did not come at the time most easily remembered. The Giambi signing, however, was a good one.

# Mike Hampton

Part of free agent lore in two ways:

1. In keeping with the baseball player tradition of not wanting to appear greedy, Hampton cited the Denver school system as the reason for accepting an eight-year $121 million deal. Please just tell us it's the money. We all understand. Really.
2. For being inexplicably terrible.

Hampton was overrated because of things not directly tied to his actual skills. He was 22–4 with the Astros in 1999 (another hapless victim of the W), and then led the Mets to the pennant in 2000. He was quite good both years, but he was overvalued. His strikeout rate was a below-average 6.5 per 9, while walking an above-average 3.5 per 9. And that was in his peak years. And yet, going into his age 28 season, Denver—and its school system—deserved better. Hampton had a 5.75 ERA in his two years with the Rockies before they gave up. He produced a WAR of 2.9 over the eight years of the contract. The horror.

# Alfonso Soriano

Not as bad as you might think. But only because it's often lumped with the worst free agent contracts of all time. .313/.489 and just about 8 WAR spread out over the eight years. Yes, this is bad, but at least it was 26-homers-a-year bad.

# Carlos Lee

This is what happens when you believe in magical things, like "RBI Machines." At six years, $100 million, the less than crippling length saves it. Lee was a nice player through his 20s:

| OB% | Slugging | OPS+ |
|---|---|---|
| .340 | .495 | 113 |

(League average being 100, 113 ain't so great.)

In the modern parlance, he was a three-win player in his prime. At the time (2007 still being the dark ages in Houston), he was a guy who "knew how to drive in runs." Here's what he did for those six years:

| OB% | Slugging | OPS+ |
|---|---|---|
| .337 | .466 | 113 |

Hey, wait a second. Stunningly, he was just about the same offensive player in his 20s and seen as a star, as he was in his 30s, when seen as a guy with a bloated contract.

Lee was durable—626 PA per season—and had the exact same OPS+. But he unfortunately went from "guy in his 20s" to "guy in his 30s." His defense and baserunning, never a strong point as a young player, slowed down enough to turn him from a three-win player in the first half of his career to a 1.4-win player in the second half.

Lee then, is an excellent cautionary tale. He did his job. He did not disappoint. He did what he was supposed to do over the second half of his career: Hit for some power, and aged normally.

The problem, here and most of the time, is paying retail for the privilege of watching a player calcify.

# Albert Pujols

My examination of big-money deals began with Pujols's entry into the free agent market. Having just arrived at MLB Network in 2011, I had sent an email of all my sabermetric ideas to VP of production John Entz and network president Tony Petitti. Given my history of slamming my head into a wall trying to get this stuff on TV, I was shocked when they told me they not only liked these ideas, they actually thought what I proposed could be its own show.

*Clubhouse Confidential!* began right after the 2011 season, running right into the big-money free agent class of Pujols, Prince Fielder, and Jose Reyes.

As with all of these deals, you need to take yourself back to the time they were happening and consider the perception of the player and market. It is hard to emphasize just how high Pujols's stock was that off-season. Pujols was not only an all-time great in our midst, but was also still seen as a franchise-changing player, two years removed from an MVP season, and just off leading the Cardinals to a World Series title. In the 2011 postseason, he hit .353, with an on-base of .463, slugging .691. He was seen as the best player in baseball.

As I got to work in my evaluation of that year's free agents, I would quickly see that this was not the case.

Let's start the process. Here was Pujols the previous three years:

|  | OBP | SLG |
|---|---|---|
| 2009 | .443* | .658* |
| 2010 | .414 | .596 |
| 2011 | .366 | .541 |

*led league

He was starting from the stratosphere of the greats, but his trajectory was clear. He was trending down.

Not only that, his postseason flash of power (five home runs, three in the one World Series game) masked something unmistakable if you were actually watching his at bats: His strike zone discipline was eroding.

Does that sentence look frightening to you? Worse things could happen, right? A player could go into bankruptcy, he could get hit in the head with a pitch, and plenty of things would sound much worse. But those are words that should buckle your knees.

Here is Pujols again over those last three years with the Cardinals. "Chase percentage" is the percentage of swings at pitches *outside* the strike zone. Chasing pitches, as any Little League coach will tell you, is a bad habit:

|  | Walk % | Chase % |
|---|---|---|
| 2009 | 16.4 | 22.9 |
| 2010 | 14.7 | 27.5 |
| 2011 | 9.4 | 31.8 |

Uh-oh. Another clear trend in the works. Walks are never exciting. I get it. But the ability to control your strike zone—and force pitchers to bring you pitches you can punish—is the foundation of your hitting. It's not just taking a base, it's also getting pitches you can drill. Pujols had a problem. And nobody wanted to hear it.

I wrote one essay after another for *Clubhouse Confidential*, pointing out the emperor's new clothes. Analysts—even the sabermetric variety— told me that this guy was different, that Pujols was an all-time great, would make adjustments, and I shouldn't worry my pretty little head over his chase rate. For God's sake, did you just see him hit three home runs in a World Series game? Do you watch the game? Do you even like baseball? It seemed blasphemous to be pointing this out, but it was staring me in the face.

We had a slugging first baseman going into his age-32 season. A slugger with diminishing physical skills and a crumbling process.

Fortunately, no one was listening to me. Pujols was underpaid by the Cardinals while hitting like Lou Gehrig, so getting a windfall seemed to be some sort of baseball justice. And overpaid he was. A blockbuster-just-above-A-Rod $254 million deal.

It was universally lauded. The Angels had gotten the best player in baseball. Viewed as a demonstration of baseball's power shift to the West, Pujols and C. J. Wilson were both introduced at a news conference outside of Angels Stadium. The mood? Jubilant.

Harold Reynolds and I were brought in on a Saturday to host the televised introductions. I stifled the urge to do hard-core analysis, as everyone seemed so damn happy. As I sat there though, I did have this thought: The Cardinals, whose offer was spurned by Pujols, had to be relieved.

I then went through not just baseball's $100 million deals, but all the big free agent deals through baseball history, and tried to spot why so many seemingly went so wrong. I went back to Catfish Hunter (seems good, but was bad), Wayne Garland (crazy long and bad), Reggie Jackson (all good), Alex Rodriguez (first deal terrific), George Foster (incredibly bad), and every big signing I could find. I found the following red flags that seemed to keep popping up in the deals that ended badly. If we could develop a methodology, it could take some of the bad decision making out of a team's hands. Here are those five red flags:

1.   Wrong Side of 30
2.   Wrong Side of the Defensive Spectrum
3.   Misreading of the Metrics

4. Contract Longer than Five Years
5. Branding over Baseball

Simplistic, sure, but have you noticed what's NOT on the list?

Money. The amount spent, oddly enough, is rarely the problem. The problems arise when the money continues to be spent year after year, and you're stuck with that player occupying space on your roster. This sparks a whole new outlook on a future wave: the big-money, short-term deal. But first, let's go through the minefield.

## 1. WRONG SIDE OF 30

If you want just one rule, this is it. You would be well served just having this one guideline. Age is everything. You will now go through your mind gathering up all the players who were great when they were old. Yes, there are exceptions—they are in the Hall of Fame, were on steroids, or both.

## 2. WRONG SIDE OF THE DEFENSIVE SPECTRUM

This one is mainly to stop buying a slugging first baseman. Bill James was among the first to say an athletic player will age better. Like you and me, a player will age, get heavier, get slower. In baseball this means leaving a defensive position for an easier one. If you're a shortstop, you have several moves—to second base, third base, maybe an outfield spot. If you're already a big dude lumbering around at first base, you have one move—leave the field and become a DH. We used to think that once a player couldn't field or run he'd still be able to hit for a few years. We were wrong.

(The DH rule was put in when Tony Oliva, Harmon Killebrew, and Hank Aaron were losing their wheels. It was expected that the DH spot would be a way station for the aging star, with the studs of yesterday hitting away for a few more golden years. This did not happen. Big Papi and Frank Thomas are the exceptions. Most sluggers lose their ability to hit right about the time they lose their ability to field. I'm sorry to break this to you.)

## 3. MISREADING OF THE METRICS

The pitching win-loss record was considered to be an indicator of pitching skill. I'm not talking about just fans, I'm talking about actual baseball executives getting paid to think about baseball.

Wayne Garland went 20–7. Mike Hampton went 37–14 over two seasons. Barry Zito was 16–10 with a good ERA. What was ignored was that Zito was in a pitcher's park, and more importantly both Zito and Hampton had about six strikeouts per nine, and four walks. This is below league average. There are a lot of ways to survive a low strikeout rate: controlling the running game, throwing a pitch that induces weak contact, and luck seem to be the primary methods. Surviving a low strikeout rate alongside a high walk rate, however, is not possible. It's a matter of time before the BABIP (batting average on balls put into play—see Glossary) gods exact their revenge.

Even in this more sophisticated age, though, evidence is ignored. The Angels ignored the hacktastic trends of both Pujols and Josh Hamilton. No one in a major league front office these days is looking at batting average or win-loss records to evaluate a player, but there is always a tendency to ignore evidence that doesn't fit your perception.

## 4. CONTRACT LONGER THAN FIVE YEARS

I was at a charity auction once where the auctioneer was egging on a roomful of reluctant bidders. He shot out the best line I'd ever heard regarding finances: "It's only money, you can make more."

Also true for baseball teams. Money of course matters, but a short-term deal that doesn't work is part of the budget. Soon it's over and you turn the page. An aging, unproductive relic however, continues to occupy a spot on the roster and forces you to make less than optimal decisions. Your hands are tied for years. Good minor league players are blocked and alternatives are ignored while teams wish for a bounce-back year that will help justify the investment. In life, and in baseball, you can make more money, but you can't make more time.

## 5. BRANDING OVER BASEBALL

This one should be subtitled "Ownership Involvement." If a signing is made to "make the franchise relevant," to "put fannies in seats," "put the team on the map," "convince other free agents to sign here," or to sell merchandise, avert your eyes from the train wreck ahead.

Here is the only good reason to sign a free agent: "He will help us win baseball games."

Signing a star to "make a splash" is a sign that an agent hoodwinked an owner who is thinking of his team's brand. What owners need to know is that winning and only winning helps the brand.

You build a methodology to help with your decision making. It's more difficult to ignore evidence if you set up a methodology, run your proposal through it, and it fails miserably. I would say two red flags out of five is a good sign that you should pass on the free agent. Three makes it an easy call.

So let's run the Angels/Pujols deal through our red flag system:

1. Wrong Side of 30. Check
2. Wrong Side of Defensive Spectrum. Check
3. Misreading of the Metrics. Check
4. Contract Longer than Five Years. Oh, yeah.
5. Branding over Baseball. You betcha.

Yikes. The Pujols deal is a clean sweep: 5 for 5.

Given all this, what happened the next two years was still surprising. Injuries, or who knows what, seemed to exacerbate Pujols's problems, and a steady slide became a cliff:

|              | OB   | SLG  |
|--------------|------|------|
| 2011 (Cards) | .366 | .541 |
| 2012 (Angels)| .343 | .516 |
| 2013 (Angels)| .330 | .437 |
| 2014 (Angels)| .324 | .466 |

That made it six straight years of a declining on-base, and four years of a declining slugging percentage. With a full seven years left on the deal, there is little evidence that this deal will be worth the money.

Teams can learn projection analysis, and the lessons of history, or they can choose to ignore them. The Angels, in their haste to spend and dominate, chose to plunge in blindly, albeit to great applause.

# Josh Hamilton

The Angels deserve their own chapter: five years, $125 million. Let's run it through the system:

1. Wrong Side of 30? Entering age 32. Yep
2. Wrong Side of The Defensive Spectrum? Had just left CF for LF. Yes.
3. Misreading of the Metrics? Big-time. Will explain below.
4. Contract Longer than Five Years? No. The only good part of the deal.
5. Branding over Baseball? No. I think they dug the star power, but I also believe they just wanted a power hitter.

So the Hamilton deal loses, 3–2. The misreading of the metrics, though, was enough to make this deal easy to predict.

As we have learned with Albert Pujols, chasing pitches outside of the strike zone is a very bad thing. Here are Hamilton's strikeout and chase percentages for the three years prior to signing with the Angels:

|      | SO % | Chase % |
|------|------|---------|
| 2010 | 16.6 | 37.3    |
| 2011 | 17.3 | 41      |
| 2012 | 25.5 | 45.4    |

Oh my. An alarming jump in strikeouts, stemming from Hamilton's startling lack of discipline. In 2011, Hamilton was in the major league bottom 10 in both contact rate and chasing pitches outside of the strike zone. By 2012, he was the worst in the league in both categories, and both by a wide margin.

It's not like this was a secret known only to FanGraphs nerds. Down the stretch in 2012, Hamilton was in a free fall before our eyes.

In the final three-game series with the A's, the Rangers needed to win just one game to clinch the AL West title. The A's stunningly won all three to force a one-game playoff. In the series, Hamilton went 2-for-13 with six strikeouts. What's most remembered is Hamilton botching an easy fly ball in the fourth inning of the final game, leading to the Oakland comeback. While this may have been symptomatic of his lack of focus, certainly anyone can miss a fly ball. It's the erosion of his plate discipline that was more alarming.

Forced to the Wild Card game against the Orioles, Hamilton then went 0-for-4, and even striking out twice, saw just eight pitches. This is some bad process. He came up four times, struck out twice, and with a first-pitch double-play he made four outs. To do that, he had to see at least eight pitches. And that's what he did.

To summarize:

1. He was turning 32.
2. He had just lost his ability to play center field.
3. He had a great start, which masked a season of offensive decline.
4. His contact rate was the worst in the major leagues.
5. His chase rate was the worst in the major leagues.
6. He had an inexplicable lack of focus with the season on the line, becoming pivotal in an epic collapse.

You don't need a Department of Decision Sciences to tell you *not* to spend $125 million on this guy. But spend it the Angels did. They would pay most of it, even after trading him to Texas in year 3 of the deal. All told they will be paying Hamilton around $73 million for *nothing*. To *not* play for them. Notice we don't have to go into Hamilton's off-field issues as a factor. The evidence needed was all on the field.

# Robinson Cano

With this one too soon to call, let's run the deal through the pre-signing checklist. For about the same money as the Pujols deal in 2011—10 years, two hundred forty million dollars:

1. Wrong Side of 30. Check
2. Wrong Side of the Defensive Spectrum? No, second base.
3. Misreading of the Metrics? No, Cano was still an elite power hitter at a position where he towered above his peers.
4. Contract Longer than Five Years? Check
5. Branding over Baseball? Possibly, but I believe the Mariners signed Cano more for his baseball skill than his personality.

A similar investment to the Pujols deal—but one with only two red flags out of five, as opposed to five for five for the Pujols deal.

Only problem is, one of those two is badly violated. A 10-year deal for a 31-year-old is likely to be a *real* problem. Even though Cano is a second baseman, where would he likely go next? Third base and the outfield corner spots are not realistic. At a certain point in his late 30s, it seems likely Cano will be an aging, eroding hitter, playing first base. This is a bad scene, man. That's age 38, 39, and 40 at $24 million a pop.

Looking back, GM Brian Cashman and the Yankees made the right call. With Derek Jeter's retirement only a year away, they had to be feeling the pressure to re-sign their star hitter. This was a club that kept its stars. Even when Jeter, Bernie Williams, and Mariano Rivera were allowed to hit the free agent market, they were hauled back into the fold. The Yankees weren't cheap, they offered $25 million a year, for seven years.

In the moment, yes, you want to keep Robinson Cano. But the Yankees, facing the fresh sting of the Alex Rodriguez, Mark Teixeira, and CC Sabathia contracts, had powerful reminders to be prudent.

# $100 Million Contract Extensions

The modern path to success is clear: Do not pay retail. Draft and develop talent. Identify that player who can start for you for a number of years. Pay that man by extending his contract while still under club control, while you still have leverage.

This is not especially difficult. Do you need to be told to throw money at Mike Trout and Andrew McCutchen? No. But beyond that, any three-win player in his early 20s is worth locking up. It's not a perfect system, but better to have a $25 million Cameron Maybin mistake than a $240 million Pujols disaster.

So let's broaden the scope to ALL $100 million deals. This now includes contract extensions—deals made when the club still has control over the player. This means the player should be younger, giving the club a much better chance of success.

At the beginning of the chapter, we saw the free agent deals of $100 million or more. Here now are the $100 million *contract extensions*.

### $100 Million Contract Extensions

|  | Span | Years | Money (Millions) | Ages | Average WAR/Year | Verdict |
|---|---|---|---|---|---|---|
| Ken Griffey Jr. | 2000–08 | 9 | $116.50 | 30–38 | 1.5 | Bad |
| Derek Jeter | 2001–10 | 10 | $189.00 | 27–36 | 4.1 | Good |
| Todd Helton | 2003–11 | 9 | $141.50 | 29–37 | 3.6 | Good |
| Albert Pujols | 2004–10 | 7 | $100.00 | 31–36 | 8.6 | Good |

(continued on next page)

| | Span | Years | Money (Millions) | Ages | Average WAR/Year | Verdict |
|---|---|---|---|---|---|---|
| Johan Santana | 2008–13 | 6 | $137.50 | 29–34 | 3.8 | Bad |
| Vernon Wells | 2008–14 | 7 | $126.00 | 29–35 | 1.1 | Bad |
| Miguel Cabrera | 2008–15 | 8 | $153.30 | 25–32 | 5.8 | Good |
| Joe Mauer | 2011–18 | 8 | $184.00 | 28–35 | 2.9 | Bad |
| Troy Tulowitzki | 2011–20 | 10 | $157.75 | 26–35 | 4.0 | Good |
| Ryan Howard | 2012–16 | 5 | $125.00 | 32–36 | −0.8 | Bad |
| Matt Cain | 2012–17 | 6 | $127.50 | 27–32 | 0.9 | Bad |
| Adrian Gonzalez | 2012–18 | 7 | $154.00 | 30–36 | 3.8 | Good |
| Matt Kemp | 2012–19 | 8 | $160.00 | 27–34 | 1.1 | Bad |
| Cole Hamels | 2013–18 | 6 | $144.00 | 29–34 | 5.2 | Good |
| Justin Verlander | 2013–19 | 7 | $180.00 | 30–36 | 2.6 | Bad |
| Felix Hernandez | 2013–19 | 7 | $175.00 | 27–33 | 5.3 | Good |
| David Wright | 2013–20 | 8 | $138.00 | 30–37 | 3.0 | INC |
| Buster Posey | 2013–21 | 9 | $167.00 | 26–34 | 5.4 | Good |
| Homer Bailey | 2014–19 | 6 | $105.00 | 28–33 | 0.7 | INC |
| Ryan Zimmerman | 2014–19 | 6 | $100.00 | 29–34 | 0.6 | Bad |
| Clayton Kershaw | 2014–20 | 7 | $215.00 | 26–32 | 7.5 | Good |
| Freddie Freeman | 2014–21 | 8 | $135.00 | 24–31 | 3.1 | INC |
| Joey Votto | 2014–23 | 10 | $225.00 | 30–39 | 4.8 | INC |
| Dustin Pedroia | 2015–21 | 7 | $100.00 | 30–36 | 2.0 | INC |
| Kyle Seager | 2015–21 | 7 | $100.00 | 27–33 | 4.3 | INC |
| Elvis Andrus | 2015–22 | 8 | $120.00 | 26–33 | 2.1 | INC |
| Giancarlo Stanton | 2015–27 | 13 | $325.00 | 25–37 | 3.7 | INC |
| Ryan Braun | 2016–20 | 5 | $105.00 | 32–36 | – | Bad |
| Miguel Cabrera | 2016–23 | 8 | $248.00 | 33–40 | – | INC |
| Evan Longoria | 2017–22 | 6 | $100.00 | 31–36 | – | INC |

Whoa. Not much better. Clearly we have a bunch that are too early to make a judgment on, but I thought these deals would be better than 50 percent.

When I think of extensions, I have a positive connotation. The Yankees locking up a 26-year-old Derek Jeter, the Cardinals extending a 24-year-old Albert Pujols. But there's also the bad calls on Vernon Wells and Ryan Howard.

Here's the box score on contract extensions only:

| | |
|---|---|
| Total: | 30 |
| Good: | 10 |
| Bad: | 10 |
| Inconclusive: | 10 |

So contract extensions, at least at this high level, have not been the universally positive move I initially thought them to be. This is telling. Not only is age a major issue, the mere act of *aging* is too. Players change. Even players with great hitting skill and plate discipline, like Joey Votto and Joe Mauer, turned into very different hitters, only a year after signing huge deals. Ken Griffey Jr. averaged 159 games a year his last three years in Seattle. He averaged 100 games a year the next seven for Cincinnati. What changed? He went from being a guy in his 20s to a guy in his 30s. That's about it.

Let's put all the $100 million contracts together:

**ALL $100 million contracts**

(Extensions and Free Agent Deals)

| | |
|---|---|
| Total: | 60 |
| Good: | 19 |
| Bad: | 22 |
| Inconclusive: | 19 |

With this group—comprising the top players in the game—there are 41 deals that can be described as good or bad.

Of the 41, only 19 of the deals can be described as successful.

*More than half of these deals would presumably not have been done, if the club could have seen the future.*

Keep in mind, these are not small problems, these are big ones. These are the mistakes that cripple you for years—a major allocation of resources, a big percentage of your budget, and with rare exceptions a player that clogs up a position because he earns too much to sit on the bench.

Here is a competitive advantage to be learned: Walk away. Don't do it. Don't sign a big-money deal.

# 11

# Hall of Fame

"Sportswriters, in my opinion, almost never use baseball statistics to try to understand baseball. They use statistics to decorate their articles."

—Bill James

Prepping for the 2012 Hall of Fame Induction Ceremony, I'm writing some notes on Barry Larkin, and thinking the sportswriters deserve some credit. Barry Larkin isn't an ironman like Cal Ripken and he's not in the 500 home run club like Ernie Banks. They're putting in a non-home-run-hitting shortstop just three years into the ballot. Good job by them.

I wrote down:

**Barry Larkin:**
12-time All-Star
1990 World Series MVP
1995 NL MVP
3-time Gold Glover
9-time Silver Slugger at shortstop
.295 lifetime batting average

So, yeah, check that thought. *This is obvious.* It's one signature career highlight after another! You'd have to not follow baseball to *not* know this was the résumé of a Baseball Hall of Famer.

It brings to mind the disclaimer that comes before most examinations of the history of Hall of Fame voting: "Throughout the decades, the baseball writers have by and large done a fine job . . . blah, blah, blah . . ."

Why, yes they have. By voting in only the most obvious candidates, the Baseball Writers Association of America has held the line in keeping the Hall a most exclusive group. Many a veterans' committee has inducted a borderline candidate, but the baseball writers have upheld strict standards.

Well, that's one way of looking at it. But how hard is it to figure out that Bob Feller and Mickey Mantle are Hall of Famers? Most of the players voted into the Hall by the writers also would have been voted in by a panel of fourth-grade baseball fans. The writers deserve credit for this?

Pre-steroids era, these calls were easy. "Hey, Johnny Bench and Carl Yastrzemski are eligible. Wonder what we should do?" Right about 1940, you could have had the Hall of Fame president make the call by himself. He could do it the Sunday after the World Series ended while having his afternoon tea, and he wouldn't even miss dinner. It would take about 10 minutes of checking out the new players on the ballot. Here's a seven-year run starting in 1977:

1977: Ernie Banks
1978: Hoyt Wilhelm
1979: Willie Mays
1980: Al Kaline
1981: Bob Gibson, Harmon Killebrew, Juan Marichal
1982: Hank Aaron, Frank Robinson, Billy Williams
1983: Brooks Robinson

How hard is that? If your interpretation of the process is to allow only the all-time greats into the Hall of Fame, you've made the job very simple. In that particular stretch, the writers made Wilhelm, Killebrew, Marichal, and Williams wait more than one year, but at least they got all of them in. Yet we continue to congratulate our baseball college of cardinals on their mastery of the obvious.

The hard part for the baseball writers is at the border. This is where they need to be *experts*. To have the ability to do *analysis*, not just vote in a 12-time All-Star. This is where they continue to fail.

# The First Vote

The people in Cooperstown had their beautiful little village named the birthplace of the sport in 1905. In the mid-1930s, they began to move toward something tangible. A gallery with some artifacts seemed like a nice idea, maybe even an old-age home for retired ballplayers. Only at the end, had there been the talk of a Hall of Fame to go with the museum. There was a Centennial Commission in charge of the whole project, but it wanted no part of deciding who deserved to be in the brand-new Hall. This would be controversial, and they could be skewered by the sportswriters. Hey, wait a second . . .

Yes, they gave the vote to the only people regularly watching and studying the game of baseball, the ones who could also provide stories on the whole endeavor: the baseball beat writers and columnists.

In the 1930s, the baseball writers were *precisely* the people to be entrusted with the duty of voting on the Hall of Fame. There was no Internet, no sabermetrics, no TV or radio analysts. Ballgames began to be broadcast regularly on radio in 1939, the year a broadcasting embargo was broken in New York. The only way to fully study baseball players back then was to go to the games. The only people going to see the games all the time were the baseball writers. Statistics were difficult to come by. The culture was still developing.

At the time of the 1939 Induction Ceremony, Babe Ruth was a retired player all of four years. In the famous photo of the first Hall of

Fame class, the men look like aged legends from a bygone era, but the Bambino was only 44 years old. Walter Johnson was just 51, the same age as Rickey Henderson and Randy Johnson when they were inducted. Eddie Collins, sitting in the front row, part of both the Black Sox *and* the "$100,000 Infield," is only 55. They lived tougher years back then. Seventy-two-year-old Cy Young is sitting right there, next to still active A's manager Connie Mack.

At the time of the first Hall of Fame vote, the National Pastime was still a relatively young professional sport. The game's all-time greats were mostly still alive. Hall of Fame founder Stephen Clark, ably assisted by Alexander Cleland and National League president Ford Frick, had gotten in early.

The Baseball Writers Association of America had the largest concentration of baseball experts anywhere, and their votes from 1936 to 1939 did a solid job of recognizing the greatest players of the previous generations.

But somewhere along the way, it had to become obvious that baseball expertise was no longer exclusive to the baseball writer. The media had developed into a deep pool of baseball authors, historians, and broadcasters. The time had come to update the voting electorate. Instead, the status quo held.

Years later, it makes even less sense. There is now an entire industry devoted to comparative analysis in baseball. Yet the *very best people* in this field do not vote. This includes Bill James and John Thorn, the two men with the most knowledge analytically and historically. Broadcaster/ historian Bob Costas does not have a vote. Neither does Keith Olbermann, nor Rob Neyer, who has written a dozen books on baseball history, nor Jay Jaffe, who writes Hall of Fame columns year-round. Until 2015 there were over 700 voters and there isn't room for the 20–30 people who follow baseball most closely?

The Hall of Fame Board of Directors finally made a move on the bloated voting rolls for 2015. Writers no longer covering the sport will not be able to keep their vote forever. They were granted a 10-year grace period before being dropped. This could cut out many of the voters no longer paying attention, or up to the task. It's a good step, but it's not the massive improvement that is possible.

The panel would not be difficult to put together. It would of course include many voting right now. You wouldn't exclude Peter Gammons, Ken Rosenthal, Joel Sherman, Tom Verducci, Joe Posnanski, Richard Justice, Tim Kurkjian, Jayson Stark, or Jon Heyman. Anyone doing the work of comparative baseball analysis on the national scene should be a vital part of the process. It's not difficult to figure out who knows what they're talking about. They're writing columns about the Hall of Fame, aren't they? Most of us could tell you within the first column if they have a good logical and analytical process. The top writers—like the ones mentioned above—obviously make the cut. They and about 50 others would join the authors and historians who pioneered this work such as James, Thorn, and others.

I'm told this would be very difficult to do. But it would take me about a month to do it, start to finish. It's easy. It's a matter of separating the wheat from the considerable sportswriting chaff.

# The Enduring Debate

Hall of Fame debates endure because they trigger so many of the things we love about baseball. They engage our opinions and memories, mixing analysis with nostalgia. A Hall of Fame discussion sharpens our focus on a particular player and period of time. The world, even the world of baseball, is wide and complex. Taking on too much information is distressing. Arguing the merits of one particular player allows us to satisfy the part of ourselves that wants to make sense of our world.

A Hall of Fame debate snaps things into instant focus. Asking if Alan Trammell is a great player doesn't yield an interesting or focused response. Asking if Alan Trammell is a Hall of Famer, however, ignites a whole new thought process that invites inquiry and comparison. The discussion on Trammell quickly brings Cal Ripken Jr. into the debate. Then

Barry Larkin. You start to go back in time—how does he stack up against Luke Appling, Lou Boudreau, Joe Cronin? The history of baseball unfolds before you, but in a sliver thin enough for you to comprehend and analyze. This is the staying power of the Hall of Fame debate.

In the 1970s and '80s, there was a dearth of Hall of Fame debate and discussion. I remember devouring anything written by Bill Madden in the New York *Daily News*. Pre-Internet, you had to hope there was a local baseball writer who cared. The columns would pop up around Christmas and New Year's, when the writers were voting, and then be put on the shelf for another year.

My Hall of Fame analysis was, at the time, unsophisticated. I looked at totals. It seemed to make sense. Who deserves to be among the top 1 percent all time? Well, who's in the top 1 percent in everything? By "everything," though, I looked at hits, batting average, home runs, RBIs, and wins. I was as brainwashed as everyone else. Why would the experts in the field not know what they were looking at? Why not work off the accepted knowledge?

In only a few years, we would learn why. Generations of experts had no idea what they were looking at. You have to remember, pre–sports talk radio and pre-Internet, the sportswriters were the critics, and it ended there. No one was there to criticize *them*. Then along came Bill James laying waste to them: "They use statistics as a club in the battle for what they believe intuitively to be correct. That is why sportswriters often believe that you can prove anything with statistics, an obscene and ludicrous position, but one which is the natural outgrowth of the way that they themselves use statistics."

James would write the book on Hall of Fame debate—*Whatever Happened to the Hall of Fame?*—in 1994. As with everything else James wrote, his powers of analysis came not from his ability with numbers, but from his endless persistence in *asking more questions*.

So let's dig a little deeper than the Masters of the Apparent do, and using a Jamesian process examine four obvious Hall of Fame careers that have somehow gone unnoticed by those with the power of the vote.

# The Missing Hall of Famers

I've been watching baseball my whole life, and covering baseball, in some form, since 1986. In joining MLB Network in 2011, though, I experienced a deeper immersion into the game.

Sitting on the *MLB Tonight* set night after night, watching every game in Major League Baseball unfold, gives one a deeper perspective. We're not churning out highlights, we're jumping into the games live, and watching them unfold one by one. It's a fascinating process, and we all learn things together as we speak over the games.

You have every game on a screen in front of you. You have producers cueing up every significant moment of every game for you to see, and then show the viewers. You have editors showing you every angle of any play, and seeing it instantly, as precisely as possible. You have researchers speaking to you to give you instant context on what each play meant to that particular game. You are sitting there with two or three ex-players or sportswriters in a fluid, ongoing discussion of what is happening, and what it all means.

If observation is the basis of scientific inquiry, then working an *MLB Tonight* is the best baseball laboratory in which to learn. A baseball reporter at a game sees dozens of plays. Working *MLB Tonight*, you will see several *hundred*. After a full six-month season, you have had the opportunity to digest the equivalent of what used to be a lifetime of baseball.

Between watching these games, we will have a constant stream of MVP, Cy Young, Rookie of the Year, and Hall of Fame discussions. It was during one of these arguments that I had a revelation: The mystifying part of the these debates was the disconnect between what we valued when we were watching the games, and what we valued once they were over.

While watching the games, defense and baserunning are seen as vitally important. Range was vital. Sloppy play—and not necessarily errors—were game changers. I would sit night after night where Bill Ripken, Harold Reynolds, or Dan Plesac would point out the important parts of the game that could easily go unnoticed: A ball knocked down and kept in the in-field that prevented a run from scoring. A tough double play wiping out a run that was otherwise crossing the plate. A runner quick enough to take two bases on a single. All these things add up, they just don't add up into one category for easy comparison. While watching the games though, ex-players recognize and value these vital components of the sport.

So, when we bring up stellar defenders for Hall of Fame consideration, I would ask a voter to take themselves back, and imagine Keith Hernandez, Dwight Evans, and Alan Trammell *actually playing the game.*

# The Best Ever

For years now, I have had Keith Hernandez at the top of the Hall of Fame–snubbed list. When I bring this up on a TV or radio show, other people say, "Keith Hernandez! Are you kidding me?"

No, I am not.

Part of Hernandez's problem as a candidate is branding. When we think "Hall of Fame first baseman," we all envision a lumbering home run hitter. This is the image imprinted in our minds, from Lou Gehrig to Harmon Killebrew. Keith Hernandez looks nothing like that, and did not play like that. But Hernandez is absolutely a Hall of Fame first baseman.

Let's start with this: Keith Hernandez is the greatest fielder, at this position, of all time. Doesn't this mean something? Not "was an excellent fielder," but "Best Ever over a 120 year period."

Fielding is difficult to quantify, and we especially lag behind at first base, where a fielder does a number of things that can impact the defense. Trying to to quantify defense retroactively, as it's being done for Hernandez, is both difficult and inexact. At shortstop, we can look back at the '80s and figure out quickly that Cal Ripken was making about a hundred more outs via putouts and assists than someone else at his position. At first base, we don't have the sample size of ground balls, or the impact of range to measure.

Bill James (of course) did a revealing study of first baseman in his 2001 *Historical Abstract*. He had what he called "the Keith Hernandez breakthrough," weaning out all the short flips to the pitcher from a first baseman's assist total. Think of any throw being made by the first baseman, except the toss to first. They are all big plays, heading off a lead runner at second, third, or the plate. This is where Hernandez excelled

When James studied 1979, he found the league average for "first base assists not to pitcher" was 22. The Cardinals, with Keith Hernandez, led the league with 44.

James found that in the late '70s the National League leaders in first base assists were the St. Cardinals until Hernandez was traded to the Mets. At that point, the Mets became the leader. Hernandez made throws to the tough bases better than anyone else.

Think of a club making 22 more outs than league average *just* from a first baseman cutting off a lead runner. This is a huge advantage. It also jibes with what we suspected while watching him; his head was always in the game, and he was always aggressive. I have seen games where other teams took off a bunt because Hernandez was not only charging, but was charging hard enough to make them think he had *the third base* side covered as well.

First base is not normally a vital defensive position. Hernandez, though, was a transformational player. He turned first base defense into a weapon few teams in the history of the game have ever even approximated. Being the best ever at anything on the field should count for a lot in a Hall of Fame case.

## Hernandez's offense

Offensively, Hernandez's rep has him to be a light-hitting first baseman. This is *not* the case. He may not have been a home run hitter, but Keith Hernandez was an excellent offensive player.

Power hitting is important, but the ability to get on base and not make an out still has the strongest correlation to scoring runs, and winning. Hernandez was an on-base machine before it was properly appreciated. He was top three in the NL in on-base percentage seven times in an eight-year stretch. In the one year he wasn't in the top three, he was seventh.

Offensively, Hernandez suffers from playing in a dead-ball era. The '70s and '80s were a low-run-scoring period. His lifetime .384/.436 on-base/slugging doesn't look special compared to others through history. Again, power is not his calling card, but he was in the NL slugging top 10 three times, and in the OPS+ top 10 six times.

A contact hitter, he had more walks than strikeouts. He didn't have speed, but he was an efficient base runner, with an extra bases taken percentage of 48 percent. This is comparable to Roberto Alomar (48 percent) and pre-bulked-up Barry Bonds (48 percent). It's better than Craig Biggio (45 percent) and Ichiro Suzuki (41 percent).

Now to the new numbers. WAR, for all its faults, does force us to consider the totality of his contribution, and not drop defense from the game. In his 12-year prime, Hernandez was a five-win player, and that's even with defensive WAR, in my opinion, not giving him nearly enough credit. But let's use what the retroactive defensive evaluation is telling us. Here's a look at some 12-year peaks of Hall of Fame first baseman:

| HOF 1B | WAR AVG (12 yrs) |
| --- | --- |
| Keith Hernandez | 4.9 |
| Frank Thomas | 4.9 |
| Harmon Killebrew | 4.6 |
| Eddie Murray | 4.6 |
| Willie McCovey | 4.5 |

I'm not saying Hernandez was better than Killebrew or McCovey for their entire careers. Those two were superior power hitters, and for a time, the best hitters in their leagues. But when looking at the totality of their contributions on the field, one should be open to the *possibility* that Hernandez was equal to these other greats for a 12-year stretch. With Hernandez's superior defense, this isn't a crazy thought.

Being a sportscaster in the New York area in those days, I thought Don Mattingly—an exceptional fielder and leader—was the best first baseman I'd ever seen. Except of course, the guy playing across town at the same time. So getting back to the disconnect in valuation—what is the one advantage a baseball beat writer—the type that has earned a BBWAA Hall of Fame vote—has over the sabermetric analyst or historian?

He's *at the games.*

I often will rail at the phrase "eye test" often used by these writers, but there is value in watching one game at a time, pitch by pitch. Numbers are an abstraction. They represent a physical act on the field. But when Keith Hernandez pegs a lead runner at third to snuff out a rally, it goes into the books as a single assist. It may have changed the game, but it's an afterthought in the box score.

Ask anyone who watched Hernandez—it's universal. A spectacular fielder, quietly superior on the bases, and on base more than almost everyone else in the league. All that is lacking are the obvious home run and RBI numbers.

Unfortunately, the sportswriters of the '80s missed a hell of game. When it came to Hernandez on the ballot, they would point to his career home runs (162), or his number of seasons with 100 RBIs (one). Stuck in a 1970s mind-set of what a Hall of Fame first baseman *should* be, they forfeited the one advantage they had over someone looking at a page in *The Baseball Encyclopedia*: being at the park to see the nuances of his game.

Hernandez spent nine years on the writers ballot, never reaching even 11 percent of the vote. He fell below the minimum of 5 percent in 2004, and was taken off.

# The Two Dwight Evanses

You will rarely see a stranger statistical profile than the one built by
Dwight Evans. For the first eight years of his career, he was the top
defensive right fielder in the game, and a decent hitter. For the next
nine years, he was one of top offensive players in the game. Had he flip-
flopped his career halves—first solidifying his offensive reputation, and
*then* declining, we would think of him very differently.

Here's what Evans did in each phase:

**1972–1979**

| OB/Slug | OPS+ |
|---------|------|
| .341/.443 | 112 |

**1980–1989**

| OB/Slug | OPS+ |
|---------|------|
| .385/.497 | 137 |

Most major league players have their best years in their 20s, and fade
in their 30s. There are exceptions, like Hank Aaron, but that's why he's
Hank Aaron, Home Run King.

Evans, though, was different, and there is a reason. Peter Gammons,
on the Red Sox beat for the *Boston Globe* in the '70s and '80s, says the
two halves came about after Evans was hit by a pitch in 1973. Gammons says Evans had three severe beanings in the '70s, at a time when
little attention was paid to neurological damage. "He had a very serious
concussion syndrome for years," says Gammons, "and at that time nobody
knew about it."

It took years for Evans to recover from the concussive effects of the
beanball, and to lose the fear at the plate. Gammons remembers the day
it happened: July 3, 1980. Gammons was shagging balls before a Red Sox
game with the Orioles. Hitting coach Walt Hriniak was throwing bat-

ting practice while Carl Yastrzemski stood behind the cage. Something clicked. "Carl Yastrzemski came out to the mound and told me, 'Peter, you'll remember this day as long as you live. He got it. He's no longer afraid.'"

For the next full decade, Dwight Evans would be *the most productive offensive player in all of baseball.*

### 1980–1989 wRC Leaders

| | |
|---|---|
| 1. Dwight Evans | 1073 |
| 2. Eddie Murray | 1033 |
| 3. Dale Murphy | 1011 |
| 4. Rickey Henderson | 993 |
| 5. Robin Yount | 989 |
| 6. Wade Boggs | 989 |
| 7. Mike Schmidt | 972 |
| 8. George Brett | 924 |

Yes, those were Evans's best 10 years as compared to anyone else in that same precise time period, but it is interesting that Evans, for a full decade, did in fact create more runs than anyone else in the game. This is not park-adjusted, and Evans was playing in hitter-friendly Fenway Park, for a full decade. Evans was fifth in total bases, first in walks, and was 9th in OPS+. All of that added up to the most runs created by a single player over 10 years.

In the pre-OPS and WAR era, Evans's renaissance went mostly unnoticed. We need categories to make sense of things, and categories that added walks and defense came into acceptance too late for Dwight Evans.

The old-school misinterpretation of statistics led to Evans being overshadowed in his own outfield. Jim Rice, Fred Lynn, and Evans are all within a year of each other in age. Evans grabbed a starting spot in 1973, the other two had spectacular rookie seasons in 1975.

Rice hit for power right away, but didn't field well and didn't run well. Fred Lynn was a great all-around player, but missed a lot of time due to injury. Rice and Lynn won MVP awards, and Rice was eventually inducted into the Hall of Fame. Evans never won an MVP, and topped out at 10 percent on the Hall of Fame ballot.

Want to guess who had the best career?

**Career WAR**

| | |
|---|---|
| Dwight Evans | 66.9 |
| Fred Lynn | 50.0 |
| Jim Rice | 47.4 |

WAR is an approximation of value, but this isn't close. So here we have another outstanding offensive player, but one who became an elite offensive player *after* his reputation had set in. We just don't see players have that kind of career, and certainly the Hall of Fame voters didn't notice it.

Gammons saw the great trio play together year after year. Always fluid in his thinking and analysis, Gammons will often say that Evans was the best outfielder of the three. This, of course, never sank into the mainstream thought.

Evans, like Keith Hernandez, was an outrageously skilled defensive player. It was obvious to the eye, it stood out. But it when it comes to awards and the Hall of Fame, voters pay lip service to defense, and vote for offense.

We can point to Ozzie Smith and Brooks Robinson getting their due, but both legendary defenders also made their mark offensively. Robinson had the good sense to have his best offensive season early, in 1964, when he led the league in total bases, and won the MVP. Brooks's offensive rep was now good enough to not just be considered a Hall of Fame candidate, but to be called the best third baseman *of all time*.

Bill Mazeroski is the best defensive second baseman of all time. In 2001, the Veterans Committee gave the light-hitting Mazeroski the votes for induction. It was a triumph for defense. It also led to a massive overhaul of the voting system. There was enough grumbling over a .260

hitter being inducted that the Hall of Fame Board of Directors changed the Veterans Committee itself, handing over its vote to the Hall of Famers. They would keep that honor for three votes over a five-year stretch, electing no one.

It is instructive that even among our greatest players—the ones actually on the field, playing at the highest level—the value of defense is largely forgotten when it comes to Hall of Fame voting.

# Alan Trammell

Here's another player from the '80s whose numbers just don't jump out because of the low-run-scoring environment. He also had the misfortune to play alongside the best live-ball shortstop of all time (Cal Ripken Jr.), and the best fielding shortstop of all time (Ozzie Smith). This is a major bummer for your Hall of Fame brand. But as I often bring up, Lou Gehrig was rarely the best player *on his own team*. You can be second best at any point anywhere and still be one of the best of all time.

Because the shortstop is the most important defender on the team, we use WAR to insure that defense is properly weighed in overall comparisons. So how about this:

### All-Time SS WAR Leaders (50% of games at SS)

|                    | Career WAR | Years Played |
|--------------------|------------|--------------|
| 1. Honus Wagner    | 131        | 1897–1917    |
| 2. Cal Ripken      | 95.5       | 1981–2001    |
| 3. Robin Yount     | 77         | 1974–1993    |
| 4. Ozzie Smith     | 76.5       | 1978–1996    |
| 5. Luke Appling    | 74.5       | 1930–1950    |
| 6. Arky Vaughan    | 72.9       | 1932–1948    |
| 7. Derek Jeter     | 71.8       | 1995–2014    |
| 8. Alan Trammell   | 70.4       | 1977–1996    |

According to WAR, Alan Trammell is the eighth best shortstop of all time, just behind Derek Jeter, who is dragged down by bad defensive metrics, and ahead of Barry Larkin, who was great but not durable. Maybe you don't want to buy into that completely, but defense and durability matter. WAR works in both.

# Shortstops of the '80s

Let's compare Trammell with his contemporaries. Keep in mind, Cal Ripken Jr. and Ozzie Smith aren't just Hall of Famers, they are the kind of players with whom you would *start* a Hall of Fame. Here they are, measuring their best 15 years:

|               | OB/Slug   | OPS+ | WAR |
|---------------|-----------|------|-----|
| Cal Ripken    | .350/.455 | 117  | 5.9 |
| Alan Trammell | .357/.428 | 116  | 4.6 |
| Ozzie Smith   | .338/.326 | 88   | 4.7 |

Trammell is the equal to Ripken in hitting, and nearly equal to Smith in overall value. Ripken is the most productive, given his durability and defensive excellence, but we knew this, right? The point here is that Trammell is comparable to two first-ballot Hall of Fame shortstops in one form or another, over a 15-year period.

The deeper you dig, though, the better Trammell gets. He rarely grounded into double plays, only eight per season on average. That's very low for a right-handed hitter. Ripken averaged 18 per season, and the extremely quick switch-hitting Smith averaged nine.

Another subtle but vital baserunning skill is taking the extra base. Trammell took the extra base at a career percentage of 53 percent. This is extremely high, the equal of Smith, who was an all-time great base stealer, and well ahead of Ripken.

Trammell, it seems, is another player, *you had to see play.* Efficient, smart. Backbone of the defense. Maybe the third best shortstop of his era, but one of the top 10 all-time. What you would call a Hall of Famer. The writers, once again, are missing a hell of a game.

# The Rock

A question: Who was the best base stealer of all time? It's not a trick question. Rickey Henderson is the all-time stolen base king. But was his base stealing worth it?

Henderson stole 1,406 bases, 468 ahead of anyone else. But bear with me.

Here is Henderson head-to-head with Tim Raines for their 12-year peak:

|  | SB/CS | Success Rate |
| --- | --- | --- |
| Henderson | 961/218 | 81% |
| Raines | 723/127 | 85% |

That leaves 238 extra steals, but 91 more times caught stealing. Henderson's extra steals came at a success rate of 72 percent. This is just about the break-even point where it's worthwhile to keep stealing. I'm willing to say I'd take the extra 200-plus steals, but it's a bit closer than most fans would think.

With a staggering career success rate of 85 percent, Tim Raines was the most efficient base stealer in baseball history; number one all-time among those with at least 500 steals. He also had a lifetime on-base percentage of .385. These two things alone make him a Hall of Famer. Here is Raines's average season for his 12-year peak:

| 1981–1992 | | |
| --- | --- | --- |
| OB/Slug | SB/CS | WAR |
| .387/.427 | 60/11 | 4.8 |

Raines's stealing 60 bases a season seems kind of exciting, doesn't it? Not easy to ignore? Yet, because he didn't produce the usual Triple Crown numbers, he will go to a tenth and final year on the writers' ballot in 2016.

# Raines vs. Gwynn

Do you think Tim Raines was as good as Tony Gwynn? Gwynn was an eight-time "batting champion," and was seen as a master of the craft of hitting. His filmed conversations with an aging Ted Williams are gold. Gwynn studied pitchers, studied video, and knew pitching tendencies better than anyone in the game. John Kruk told me that when he was with the Padres, he started to ask Gwynn what he thought of the team they were about to face in the next series. He said Gwynn, off the top of his head, gave him a detailed scouting report on each of the starters and key relief pitchers they were likely to face. From that point forward, Kruk said he could stop studying, and just ask Tony. His report was better than anything the team produced. Gwynn would spend his career being lauded for his approach, and would rightly sail into the Hall of Fame on the first ballot.

Yet, Tony Gwynn and Tim Raines reached the same level of production in their careers. We don't think of it that way, because of the way we were trained.

Check out their careers:

|  | BAvg/OB/Slug | OPS+ | SB/CS | WAR | oWAR |
|---|---|---|---|---|---|
| Raines | .294/.385/.425 | 123 | 808/146 | 69.1 | 68.4 |
| Gwynn | .338/.388/.459 | 132 | 319/125 | 68.8 | 66.2 |

The on-base is about the same, with Gwynn having a sizable advantage in slugging. Raines, though, has nearly 500 more stolen bases, while getting caught nearly the same number of times as Gwynn.

Once again, the perception gap comes down to the decision made in the nineteenth century: batting average over on-base percentage. Gwynn got his on-base from a .338 batting average, Raines from a .294. It is better to get hits than walks, but Raines makes up for it with his baserunning. Even their fielding is about even.

Raines has the better career WAR, offensive WAR (oWAR—see Glossary), and WAR over their best seven seasons. These two had the same production, they just got it differently.

In 2007, Gwynn sat on the stage with Cal Ripken, and was inducted into the Hall in front of 75,000 people. Raines is likely headed to the Veterans Committee.

# The Vote

The maddening thing is you can't actually get into a legit Tim Raines/ Hall of Fame argument these days. When Raines was first getting on the ballot, I would speak to the regulars on ESPN Radio—Peter Gammons, Jayson Stark, Tim Kurkjian. All take their votes very seriously. All without hesitation said Raines had their vote. Fortunately or unfortunately, all I had access to was outstanding analysts. This is still largely the case. On an MLB Network Hall of Fame Roundtable in 2015, everyone— Gammons, Ken Rosenthal, Harold Reynolds, Tom Verducci, Al Leiter, and Dan Plesac—was in favor of Raines. Almost anyone paying attention nationally knew that Raines is well above the line. But that's not who has the majority of the vote.

Jon Heyman of MLB Network is famously old-school enough to be endearingly called my Arch-Nemesis. He's a writer who values RBIs and grit. He also for years voted for both Don Mattingly and Dale Murphy. He was in the distinct minority, but he's not out of his mind. He just values the player with the high peak years. You can have good reasoning and still come up with a ballot different from the norm.

Speaking of controversial candidates, the last year he was on the writers' ballot, Jack Morris was a major topic of conversation. His career—

not the man himself—had become polarizing. Sabermetric types would be openly baffled by the high ERA and the inflated reputation. Old-schoolers would say he "pitched to the score," allowing meaningless runs to score when the Tigers were far ahead. The excellent sabermetrically minded Joe Sheehan of Baseball Prospectus did the labor to disprove that assertion years ago, but somehow the fading narrative survived.

It got to the point where I finally stopped talking about whether Morris deserved to be in the Hall of Fame. It was a fascinating debate—whose perception was closer to the truth?—but at a certain point I realized, why am I always going after this guy? If he gets in, he'll be happy. His family will be happy. If anyone has noticed, I normally don't write the painful "This guy doesn't belong in the Hall of Fame" essay. These are human beings with families—I don't need to be the guy keeping someone out, when I can use my energy to get someone else *in*. You can see this in my comparison of Mickey Lolich to Morris in Chapter 2.

On the last year Morris was on the ballot, John Thorn made a guest appearance on *MLB Now*. We asked him, "Is Jack Morris a Hall of Famer?" Certainly the sabermetric pioneer and official historian of Major League Baseball would deliver a final shot to end the silliness.

Instead he said, "Sure he is—he's famous. It's a Hall of Fame." I might disagree with the conclusion, but I had to admit, it's one of the best Hall of Fame arguments I've ever heard.

# 12

# Triple Crown —
# A Love Story

"It is difficult to free fools from the chains they revere."

—Voltaire

Somewhere during the stretch run of 2012, I remember having the thought: Can you win the Triple Crown, and not win the MVP? As I said that to Harold Reynolds on the set of *MLB Tonight*, we both sat in silence for a few seconds. It was something we never had to think through.

Harold recovered: "It's the Triple Crown! Of course Cabrera wins it."

Think of where we were at the time. Bill James already had two World Series rings as a Red Sox executive. The Houston Astros were being run by a former engineer—Jeff Luhnow—who had hired four PhDs and a director of decision sciences for his front office.

The Rays, using an integrated sabermetric and scouting approach, would win 90 games for the third straight year. The A's, led by saber-pioneer Billy Beane, were about to run down the Rangers on the final weekend of the regular season to win the AL West title.

The Analytics Revolution had swept through the front offices of the game. Almost every club had an analytics staff. The teams themselves spoke the same language as the young stat nerd on FanGraphs and Baseball Prospectus.

But a certain group was late to the party. And that group still did the voting for MVP, Cy Young, and Hall of Fame. The BBWAA, the baseball writers.

In 2012, there was a confluence of the old and new. Mike Trout was the talk of baseball. He was not only a star rookie, he was a power-hitting speedster who was probably the best fielding center fielder in the game. Only 20 years old, he drew favorable comparisons to Mickey Mantle and Willie Mays at the same age. It all happens so fast now. In 2012, things traveled fast. Sports cable shows run 24/7, websites need content, and Trout provided for plenty of "Best Player in Baseball?" and "Best Age 20 Seasons Ever" columns. Trout was a star by the end of the season.

Meanwhile, Miguel Cabrera was having his usual excellent season, *and* just happened to lead the American League in batting average, home runs, and RBIs.

Cabrera led his league in three categories we once thought to be a good measure of a ballplayer. The Triple Crown had good branding. It was part of history. But we knew better, right?

I was so naive. A regressive piece of nostalgia had been lying dormant. The Triple Crown was like a dragon, asleep in its lair since the 1960s. Until Miguel Cabrera woke it up.

The dragon awoke to a brand-new world, one that some of us thought had moved on and left the dragon for dead. But the Triple Crown was back in business, and would crush all the new math in its path. We would all bow to its power.

# Origins

I hate to rain on yet another parade, but where did this Triple Crown come from anyhow?

The invention of clever sportswriters, it was lifted from the horse racing Triple Crown. Horse racing isn't as big these days, but in ye olde times (like when I was a kid) the Triple Crown—the Kentucky Derby, Preakness, and Belmont—was a huge deal. In the first half of the twentieth century, only baseball and perhaps boxing, were more popular than horse racing.

It is easy to see how these three categories were chosen as a shorthand for a hitter's value. Batting average comes from the 1-for-4 in the box score. It's easy math, and as I've said earlier, it made sense when it was all singles, all the time. Home runs are obviously the most rare and most celebrated act on the field, and runs being driven in are what decides the game. Scoring that run also decides the game, but again, it's a *Triple* Crown, so having four categories messes it all up. Runs scored didn't make the cut.

Let's quickly go through what's wrong with the Triple Crown categories.

## Batting Average

A single is worth the exact same amount as a home run. This, of course, is not the case. I discuss the strange dominance of this most rudimentary stat elsewhere.

## Home Runs

Home runs are valuable, and worthy of counting. But in that Triple Crown season of 2012, Adam Dunn had more home runs than Robinson Cano, Andrew McCutchen, and Trout. You want to tell me you'd take Dunn over any of those three? Not a chance.

So while it's obvious we shouldn't show blind allegiance to the arbitrary grouping of these three stats, let's also realize the limitations of following the seemingly most important one.

## RBIs

If you asked someone what the biggest moments were in any single base-ball game, he would likely point to a player driving in some runs. Where it loses its value, though, is the precise way it has been used for decades—for comparing players.

RBIs are an excellent example of the myopic view of sportswriters. Having watched many ballgames, they saw that driving in runs was im-portant. Somehow they never fully understood the idea of RBI opportu-nities, and just how widely varied these opportunities could be.

The RBI also calls into question our bias toward the man *driving in the run*, over the man *scoring the run*. To drive in a run, you need a man on base. Yes, the man batting with a man on base *knows* it's a big moment, and an opportunity to "come through." But the player up with no one on base knows his at bat is important as well. Isn't it to the credit of the man up with no one on base to know that this, too, is an opportunity? That nothing can happen without him starting a rally?

Yet when a run is driven in, our focus goes to the batter. He is the one who came through for his team. It's just more *visual*. It stirs us emotion-ally to see a player succeed so directly. The player scoring the run may have worked a walk on a 10-pitch count, stolen second base, and taken third on a fly ball to center. Next hitter steps up, slaps a seeing-eye single, and *that* guy is somehow the hero.

Among the many things wrong with boiling down baseball to these three categories are:

1. Doubles and triples don't exist, if they don't drive in a run, and that happens a lot.
2. A single is as good as a home run (in batting average).
3. There can be big differences in RBI opportunities.
4. Walks don't exist.
5. Grounding into double plays doesn't exist.

6.   Defense doesn't exist.

7.   Baserunning doesn't exist.

And yet somehow, 70 years later, we are still taking the Triple Crown seriously.

# Heroes of a Bygone Age

The Triple Crown is connected to some of the giants of the game. Whether it showed the player's true value or not, it is a rare feat. A quick trip to the books brings out the names Rogers Hornsby, Lou Gehrig, and Ted Williams.

By the time we get to a Triple Crown anyone alive today had actually seen, we're talking the Mick.

One of the game's mythic figures, the 1956 version of Mickey Mantle is the postwar American ideal, escaping the coal mines and emerging in Yankee Stadium like a supercharged engine of baseball democracy.

Our late memories of Mantle were of a man broken by his own misdeeds and failings. Memories of his Triple Crown season erase the aging Mick, and bring us back to the pure and awe inspiring: a blond hero packed with muscle, stately in pinstripes.

In the Triple Crown season of 1956, Mantle was a baseball god; 52 home runs, 130 RBIs, with a .353 batting average. He led the league in slugging, total bases, and WAR, and led the Yankees to the World Series title.

The next Triple Crown came from Frank Robinson in 1966. Robinson also had an unreal season, leading the AL in on-base, slugging, and total bases. He also led the Orioles to a pennant, and then a World Series sweep of the Dodgers. Robinson is a vastly underrated all-time great, and here he was at the height of his powers.

One reason Robinson stayed underrated was that the very next year there was another Triple Crown. This one, incredibly, was even better.

In 1967, Carl Yastrzemski led the American League in WAR, on-base, slugging, OPS+, and total bases. In a very low-run-scoring season, his numbers were immense. He also ate clutch for breakfast, and again at lunch; leading the AL in win probability added and run expectancy.

Oh yeah, he also led the league in batting average, home runs, and RBIs.

Beyond this, he also led the Red Sox to the pennant. This was not Boston sportswriter fiction. Yaz in September hammered out a .504 on-base percentage, slugging .760.

In modern baseball, here are the greatest seasons of all time, using wins above replacement:

### Single Season WAR Position Player Leaders, 1901–2014

| | | |
|---|---|---|
| 1. Ruth | 1923 | 14.1 |
| 2. Ruth | 1921 | 12.9 |
| 3. Yastrzemski | 1967 | 12.4 |
| 4. Ruth | 1927 | 12.4 |
| 5. Hornsby | 1924 | 12.1 |

I mean, a season like Yastrzemski's *deserves* more than just a batting title, or even an MVP. There had to be a sense that the season was better than that. And it was. The Triple Crown, a throwback to the days of Ted Williams, filled that desire to properly reward this feat.

A full 30 years later, sabermetrics was taking hold, and stats like batting average and pitcher wins began taking direct and regular fire. They would wither under the scrutiny.

But the sabermetric era and the Triple Crown never had to duel. Had there been an annual run at the Triple Crown, it could have been exposed for the anachronism it was. But that had not yet happened.

It lay in our minds, embedded as a piece of history, language, and branding. The words "Triple Crown" translated to "Greatness that can be measured only by the eons." It conjured up Mantle, Robinson, and Yaz.

In 2012, Miguel Cabrera triggered the nostalgia and tradition still carried by the Triple Crown.

# Triple Crown!

In 2012, Miguel Cabrera was having his typical season. His batting average dropped 14 points from the previous year. His on-base dropped a whopping 55 points. He would set a new personal best in home runs, but it was only the second best slugging percentage of his career. It was a great year, just not his best. Compare 2011, with no Triple Crown, to 2012—Cabrera's Triple Crown season:

**Miguel Cabrera**

|        |                  | wRC+ | oWAR |
|--------|------------------|------|------|
| 2011:  | .344/.448/.586   | 177  | 7.9  |
| 2012:  | .330/.393/.606   | 166  | 7.7  |

Miguel Cabrera was better in 2011 than he was in 2012. Weighted runs created plus (wRC+) (see Glossary) is based on a league average of 100. In 2011, Cabrera was 77 percent better than the league average in the AL. In 2012, he was 66 percent better.

Win Probability Added—what Cabrera did to change the Tigers' chances of winning with each at bat—is not even close. If "clutchiness" is something you value, this is the stat for you. The 2011 Miggy crushes the 2012 Miggy.

And yet . . . in 2011, Cabrera was fifth in the MVP voting, getting just two of 28 first-place votes.

The point here is not that Cabrera should have won the MVP that season. The point is that the very next year, he had a worse offensive season and won the MVP by acclaim over a more deserving player.

And we know why he won the MVP, don't we? Because he happened to lead the league in the Triple Crown: three disparate offensive categories slapped together by sportswriters who knew no better.

You could *say* the performance was close enough, that Cabrera was *just about* the best hitter in the league.

You could also say the earth seems *just about* flat. It certainly can seem like it, it just actually isn't.

The sportswriters who voted in 2012 chose to be deliberately and belligerently ignorant.

I know they mean well, but too bad. This is your full-time job. Do some work. Keep up with the advances in your industry. If the stock-in-trade is analyzing numbers, spend a little time gaining a fundamental understanding of those numbers. At the very least stop making fun of those who have. Not only that, you are given the privilege of putting your imprint on history by naming the award winners. Have some respect for that responsibility.

Here's where we introduce the best player of 2012: Mike Trout.

# Mike Trout

The argument for Cabrera over Trout took quite a reversal for the mainstream baseball media, as it flouted the basic principles of the old school's beef with the SABR set, which is:

*You can't judge everything by the numbers.*

So on what basis did the writers hand Cabrera the MVP? Three hitting numbers. That's it. The old-schoolers defending America were blinded by the beauty of the metrics they saw on the back of their schoolboy baseball cards—but metrics nonetheless.

Another old-school complaint commonly made against sabermatrics is this:

It's the "little things" that matter. There's more to winning baseball than hitting. There's hitting the cutoff man. Taking the extra base. Making a great running catch.

And which player did that, exactly? You had the best base runner and best fielding center fielder in the game up against an immobile slugger who was about the worst-fielding third baseman in the game.

Let's ask the basic question that is pertinent to the MVP: If you could choose among all the players in the league, and select one player for that full season, which one would you choose?

## Hitting: Two Ways to Measure

This is about to get wonky. It'll just take a minute, relax!

There are two main ways to measure hitting; context neutral and context dependent (see Glossary). Neutral means what you did on the whole, regardless of situation. This is mostly everything we have been measuring for over a century: batting average, on-base percentage, total doubles, and everything else.

### Context Neutral

**wRC+ 2012**

| | |
|---|---|
| Trout | 167 |
| Cabrera | 166 |

**OPS+ 2012**

| | |
|---|---|
| Trout | 168 |
| Cabrera | 164 |

Weighted runs created plus is more precise. I used both categories since this is close. Given the adjustment for park effects (that's the "+"), this is as good as even. Let's be clear: Trout doesn't lose in the hitting comparison.

## Context Dependent

Context dependent measures what you did given the context; early or late in the game, men on base, no outs, two outs, no one on base, and so forth. If you're into "clutch," then context dependent is for you.

Run expectancy measures each base and out situation, and what the hitter does to change the chances of scoring a run. In this measurement, Mike Trout was a better offensive player than Miguel Cabrera in 2012:

**2012 AL Leaders—Run Expectancy**

| | |
|---|---|
| Trout | 53.4 |
| Cabrera | 46.8 |

Driving in runs, coming through with two outs, and playing a lot of games, are all big factors in RE24. But so is a leadoff walk. So is a stolen base. And here, Trout had more of an impact than Cabrera, even though he missed nearly a month of the season.

# Win Probability Added

Now we're deep into the clutches of clutch. WPA, or win probability added is a measurement of how you changed the odds of your team winning. Ergo, the most "clutch."

Here, as opposed to RE24, the score matters. In RE24, a leadoff walk is worth the same in the first inning or ninth, leading by a run or trailing by 5.

In win probability added (WPA), the inning and the score matter a great deal. The name explains what it measures: How much have you *added* to the *probability* of your team *winning* the game?

Here's an example. August 5, 2012, Tigers hosting the Indians, the game in the bottom of the 10th, two outs, man on first. The odds of the Tigers winning at this point in the game are 56.4 percent.

Miguel Cabrera hits a home run, ballgame over. The victory now 100 percent in hand, Cabrera added a 43.6 percent probability of winning. His team wins as a direct result, so of course Miguel Cabrera was clutch. WPA gives enormous credit to Cabrera for his home run.

June 11, Angels at the Dodgers, Top of the ninth, score tied, one out. Mike Trout draws a walk and steals second base. The Angels' chance of winning goes from 44.9 percent to 56.5 percent.

This obviously is not as huge a swing as Cabrera's home run, but it's still a major contribution in a big moment. Whether they go on to win or not has no bearing on the "clutchiness" of Trout's actions. You'll more likely remember the game if he's then driven in by a teammate to win the game (which happened), less likely if his teammates come up empty. Either outcome doesn't change the fact that Trout did his job.

Being clutch in late innings changes the chances of winning a great deal. "Clutch" was the battle cry for Cabrera MVP supporters in 2012.

So check this out:

**WPA 2012**

| | |
|---|---|
| Trout | 5.2 |
| Cabrera | 4.8 |

As Oscar Gamble once said, "They don't think it be like it is, but it do."

Mike Trout had more to do with changing his team's chances of winning games in 2012 than Miguel Cabrera did.

Yes, Cabrera did hit a lot of home runs and win a lot of games. No question. But the probability of winning is always in flux. The game is always on the line.

This is an example of how limited our memories are in these cases—the disconnect between what matters and what we remember.

Data cuts through that. Data is more accurate than our impressions or memories. We've now established pretty clearly that when it came to hitting in 2012, Mike Trout was, at the very least, the equal of Miguel Cabrera.

# Baserunning

You don't need a scout to tell you that Trout ran better than Cabrera.

Going from first to third, first to home, or stealing a base is not as important as getting on base or hitting for power. But it *is* very important. In playoff games, the Tigers' powerful but ponderous offense was criticized for being so station-to-station.

Cabrera himself would make key outs on bases in the postseason, and his teammate Prince Fielder was thrown out at the plate in Game 2 of the World Series in a Series-changing play (the Tigers would be swept by the Giants).

The Tigers were called a "slow pitch softball team" by some of my MLB Network colleagues. It's not bunk; having a slow team has an impact. Can we just remember this impact come awards time?

Anyway, here's the shorthand:

| Baserunning Runs (FanGraphs) | |
| --- | --- |
| Trout | 12.0 |
| Cabrera | −2.9 |

Trout led MLB in this category, which calculates the estimated extra runs produced by excellent baserunning. By our best measurement, Trout was nearly 15 runs better than Cabrera—in baserunning alone.

# Defense

Trout actually represented all that the old school purportedly loves: a fleet center fielder covering the gaps with electrifying speed, and climbing walls to take back home runs (he took back three).

On the other side, Cabrera deserved credit for "taking one for the team," and moving back to third base to make room for free agent addition

Prince Fielder. Cabrera, though, was no longer a good fielder anywhere on the diamond. There are no metrics or scouts who would tell you otherwise.

I don't mean he can't field. Miguel Cabrera in 2012 was likely a much better third baseman than anyone in the history of your high school. Even the guy who made All-County before going to fight the Germans and still has a uniform hanging in the showcase. But compared to other major leaguers, Miguel Cabrera was way below average. Compared to Mike Trout, he was awful.

Here are the two main defensive measurements:

### Defensive Runs Saved

| | |
|---|---|
| Trout | +21 |
| Cabrera | −4 |

### Ultimate Zone Rating [see Glossary]

| | |
|---|---|
| Trout | +13.3 |
| Cabrera | −7.5 |

It's difficult to quantify precisely how many runs Trout prevented for the Angels and Cabrera cost the Tigers. But the case is open-and-shut. It's a wide, wide gap.

To recap our finding so thus far in Trout vs. Cabrera:

Hitting: Even.

Baserunning: Trout by as wide a margin as possible given it's the major leagues.

Fielding: Trout by as wide a margin as possible given it's the major leagues.

So *how* exactly did these rocket scientists figure the MVP had to go to Cabrera? Let us count the reasons actually given in the MVP debate of 2012:

## 1. TRIPLE CROWN!

The wrong categories, and not enough categories. A publicity stunt simple enough to catch on, and with the staying power to brainwash a generation who actually had the information to know better.

## 2. CLUTCH.

I was asked many times "Gun to your head, in the ninth with two outs, who do you choose?"

I think this question was popular because Cabrera was quite good with two outs late in games that year. And of course sportswriters usually dream of putting a gun to my head.

## 3. CABRERA CAME THROUGH LATE IN THE SEASON, *WHEN IT MATTERED THE MOST.*

To which I have a question: Which is worth more: a win in April, or a win in September?

The answer: They are worth the same. Each is worth one win.

The main reason we feel a win in September is worth more than a win in April is that we are usually doing this assessment in October.

What has just happened to us looms larger in our emotional memory. Awards discussions come just after the last part of the season. So of course September looks more important. It just happened.

Recency bias is a normal phenomenon. For a baseball fan, it makes sense to think, "Chambliss was big down the stretch, that's where we won the division."

For a voting baseball writer, however, it's your job to be an *analyst*. An analyst uses his training and intellect to separate himself from obvious bias and avoid sloppy narrative-driven conclusions.

## 4. SAYING "IT'S THE MOST *VALUABLE* PLAYER, NOT MOST OUTSTANDING PLAYER."

This was the cop-out of choice for the reasonably intelligent writer who had come to the conclusion that—uh-oh—Trout *was* better. When one needs an escape route, this whopper could buy time, and obfuscate. I was told often, "There's no one definition for 'value.'" This is the case with almost every word in the English language. There is however, a *primary* definition:

Valuable: 1. *Having considerable monetary worth.*

So look at it this way: If you were a GM in 2012, which season would you pay the most for?

One player can hit for more power, but the other is his equal in hitting on the whole, can run much better, and field much better.

### 5. CABRERA LED HIS TEAM TO THE
### PLAYOFFS, TROUT DID NOT.

The classic stupidity, latching on to the value of teammates when assessing an individual award. The best part about this ruse is that Trout with his teammates won 89 games, while Cabrera and his teammates won 88. The Tigers being in a weaker division enabled them to make the postseason. The relative weakness should not bolster Cabrera's MVP case.

# WAR: What Is It Good For?
# Absolutely Something

I'm not a blind devotee of wins above replacement, but I do enjoy the different baseball language. Instead of saying a player is a "100 RBI guy," or "a .320 hitter," you can say he's a "five-win player." This not only tells you he's an All-Star, it tells you he reaches this level by adding together his hitting, baserunning, and defense. Numbers tell a story, and WAR gives you a lot more information than the run-of-the-mill stats from 1910.

The value of WAR is that it forces you to confront the totality of the player's contribution. It's one thing to say, "he can hit 25 homers and also play great defense," but the "and also plays great defense" is too often left by the side of the road. With WAR, everything is added into the mix.

Here is what WAR said about the AL in 2012:

### 2012 American League WAR Leaders

| | |
|---|---|
| 1. Mike Trout | 10.8 |
| 2. Robinson Cano | 8.5 |
| 3. Justin Verlander | 7.7 |
| 4. Adrian Beltre | 7.3 |
| 5. Miguel Cabrera | 7.2 |

WAR is an approximation. It is not telling you that someone who is a 7.3 is better than a player at 7.2. But if the gap is 3.6 wins—which it is between Trout and Cabrera—then it is telling you Trout is a better player, and by a convincing margin.

Old-school columnists at the time mocked the WAR list that year, saying a man who won the Triple Crown could not possibly be just the fifth best player in the league. But is that crazy? Robinson Cano was fifth in wRC+, while Adrian Beltre was sixth. Both also played superior defense at vital defensive positions. Beltre was +13 runs in defensive runs saved at third base, fourth best at the position in the majors, while Cano was +15 at second base, second best at his position.

So Cabrera was not only *not* the best player in the American League that season, there is a good chance he wasn't even the best player *at his position* in the American League that season.

If I had a season to pick among third basemen, I'd probably go with Cabrera's. But if I'm watching Beltre field all season, I might feel differently. I'm just saying, it's not so farfetched.

# Final Call

Using objective methodology, the conclusion is inescapable: In 2012, Mike Trout was a better offensive player than Miguel Cabrera.

Defensively, it's a blowout. Trout was approximately 20–30 runs better than Cabrera in the field. We can dispute the exact difference, but not the outcome.

Mike Trout, slicing it every way we can logically, was a better player in 2012 than Miguel Cabrera, despite playing three fewer weeks through no fault of his own. He also did so playing for a team that won more games than Cabrera's.

We had all been trained to think of a Triple Crown winner as the undisputed Champion of Baseball. Having not had to confront even the *possibility* of a Triple Crown winner NOT being an MVP, our collective heads snapped. Lou Gehrig and Ted Williams had won Triple Crowns and not won the MVP, but that was lost to memory. The Mantle/Robinson/Yaz years had wiped out that memory. We had not had to deal with such a thing.

The vote parallels the BBWAA itself. Once the best analysts of the game, the writers grabbed power, and held it long after their exclusive run should have ended. They created the Triple Crown, and built its narrative power. Their dragon woke up for one more run in 2012, ransacking logic and reason.

# 13

# The Mis-Education of the Voting Sportswriter

"Stupidity carried beyond a certain point becomes a public menace."
—Ezra Pound

I became a sportscaster in 1986. In the 30 years since, controversial MVP votes have been a way of life. I've gotten used to picking apart the annual MVP and Hall of Fame votes and as sabermetrics enabled some of us to get smarter, I've have been unsparing in my criticism of what I think are poor decisions. Comparative analysis is really not all that complicated, and I've been dumbfounded that those who are charged with handing out these awards—and thereby creating a first draft of history—have refused to elevate their analysis. Given that one could always go back through the years and find the occasional controversial vote, I took for granted that the baseball writers have been botching votes since the dawn of time. I am both pleased and shocked to say that is just not the case.

The Trout-Cabrera controversy scarred my analytic psyche. Sportswriters aren't completely to blame for being stretched beyond their capabilities. They're just doing what they were trained to do: tell stories, build narrative, and crown heroes for public consumption and entertainment. This doesn't make them bad people, it just makes them bad analysts.

I began to go through the votes year by year, figuring I'd be exposing one ridiculous narrative-driven voting result after another, when a funny thing happened; most of them, when subjected to rigorous modern analysis, held up just fine.

There are four basic categories for a bad MVP vote:

1.  RBIs
2.  Team Success
3.  Meritorious Service
4.  Representativeness

Representativeness in this case means physical appearance, which, as we have learned, is a big part of perception. In our minds, we envision a representative MVP as a big, strapping power hitter. If a decent, but not great hitting first baseman or outfielder wins an MVP, it's usually because of what he looks like.

# The Way of WAR

Let's try to judge MVP voting objectively. Not that WAR is a perfect stat, but it does boil things down to one number, and gives us a starting point. From 1931 through 2014, the leader in WAR won the MVP only 32 percent of the time. There are many years, of course, where a seemingly legit MVP is merely among the WAR leaders. The MVP has been in the top five in WAR 65 percent of the time.

What we're looking for here is not the reasonable close call, but the truly botched vote. How many MVP's have not even made the top 10 in WAR? An MVP, with a few extenuating circumstances, should at least be in the top 10. Turns out, of the 168 MVPs between 1931 and 2014, only 31 have not made the top 10 in WAR. Only 18 percent.

Not all the 31 are actually bad calls. Let's start by agreeing that WAR may not capture the full value of catching. The man behind the plate is in on every single play; framing pitches, blocking pitches, calling pitches, and controlling the running game. That's an enormous amount of hard-to-quantify responsibility. Yogi Berra and Roy Campanella were both big-hitting catchers (often in the top 10 in slugging, total bases, or offensive WAR) who were outside the top 10 in WAR. I'm not lumping them in with the bad MVPs because of retroactive defensive catching metrics.

That's six catchers. Here are some more instances where being out of the WAR top 10 doesn't make a player a bad MVP choice:

**Jim Konstanty, 1950** Phillies reliever led NL in win probability. 152 great relief innings, properly applied, can make you the most valuable player. Good call by writers (see Chapter 8).

**Joe Torre, 1971** Led NL in total bases, third in OPS+, while playing third base. Hank Aaron may have been better, but it's not a bad vote.

**Jeff Burroughs, 1974** An RBI vote, but also led league in Win Probability (clutch), and run expectancy. If this is what voters were responding to, not a bad call.

**Rollie Fingers, 1981** Yes, a relief year, but in a shortened season, pitched in nearly half the Brewers games, with a staggering 1.04 ERA. Next closest was Dan Quisenberry at 1.73. Understandable.

**Willie Hernandez, 1984** 140 innings of relief is a different animal. Hernandez pitched 80 games, nearly half of Tigers games that season. Led AL in win probability added by an incredible margin. Correct choice.

**Ryan Howard, 2006** Bad defender and base runner, but a .425/.659? Howard also led league in total bases, and was second in OPS+ to Pujols. Not going to quibble.

Of the 31 on the non–top 10 WAR list, 12 are now explained: Six catching seasons, and six where wins above replacement did not do their seasons justice.

That's 19 bad MVP votes via our WAR methodology. I have taken the liberty of adding four more to the list that were still terrible choices despite making the WAR top 10. We now have 23 inexplicable and unforgivable votes. Remember, there are four basic categories for choosing a bad MVP: RBIs, Team Success, Representativeness (looking the part), and Meritorious Service. There is a fifth category: No Freaking Clue.

**1931, Frankie Frisch** Meritorious Service/Team Success. Great player coming off a great 1930 season, but was 33, and 1931 was his worst year in a decade.

**1940, Frank McCormick** Representativeness/Team Success. Good but not great power hitter with an excellent Reds club. Overperformed in MVP voting; three straight top five finishes without ever slugging .500. A big-for-the-time 6'4", 205 pounds (described as "huge," "plodding"), he looked the part of a strapping MVP first baseman, whether he hit like one or not.

**1944, Marty Marion** Team Success. Cards won pennant, and I'd love to give a good fielding shortstop the credit. But a young, good-fielding Stan the Man led NL in on-base and slugging. Writers had just voted for Musial in 1943, and looked to spread the Cardinals' credit.

**1947, Joe DiMaggio** Team Success/Meritorious Service. Deserved it over Ted Williams in 1941 (see Chapter 14), but this was an older, slower version of the Clipper. Sportswriters not as swayed by Triple Crown back then, as Williams led league in basically everything.

**1952, Hank Sauer** RBIs/Meritorious Service. Jackie Robinson had .440 on-base percentage, with great base running and defense, Musial had usual best-hitting season in the league, but Sauer led the NL in homers and RBIs. This even defies normal voter pattern, as the Cubs were a .500 team, with the Dodgers winning the pennant.

**1956, Don Newcombe** Wins (pitching version of RBIs). Newk was third in ERA, third in innings pitched, but finished with a 27–7 "record." Duke Snider was the best hitter in the league, led the league in on-base, slugging, WAR. The Duke never won an MVP, and this was his year.

**1958, Jackie Jensen** RBIs. Mickey Mantle beat Jensen by 47 points in on-base, 57 points in slugging, 30 walks, and 14 Total Bases. Mantle also the better base runner and fielder. What gives? Ninety-seven RBIs for Mantle looks bad compared to 122 for Jensen. What's funny is Mantle scored 127 runs to Jensen's 83. For every RBI, there is a run scorer, but the voters missed that.

**1964, Ken Boyer** RBIs/Team Success/Meritorious Service. Not an embarrassing vote. Boyer had been a top player in NL for years; top five in WAR three times. Played all 162, and *was* an excellent fielder, just not that year at age 33. Was actually third-best at third base in the league that season, behind Ron Santo and Dick Allen.

So there we have the pre-divisional era. Some bad votes, but between 1931 and 1969, there were 78 votes. In the days before *The Baseball Encyclopedia*, in-depth stats, and deep comparative analysis, 70 for 78 is pretty remarkable. It's hard to pinpoint precisely why, but it's possible that pre-cable and widespread TV coverage beat writers were actually at the games. They had a small league to cover; only 10 teams. Perhaps they just had a better sense of what was happening in front of them. I hereby apologize to the sportswriters of the Golden Era. They did an excellent job.

Hold on, though, things are about to get rocky.

**1970, Boog Powell** Team Success/Representativeness. Frank Howard led league in homers and RBIs, but for a last-place team. Carl Yastrzemski led league with .452 on-base and 335 total bases. A good hitter for the best team, Big Boog, like Frank McCormick, is what an MVP is supposed to look like.

**1974, Steve Garvey** Team Success/Representativeness. Speaking of what it's supposed to look like. Garvey was a baseball model, and in 1974 the 12th best hitter in the NL. Back then, 200 hits and 100 RBIs were benchmarks, the Dodgers infield was excellent, and Garvey was the one who could hit for power. Schmidt, Morgan, Bench, Stargell all better, but this wasn't controversial at the time. We knew no better.

**1979, Don Baylor** Team/RBIs/Representativeness. Led league in RBIs and runs, played in all 162. Solid year, just not the best. Eighth in OPS+, fourth in total bases, played 65 games at DH.

**1982, Dale Murphy** RBIs/Representativeness. Led league in RBI's, and was a tall, handsome centerfielder. The All-American type. Deserved the MVP the next year, but in 1982 was out-hit by Mike Schmidt and Gary Carter, with both Schmidt and Carter playing historic levels of defense.

So that's four clunkers in just 13 years. The sportswriters are starting to disconnect from the game. It's a bigger league, having expanded in 1961, 1962, 1969, and 1977. Television has arrived, and it's more of a coast-to-coast game. Reputation and narrative are starting to take over for the actual production.

Pitchers with big seasons had also stopped winning. In the 1930s, five starting pitchers won an MVP. There were four in the '40s, three in the '50s, and three in the '60s. In the decades where the voters had a good track record, there were 15 in 40 years. In the '70s, '80s, '90s, and aughts—40 years—we have just two: Vida Blue in 1971, Roger Clemens in 1984.

Certainly lighter workloads have something to do with it, but there were a number of big-inning seasons in the '70s and '80s. Voter logic is beginning to fray. We are about to enter into the Dark Ages of sports-writer voting.

**1987, Andre Dawson** Meritorious Service/RBIs. After years of excellence in Montreal, an age-33 Dawson puts up eye-popping power numbers at Wrigley Field. Led league in home runs, RBIs, and total bases. Yet he is just 15th in wRC+, sixth in slugging, and had a dismal .328 on-base percentage. Tony Gwynn and Tim Raines had monstrous years. Eric Davis out-slugs Dawson *and* steals 50 bases. Dale Murphy out-slugs Dawson, and walks 83 more times. Ozzie Smith had a .392 on-base and an all-time-great fielding season at shortstop. Myopic vote that starts a trend.

**1987, George Bell** RBIs. Had big 47/134 homer/RBI totals, and led left fielders in assists. Hitting home runs and throwing guys out are attention-getting. Did lead league in total bases, but Wade Boggs had a .461 on-base, slugging .588. Alan Trammell had a .402/.551, while playing an excellent shortstop. Dwight Evans had a great year. But this was before writers knew walks helped score runs. Bad vote.

**1992, Dennis Eckersley** No Clue. I've demonstrated I'm willing to go with an MVP reliever if he pitches enough innings. Eck doesn't make it. His 1.91 ERA is only 10th best among those with 60 innings, though his 93 Ks and five walks (unintentional) were unreal. Clemens, Frank Thomas, and Kirby Puckett all had monster years.

**1993, Frank Thomas** RBIs/Representativeness. The Big Hurt deserved it in '92 and '94, but not here. Was second to John Olerud in OPS+, while Griffey led league in WAR. Olerud's 35-point edge in on-base didn't register with voters in '93, but what about the 47-point gap in batting average? White Sox won AL West, but Blue Jays won East. Big Frank looked the part, and I count RBIs because he was second in ribbies to Albert Belle. Belle was so unpopular with the media that the BBWAA voters evidently ruled Belle ineligible.

**1995, Mo Vaughn** No clue. Big Mo was ninth in OPS+. I would go with Edgar Martinez (.479/.628), but for the sake of a direct comparison, stack up Vaughn with Albert Belle:

|  | PA | BA/OBP/SLG |
|---|---|---|
| Belle: | 631 | .317/.401/.690 |
| Vaughn: | 636 | .300/.388/.575 |

Vaughn is not a good defensive player, so where exactly is Vaughn better? Belle (ineligible) led AL in home runs, RBIs, and total bases. Red Sox won the East with 86 wins, but Belle's Indians went 100–44. There's no logic, even by normal '90s sportswriter's standards. Inexplicable.

**1996, Juan Gonzalez** No Clue. Had big "numbers," 47 HRs and 144 RBIs, but in steroid era this was only good for fifth and second, respectively. Was just 12th in OPS+. Griffey led league in WAR, playing sensational center field. A-Rod led league in total bases while playing a great short-stop, and Belle (ineligible) had a typical 48 HR/148 RBI year. Doesn't make JuanGone a bad guy, just not the MVP.

**1998, Juan Gonzalez** RBIs. So many great candidates; Jeter, Nomar, A-Rod all incredible years at shortstop. Bernie Williams, Edgar Martinez, Albert Belle (ineligible), Griffey (56 HRs), and even Roger Clemens. JuanGone was ninth in OPS+, but number one in RBIs. Writers had just stopped trying.

**1998, Sammy Sosa** Meritorious Service (for one season). Also ridiculous. See page 252.

**2002, Miguel Tejada** Team Success. Nice year, it's just that another short-stop in his own division blows him out:

|  | HR | RBI | TB | OBP/SLG |
|---|---|---|---|---|
| A-Rod | 57 | 142 | 300 | .392/.623 |
| Tejada | 34 | 131 | 308 | .354/.508 |

So where exactly is Tejada better? Oh, his *team* is better. And that matters . . . how?

**2006, Justin Morneau** See page 255.

**2012, Miguel Cabrera** Under normal circumstances, this is fine. Cabrera was close second to Trout in wRC+, and led league in total bases. But you know what, this isn't 1952. We now *know* the baserunning and defensive metrics. We have instant access to all sorts of stats voters could not even dream of in the old days. Those stats told us *clearly* that Mike Trout was the MVP. If you're still unsure, please see Chapter 12 on obsessive Triple Crown behavior.

Have you noticed something? In the first 40 years of MVP voting, there were only eight bad choices. Yet there were another eight in just a 12-year period—1987–1998.

It is an isolated run as well. In the post-*Moneyball* era, the voting has been much better—the Triple Crown's Last Gasp in 2012 notwithstanding. Justin Verlander, Buster Posey, Ryan Braun, Andrew McCutchen, Joey Votto, Clayton Kershaw, and Mike Trout—all choices in the last five years—have been excellent. Scrutiny has intensified, and more objective analysis is being done. Younger writers, exposed to sabermetrics, have started to break through and get votes. One would expect the trend of smarter voting to continue.

So the early sportswriters were close to the game and got it right. Today's sportswriters exposed to sabermetrics are getting it right as well. So what happened in between? The sportswriters weren't as close to the game as their forebears, watching every pitch and having an appreciation of how games were won. They also weren't accepting the latest advances in their own business. Right in front of them was a group showing a better way of quantifying performance. Bill James was writing his *Abstracts*, and the value of on-base percentage became public and obvious. It was the worst of all worlds; things that *seemed* important during the game—

RBIs and pitcher wins—were taken into account, while things that *were* important—defense and baserunning—were not.

Middle infielders Phil Rizzuto, Nellie Fox, and Marty Marion were MVPs in the '40s and '50s. Defensive stalwarts Brooks Robinson, Zoilo Versalles, and Dick Groat won in the mid-'60s. Not all were great calls, but at least defense factored in.

In the '90s it was JuanGone, Mo Vaughn, and Frank Thomas—obvious, plodding sluggers. The greatest fielder in baseball history—Ozzie Smith—didn't win. On-base machines Wade Boggs and Tony Gwynn didn't win. Greg Maddux and Pedro Martinez, having historic pitching seasons in a high-run-scoring era, also could not win an MVP.

# WAR Leaders

What would happen if we made the MVP a completely objective, data-centric award. Let's say 1930s mad scientists, instead of arming a world for war, armed baseball with WAR. Let's also say sportswriters of the day decided to name the MVP based on WAR, in the name of a logical, utopian future. Hey, it could have happened. Here's a view of the multiple WAR MVPs, with their BBWAA MVP number listed beside:

|                   | WAR MVP | BBWAA MVP |
|-------------------|---------|-----------|
| Willie Mays       | 10      | 3         |
| Ted Williams      | 6       | 2         |
| Barry Bonds       | 6       | 7         |
| Mickey Mantle     | 5       | 3         |
| Stan Musial       | 4       | 3         |
| Albert Pujols     | 4       | 3         |
| Cal Ripken        | 3       | 2         |
| Carl Yastrzemski  | 3       | 1         |
| Mike Trout        | 3       | 1         |

*(continued on next page)*

| | WAR MVP | BBWAA MVP |
|---|---|---|
| Bob Gibson | 3 | 1 |
| Greg Maddux | 3 | 0 |

Interesting, isn't it? In this alternate reality, Willie Mays is a 10-time MVP. (In the pre-BBWAA MVP era, Babe Ruth is also a 10-time WAR leader.) Ted Williams picks up four more, and Maddux goes from zero to three. Not that Ripken, Yastrzemski, and Gibson need more accolades, but "three-time MVP Bob Gibson" adds another level to the legend. Of those on this list, only Barry Bonds loses an MVP.

The WAR MVP list also features Ben Zobrist and Nick Markakis. I wouldn't have voted for either, but they are two very good all-around players with varied skill sets. It also features the following players who never won an actual MVP: Tony Gwynn, Dave Winfield, Gary Carter, Wade Boggs, Dwight Evans, Todd Helton, Duke Snider, and Minnie Minoso.

Didn't you think a few of those players *did* win an actual MVP? They didn't.

The WAR MVP also goes to a lot more pitchers. Here's a list of pitchers who led their league in WAR, but never won a BBWAA MVP: Bob Feller (2), Warren Spahn, Robin Roberts (2), Fergie Jenkins, Steve Carlton, Tom Seaver, Mark Fidrych, Jim Palmer, Ron Guidry, Dwight Gooden, Greg Maddux (3), Pedro Martinez (2), Zack Greinke.

These are some of the most memorable seasons in baseball history:

| | | ERA | IP | ERA+ |
|---|---|---|---|---|
| 1972 | Steve Carlton | 1.97 | 346.1 | 182 |
| 1978 | Ron Guidry | 1.74 | 273.2 | 208 |
| 1985 | Dwight Gooden | 1.53 | 276.2 | 229 |
| 1994 | Greg Maddux | 1.56 | 202 | 271 |
| 1995 | Greg Maddux | 1.63 | 209.2 | 260 |
| 1999 | Pedro Martinez | 2.07 | 213.1 | 243 |
| 2000 | Pedro Martinez | 1.74 | 217 | 291 |

Not one sportswriter MVP in the bunch. League average for ERA+ is 100. Pedro's 291 is the all-time single-season record.

Looking back at the old days, it does make more sense that a pitcher deserved the MVP. Here are a few more WAR MVPs. Check out the innings pitched column, and keep in mind over the last 10 years, only three pitchers have topped 250 innings:

|      |              | ERA  | IP    |
|------|--------------|------|-------|
| 1940 | Bob Feller   | 2.61 | 320.1 |
| 1947 | Warren Spahn | 2.33 | 289.2 |
| 1953 | Robin Roberts| 2.75 | 346.2 |
| 1971 | Fergie Jenkins | 2.77 | 325 |
| 1973 | Tom Seaver   | 2.08 | 290   |
| 1975 | Jim Palmer   | 2.09 | 323   |

Does a pitcher deserve the MVP? Not an easy answer, but at least in the old days, with a larger volume of work, it made more sense. In the early days of the MVP vote, the BBWAA actually did an excellent job of recognizing when a pitcher was deserving of the MVP. Lefty Grove, Carl Hubbell, Dizzy Dean, Bucky Walters, Mort Cooper, and Hal Newhouser—all MVP winners in the '30s and '40s—were at or near the top of the WAR charts while taking first place. The voters did a creditable job of figuring out when a pitcher deserved the nod.

# Ineligible

One thing a WAR MVP doesn't care about is how the candidate's team is playing. This is a good thing, because sportswriters sure do.

In August of 2013, our MLB Network producers thought it would be a good time to have a little MVP debate. In the National League, we were going to focus on Buster Posey, Andrew McCutchen, and Yadier Molina.

I asked, "What about Ryan Braun?" (This is before the failed drug test.) Jon Heyman, longtime BBWAA member and voter, said, "The Brewers are out of it."

In the ensuing hallway debate (we have plenty of them), I asked why it mattered what Braun's teammates were doing when he had almost exactly the same numbers as the previous year, when he did win the MVP. Heyman and a few others told me, "His team is out of it, these aren't meaningful games."

I asked, "So, he's basically ineligible?"

Heyman answered, "Your word, but yes, ineligible." I love Jon, at least he doesn't try to confuse the issue.

Shoot ahead to the end of September, and another MVP debate. The Brewers have made a run, and are just three and a half games out of the NL Wild Card.

I asked Heyman, "Is Braun eligible *now*?" Heyman: "Yes, he is now eligible."

It's a wonder I get any work done.

I went to check things out, just to see if there was any variation of performance. Maybe Braun was *now* leading Milwaukee to playoff contention. That would give some credence to his change of "eligibility" in an MVP race.

### First Half

| Brewers | Braun OB/Slugging |
|---------|-------------------|
| 40–43   | .391/.599         |

### Second Half

| Brewers | Braun OB/Slugging |
|---------|-------------------|
| 43–34   | .392/.591         |

Whether his team was struggling or playing well, Ryan Braun was the same guy. Yet he went from being totally outside the MVP discussion to actually finishing second to Posey at the end of the season. With Milwaukee's late run, his team had evidently gotten close enough to gain "eligibility" for the league's best player award.

It illustrates the silliness of judging a player's individual performance by what his team is doing. It might seem like teams in the pennant race, playing in full ballparks, are playing the games that matter. But in the major leagues, *all* games are meaningful.

Mickey Mantle said during the Yankees' run of dominance, he and his teammates would wonder what they would be able to do individually if they didn't have the searing pressure of the pennant race each year. When they got to the mid-'60s and felt what it was like outside of the race, Mantle said it was *more* difficult to stay focused.

This is just one anecdotal case, but it is not necessarily easier to put up numbers in "meaningless" games. Anytime you watch a major league game—at least these days—I defy you to show me players just giving away hits or outs. It's very rare, if it happens at all. There is just too much at stake.

# The WAR King

WAR takes into account defense and baserunning, so it should be no surprise Willie Mays led the NL in WAR 10 different seasons. Doing so while going up against—in various years—Stan Musial, Hank Aaron, and Frank Robinson makes it all the more remarkable. So how did he win just two MVPs? The writers in those days *loved* Mays, writing one homage after another, so the usual overstated nonsense of the player "not being good with the media" doesn't even enter the equation. This is a good thing. In fact, a closer look shows Mays getting jobbed is not nearly as bad as some of the later votes.

**1954:** Mays leads the NL with a 10.6 WAR, the Giants win the pennant, and he wins the MVP. All good.

**1955:** Mays leads NL with 9 WAR, but Roy Campanella (5.2 WAR) gets the nod. Defensive metrics for catching are tricky, and *retroactive* defensive metrics are downright sketchy. A catcher with a .395/.583 can't be dismissed, though Campy played only 123 games. Dodgers winning the pennant is likely the reason.

**1957:** Mays (8.3 WAR) loses to Hank Aaron (8.0 WAR), the Hammer's only MVP. Mays had the better on-base and slugging, but Aaron led the league in home runs and RBIs while playing for the pennant winner. You know how that goes.

**1958:** Mays had a 10.2 WAR, but Ernie Banks (9.4) is close, playing shortstop while hitting an eye-popping 47 HRs and 129 RBIs. Banks leads the league in slugging and total bases while not missing a single game. I'm giving credit to the writers for valuing a power-hitting shortstop on a mediocre team.

**1960:** The Pirates win the pennant, while MVP winner Dick Groat (6.2 WAR) leads the league in batting average on a 95-game winning team, but also has a great defensive season. Mays leads in WAR, but Aaron, Banks, Ken Boyer, and Frank Robinson all have a legitimate beef here.

**1962:** Mays (10.5 WAR) was famously shafted as writers go with Maury Wills (6.0). But you know what? I'm going to defend it. Ty Cobb's single season record of 96 steals was the stuff of ancient (1915) legend. Since that year, no one had even topped 70 steals in a single season. Since 1945, the best was 56, by Luis Aparicio in 1959. So 104 stolen bases by Wills had to be *mind-blowing*. It just wasn't done in the modern game. Wills was also caught stealing just 13 times, played shortstop, and also had a .299 batting average, which was what everyone paid attention to. The writers deserve a pass. (Remember this kindness, please, when you see sportswriters attack me.)

**1963:** Mays (10.6) loses to Sandy Koufax (9.9) in a year where Koufax delivers 311 innings of a 1.88 ERA, and led the league with 306 strike-outs and 11 shutouts. Fair enough.

**1964:** Willie churns out an 11 WAR, with a .383/.607. Ken Boyer (6.1 WAR) wins, with a .365/.489. There's really no justifying this one, as the writers went with the RBI league leader on the pennant-winning club. Boyer was an excellent fielder, and played all 162 games, but this was a fantastic year for Mays: led NL in home runs, OPS+, run expectancy, and win probability. I don't expect the 1964 voters to know that, but there had to be a lot of "clutchiness" going on that year. They just missed it.

**1965:** Two out of 10 ain't bad! Mays (11.2 WAR) wins over the second place finisher Koufax (8.1). Juan Marichal had 10.3, but this was a 34-year-old Mays still at the height of his powers. He led the league in everything important, and did it in a pitcher's park.

**1966:** Roberto Clemente (8.2 WAR) wins over a slightly diminished Mays season (9 WAR). Clemente is close in on-base and slugging. Most deserving was Koufax in his final year: a staggering 1.73 ERA over a more staggering 323 innings.

In all, there were only three seasons where the writers lost their way: with Groat in 1960, Wills in 1962, and Boyer in 1964. All three, though, were infielders who had excellent seasons for a pennant-winning club. All three, while maybe not having great fielding seasons that year, were once top-flight defenders, and back then it was hard for the eye to see when the aging process took the range away. Two other times—with Campanella and Banks—you had fabulous offensive production from the toughest defensive positions. All things considered, Mays was more a victim of circumstance than voter ignorance.

# The Lost Summer of Love

In the midst of the bad vote era comes a truly absurd vote that defies any type of logic.

Sportswriters would now like to forget the fawning attention they poured over Mark McGwire and Sammy Sosa in 1998. It is rarely revisited, having been robbed of all nostalgic value by steroids.

In the history of baseball, there have been few MVP story lines that have gotten more attention than the 1998 McGwire-Sosa home run chase. DiMaggio and Williams in 1941 (see Chapter 14), Maris vs. Mantle in 1961, and Cabrera vs. Trout in 2012. You would think a robbery is less likely to happen when everybody is paying close attention, but here is proof: It ain't!

Both men, evidently fueled by magic elixirs, broke one of the sport's most sacred records, Roger Maris's single-season home record of 61 that had stood for 36 years. In one summer, the record was not only broken, it was shattered. By *two* men.

It was McGwire who ended the season with the new record, hitting 70, while Sosa ended with 66. Do you recall how the MVP went that year?

**1998 NL MVP**

|            | Points | 1st Place Votes |
|------------|--------|-----------------|
| 1. Sosa    | 438    | 30              |
| 2. McGwire | 272    | 2               |

Well *that* doesn't look very close now does it? So how did that happen?

First off, it was 1998, and these trained analysts were still calling Bill James a crackpot. So let's examine the numbers they were looking at:

|          | HR | RBIs | BAvg |
|----------|----|------|------|
| McGwire  | 70 | 147  | .299 |
| Sosa     | 66 | 158  | .308 |

So it makes sense if you're 12 years old. Sosa has more RBIs and a higher batting average. If you are a professional baseball writer, though, covering the game for money every single day, perhaps you could also be looking at these numbers:

|          | OP    | SLG   |
|----------|-------|-------|
| McGwire  | .470  | .752  |
| Sosa     | .377  | .647  |

These numbers were readily available. McGwire has about *100 points* on Sosa in both on-base and slugging. It's not close.

You can also forget defense, because Sosa, while a better runner and defender than McGwire, rated below average that season in right field. He did steal 18 bases, which looks nice, but getting caught nine times negates most of that. WAR, which was not yet in vogue in '98, still favors McGwire—7.5 to 6.4. This isn't Trout vs. Cabrera. This is Cabrera vs. Cabrera. *On steroids!*

Sorry about that.

You might remember that the first home run chase also resulted in a controversial MVP result: Roger Maris over Mickey Mantle. We know that Mantle had the better season in 1961. He had 76 points on Maris in on-base percentage, and 67 points in slugging. But two things: It was a close vote, 7–6 Maris in first-place votes, and they also gave it to the guy who won the home run race. The summer was dominated with the home run, and they gave it to the guy that won it. In 1961, no one was talking on-base percentage. There's a difference between lacking information, and *resisting* information. In 1961, they knew no better.

Back to 1998. Other than the Cubs finishing seven games ahead of the Cardinals in the NL Central race, there is really nothing to point at that could give you the excuse to vote Sosa over McGwire. The BBWAA's inability to isolate individual production is their calling card, and this is likely the explanation in 1998. While doing shows at ESPN, some of our producers joked that the MVP was a consolation prize for Sosa, since

McGwire was being treated like Neil Armstrong coming back from the moon.

What the sportswriters missed—fantastically enough while writing about it almost every single day—was one of the greatest offensive seasons ever. Beyond on-base and slugging, there are two main ways to measure hitting results: how you affected the chances of scoring a run, and how you affected the chances of your team winning.

Let's look at win probability: How did McGwire's at bats affect his team's chances of winning? The data necessary to calculate win probability goes back only to 1938. That takes Babe Ruth and other greats out of the equation, but it still shows some of baseball's legendary seasons:

**Best Win Probability Added, Single Season, Through 1998**

|  | Year | WPA |
|---|---|---|
| 1. Willie McCovey | 1969 | 10.1 |
| 2. Mark McGwire | 1998 | 9.6 |
| 3. Mickey Mantle | 1957 | 9.3 |
| 4. Mickey Mantle | 1961 | 9.0 |
| 5. Joe Torre | 1971 | 8.9 |
| 6. Stan Musial | 1948 | 8.5 |
| 7. Mickey Mantle | 1956 | 8.4 |
| 8. Carl Yastrzemski | 1967 | 8.4 |
| 9. Ted Williams | 1957 | 8.4 |
| 10. Will Clark | 1989 | 8.3 |

The writers that 1998 season knew, of course, they had witnessed a very special season. They did not know they had seen the second best hitting season since the Depression, but the 70 home runs and 162 walks should have been an indication. Yet McGwire only got two of 32 first-place votes. TWO!

The irony is that no one cares McGwire got jobbed. No one wants to remember this home run race even happened. The most heavily publicized race in baseball history is being purged from history.

# The Mystery of Morneau

It's 2006, it's the day of the American League MVP vote, and I'm doing the six o'clock ESPN *SportsCenter*. In our meeting, the producers prodded me, asking who was *supposed* to win, given my mysterious mathematical prowess. I really didn't have a strong feeling about it. I swear, I wasn't gunning for a fight. I remember saying I wasn't sure, but I was good with Derek Jeter, Joe Mauer, or Johan Santana.

Jeter came in with a .417/.483 OBP/SLG playing shortstop. Mauer had a .429/.507 playing catcher. These are fantastic seasons for players at defensive positions. There were two other excellent seasons from players at key defensive spots: center fielder Grady Sizemore of the Indians, and shortstop Carlos Guillen of the Tigers

Santana led the league in ERA, FIP, innings pitched, and strikeouts. It's never easy comparing the value of pitchers and position players, but Santana did lead the AL in WAR.

That afternoon, of course, Justin Morneau wins. Everyone in the ESPN newsroom is smiling, because I'm forced to confront this. How does this happen? Who are these guys who vote? What are they looking at? *Moneyball* came out three years ago! The Red Sox have already won a World Series with Theo and Bill James! It's one of those moments where you're speaking and you realize you're ranting because people are backing away from you wide-eyed and slightly frightened. It was one of those days.

Morneau had a very good year. But according to WAR, he was the 24th best position player in the league, and the fourth best player *on his own team*. Santana, Mauer, and Francisco Liriano ranked higher.

WAR incorporates the defensive metrics, and at first base I'm not sold on their accuracy. So let's just talk hitting. According to park-adjusted OPS (OPS+), Morneau was the eighth best hitter in the American League. Fifth in total bases. Sixth in slugging.

So even in 2006, it still came down to RBIs. Except he didn't lead there, either. David Ortiz, who outslugged Morneau by 77 points, led the league that year with 137 to Morneau's 130.

No, this was a composite of the convoluted logic of the MVP voter. Where the criteria are:

1. Not a pitcher, unless he has 24 or more wins, and single-digit losses.
2. Most RBIs.
3. But only with a division champion.

I blew off some steam, demanding that Jayson Stark tell me by what reasoning Morneau could have been the best player in the league. Jayson, being a logical fellow, said something along the lines of "Brian, I hear ya. But you know these guys, blah, blah, blah . . ."

I didn't know it at the time, but there was a reason. Representativeness. When voters don't have a player with overwhelming numbers, they vote for a power-hitting first baseman. Perhaps it comes from reading about big, solid Lou Gehrig, and seeing Gary Cooper play him in *Pride of the Yankees*. This is what an American male looks like, and dammit, what an MVP is supposed to be all about. Some of the least explainable MVPs are in this subcategory: Frank McCormick, Steve Garvey, Mo Vaughn, Justin Morneau. I know, I know, a five-foot-nothing Yogi Berra won three MVPs. I'm not saying it happens every year. But when confused by too much choice, something unexplainable can happen to an otherwise disparate voting group. A representative-looking MVP choice emerges: Dale Murphy, Jackie Jensen, Don Baylor, Juan Gonzalez. If you have a better theory, let me know.

When I interviewed Morneau the next day, my producers asked if I was going to question the vote. To Morneau? No, I congratulated him. I had no beef with Morneau—is he supposed to refuse the award on sabermetric principles? His job is to play, and collect anything given to him.

This is strictly between me and the sportswriters.

So I take it all back. Okay, *most* of it back. The writers weren't always missing a hell of a game, just for a certain period of time. Oddly enough, their spate of bad votes came at the precise time when sabermetrics came of age. They chose to ignore what was happening on the field and cling to the traditional stats, at the same time those stats were being devalued. I'm not advocating a WAR MVP, or even a Win Probability Added MVP, but it sure is a place to start. It's time we got there.

# 14

# The 1941 MVP — Blind Squirrels Find Nut

"One of the most endearing things about baseball history is that it's so packed with bullshit."

—John Thorn, MLB Official Historian

I first heard the voice driving north on the New York State Thruway. Finishing my sportscast, I would head north and drive home through the countryside. I remember one night flipping on the radio and getting a sports talk show. Not many of those at the time. I remember hearing a crazy person.

It was the first time I had heard the voice of Christopher "Mad Dog" Russo. It had to be around 1987, before he was paired with Mike Francesa, and they became the biggest local sports radio show in the country. The Dog was unfettered, and he was hilarious. I didn't listen every night, but when he sprang up later on WFAN, I remembered precisely who he was. He was that distinctive.

The Dog loves his baseball history, so we always hit it off. He is, though, as anti-sabermetric as it gets. To him, I guess it complicates things. In 2014, he came to the MLB Network, where we would guest on each other's show. It became an in-house highlight. You know you have something good when the producers, who concoct sports arguments every day, stop cold to watch a particular segment. Even with our shared love of baseball history, we saw the game *very* differently.

During the 2014 season, with the Royals on their run to the American League pennant, I posed the following question to Russo: Is Alex Gordon a superstar?

Okay, so I'm baiting the Dog a bit. Gordon does not have the offensive firepower to be among the top hitters in the game. I admit I'm taking a polarizing position to spark a debate, and of course, Mad Dog's head came near spinning off his shoulders. "NOOO! He's a left fielder for gosh sakes! He makes one catch a game! He doesn't drive in a hundred! He's not Reggie Jackson!"

But let's think this through. Baseball is more than hitting. Say there is room for about 10–15 superstars in the game at any point. It's a reasonable number. It's the top starter at each position, with a few pitchers.

A superstar doesn't have to be a home run hitter. I'm looking for the *best players*. The players that help you win. Here are the WAR leaders among position players from 2011 to 2014:

**MLB WAR Leaders, Position Players, 2011–2014**

|   | WAR |
|---|---|
| 1. Mike Trout | 28.6 |
| 2. Robinson Cano | 28.3 |
| 3. Andrew McCutchen | 27.2 |
| 4. Miguel Cabrera | 27 |
| 5. Adrian Beltre | 25.7 |
| 6. Alex Gordon | 24.4 |

(continued on next page)

|                      | WAR  |
|----------------------|------|
| 7. Ben Zobrist       | 24.3 |
| 8. Dustin Pedroia    | 24.2 |
| 9. Jose Bautista     | 21.8 |
| 10. Joey Votto       | 20.7 |

Alex Gordon, according to WAR, was the sixth best position player in the major leagues, over a full four-year period. If that's not a superstar, I believe you need to redefine the word.

I realize WAR isn't the decider on these cases. I will say it many times in this book. It does, though, force us to confront and count all areas of the game.

Watching Gordon through the 2014 season, he would continually show his broad range of skills. He was the best fielding left fielder in the game—the MLB leader in defensive runs saved for outfielders over a four-year period. He would take an extra base (an excellent 52 percent XBT—extra bases taken—see Glossary), in 2014, and occasionally steal a base.

Offensively, no one thing stood out. In 2014, he hit just .266, but with 65 walks, he had a .351 on-base. Even if his hitting was just above average, the total result was something few in the game could achieve.

WAR, flawed though it may be, adds up all components of the game and gives us a number that represents all facets of a player's game. In the 2014 playoffs, the number matched up with what you would see inning for inning. Gordon would turn what should have been a single into a double, then tag up and take third, and later score on a sacrifice fly. Most runners would still be standing on second. Gordon had scored. A Gordon catch would snuff out a rally. A triple would clear the bases. His end-of-season numbers didn't say superstar, but his inning-to-inning play was extremely valuable when you studied his every move.

Remember, the biggest disconnect in baseball is what we value while watching the games and what we remember after them. WAR might be a good reminder of that.

Which brought forth some froth from the Dog: "Brian I love ya, but you and your cockamamie statistics, I just don't know what game you're watching! This guy's a nice player, he is *not a superstar!*"

Our next topic of discussion concerned Joe DiMaggio. Russo is a huge DiMaggio fan, usually throwing the name in some young player's face when they start bat flipping a bit much for the Mad Dog's taste: "Hey kid, whaddya think, *you're DiMaggio now!*"

As I sat on the set, trying to put DiMaggio into historical perspective, I felt a connection between the current and historical subject matter. I thought about all the things I was saying about Alex Gordon. It's basically a New Age version of "You had to see him play."

And that is one thing everyone always said about Joe DiMaggio.

## The All-Around Star

A five-tool player with a high baseball IQ can beat you in a lot of ways. When you can field, run, and throw, it adds dimension to your game that doesn't quite translate *fully* into your stat line.

Not that DiMaggio needed anything more than hitting to be a Hall of Fame player. But players like DiMaggio, and of course Willie Mays, were more than respected. For people who saw them, they were held *in awe.*

It's part of baseball lore: DiMaggio never threw to the wrong base, never got thrown out on the bases, and never made a mental error. He exuded intensity and confidence. Phil Rizzuto would say the mere sight of him lacing up his cleats would inspire everyone in the clubhouse. Joe Page finished off the Dodgers in Game 7 of the 1947 World Series, saying "I knew I had to do it for Joe."

After so many years of tributes and specials, the DiMaggio stories begin to sound like an ancient myth. It just *had* to be hokum. He was a great player who played on nine World Series champions. I'm buying his standard of excellence, but through the years it seemed more likely that Yankee success bestowed a stadium-sized halo effect.

But as I sat there extolling the virtues of Alex Gordon, it occurred to me: DiMaggio was an excellent center fielder. It wasn't an era where players stole many bases, but DiMaggio could run. Yankee teammate Tommy Henrich said no one slid harder than DiMaggio. Nice observation, but what does it mean? In this case, it means quite a bit. Pete Palmer said one of his chief observations in the pre-sabermetric days was that "a lot of people talked about the fighting spirit, but not what the fighting spirit *brought about*."

In this case, DiMaggio's speed brought about wins. He hit 43 triples his first three years in the majors. From the data that can be found, he took extra bases at a very high rate. His all-around game was not fiction, it came from a day-to-day intensity that showed itself in one of the most famous plays in World Series history.

In the 1939 Series, the Yankees were up three games to none on the Reds, trying to finish off a sweep, and win a then record fourth straight championship.

Cincinnati, though, was up 4–2 in the ninth. With Charlie Keller on first, DiMaggio singled, and it was first and third. Hall of Famer Bill Dickey then hit a bouncer to Reds shortstop Buddy Myer. The throw went to second, and DiMaggio slid hard and wiped out Myer, dislodging the ball. Everybody safe, Keller scored, and instead of a double play, there were men on first and second, still nobody out.

George Selkirk then hit a fly ball to right field, and DiMaggio tagged up and took third. This is a huge base because on the next at bat, Joe Gordon hit a ground ball to third. The throw went to the plate, but DiMaggio slid around the tag to tie the game.

Follow this now. After the DiMaggio single, the Yankees didn't get a hit. But DiMaggio took out the shortstop to get second, tagged up to get third, and scored on an aggressive dash to the plate. He took *three extra bases*. That's not going into his OPS. Even in the box score, the tag-up and run scored don't tell the story. This is the hidden game of baserunning. Today, he well might have a good baserunning runs stat, but it's still not giving him the proper credit. Many sluggers would have singled, and been snuffed out at second. Or stayed at second on the fly ball. Or stayed at third on the ground ball. *DiMaggio scored.* Game 4 of the World Series went to extra innings.

DiMaggio wasn't done. Now 4–4 in the top of the 10th, the Yankees have first and third, nobody out, and DiMaggio rips a base hit. This drives in the go-ahead run, and the ball is then misplayed in right field. Charlie Keller, who was on first, tries to score and crashes into Reds catcher Ernie Lombardi. Lombardi is out of it for a second, in that he was kicked in the groin in the collision. DiMaggio breaks for the plate. Lombardi recovers and dives back to tag him. DiMaggio is dead to rights. No doubt he will be out.

Mind you, this is on film, it's not some tall tale.

DiMaggio was starting his slide as Lombardi dives in front of him. DiMaggio veers toward the front of the plate, *kicks his right leg into the air,* avoiding the tag, and taps his foot on the plate from directly overhead. He does this in one motion, while he is still coming in full speed on a slide.

DiMaggio cleared the bases, scored on his own single, making it 7–4 Yankees. This is how he and the Yankees won their fourth straight World Series title.

Think of all the wreckage done by DiMaggio in just two innings, most of it on the bases. Earlier he had made two crucial plays in the outfield to save runs. In the inning-to-inning play-by-play, the man gets better and better. Baserunning matters, defense matters.

DiMaggio now had four World Series titles in his first four years. Something never done before, something never done since. This is how you become a baseball god. But that very year, another brilliant—but very different—player had arrived in the American League to challenge him.

# Teddy Ballgame

Wow, the sportswriters hated Ted Williams. As we have noted, he led the American League in WAR six times, and won just two MVP awards. He was the league's top player six times, even though he lost *five seasons* to World War II and the Korean War.

Williams was an irascible genius, and must have been tough to be around. But he was dedicated to his craft. He wasn't in barroom brawls. He famously went around drinking milkshakes trying to gain weight. He later became a United States Marine Corps fighter pilot, seeing actual duty, actively and physically defending his country.

Why did they hate this guy again? Oh yeah, he was "selfish."

Williams fought back, sarcastically calling the writers the Knights of the Keyboard. He was loud and intimidating. He would seek retribution for any slight. Part of the problem was that the press thought Williams considered himself better than everyone else. Part of the problem with that is that in Williams's case, this was a defensible position.

When TV host Maury Povich was a guest on *MLB Now*, he told me his father—the legendary sportswriter Shirley Povich—befriended Williams. Williams thought Povich gave him a fair shake. Shirley would see Williams chide the Boston beat writers, telling them, "If you guys were any good, you'd be in New York." Keep in mind, this was a time when Boston had *nine* newspapers. These were the days when there was no one to tell Ted that this was "not good for his brand."

Years later, the narrative was still firmly planted. Even Mad Dog Russo threw a Phil Rizzuto line from years earlier: "Williams cared about hitting, DiMaggio cared about winning."

DiMaggio was cool and aloof. He also helped win nine World Series and 10 pennants.

Williams was angry and selfish. He played in one World Series and hit .200 in it.

These things are unfair, but this is how it played out. At least, for years after their retirement.

# The Second Act

A strange thing then happened in the shaping of our fading legends. DiMaggio's "cool" began to change to "paranoid." The public was always fascinated by both men, and books were churned out year after year. DiMaggio remained intensely private, leaving the writers to their own interpretation. Williams was talkative and interesting. His persona shifted from "angry young man" into "crusty old genius." In his twilight, Ted Williams was still compelling.

When I was growing up, the players in the conversation for "Greatest Ever" seemed to be: Babe Ruth, Ty Cobb, Willie Mays, and Joe DiMaggio. Honus Wagner was for hard-cores fans only, and Mickey Mantle was seen as too injury prone. Musial, Gehrig, and Williams were in a slot just below the top.

Among those who had seen them play, the perception was that DiMaggio was one of the *greatest ever*. In 1969, he was famously voted by a sportswriters panel to be "The Greatest Living Ballplayer." It was considered a great honor. Years later, he reportedly asked for this to be part of his standard introduction at public events. If one were ever voted the "greatest living" anything, I doubt any one of us would avoid including this in our standard intro. For DiMaggio, though, it was seen as an act of hubris. Once regarded as a man of remarkable class and grace, he was gaining a reputation as a pompous narcissist, seeking constant adoration from the masses.

This occurred as sabermetrics took hold of the game. There were new ways of quantifying production, and a closer statistical inquiry into Ted Williams's record yielded a new view: Williams was the *real* war-era God of baseball.

Although Williams actually *did* win a Triple Crown, it was the move *from* the Triple Crown numbers that elevated his record. As we moved to the slash line, Williams looked like he had been dropped into the baseball world from outer space. Like one of these Old Hoss Radbourn types who pitched 500 innings a season in the 1800s. Except Williams did this in the '40s, '50s, and '60s, playing a modern game, right alongside the players we all knew. Here is Williams's Career slash line:

| PA | BA | OBP | SLG |
|----|----|-----|-----|
| 9,788 | .344 | .482 | .634 |

This is the second best hitter of all-time. Only Babe Ruth was better. To put it into a modern perspective: Joey Votto, Miguel Cabrera, and Mike Trout have never had a *single season* with an on-base percentage that high. Only Cabrera has had *one season* with a slugging percentage as high as Ted Williams had *for his entire career*. Williams's on-base is number one all-time, his slugging is second only to Ruth.

The new math—and we're really just talking on-base and slugging—made it clear. The greats of the mid-twentieth century—DiMaggio, Musial, Mays, Mantle, and Aaron—had *nowhere near* the awesome offensive capability of Teddy Ballgame.

Even with five seasons lost to military service, Williams led the AL in on-base percentage 12 times, and slugging nine times.

Sabermetric study is able to flatten out the fluctuation of run scoring through different eras, measure production, and cut through the myth-making. The first phase of sabermetrics realigned the order of the greats. Linear weights made it possible to properly measure the run values of all offensive results. Not just home runs vs. singles, but walks, doubles, double plays, everything. And when everything was requantified, it was Ted Williams who benefited the most.

It was not the only reevaluation of Williams's life. By the late '90s, as the "Greatest Generation" was getting its due for its war service and sacrifice, Williams's fighter pilot record was given a fresh look. This man was in combat missions over Korea, not playing baseball safely on a military base, like DiMaggio. *This* was the American hero.

As he aged, Williams was treated—correctly—as baseball royalty. The 1999 All-Star Game at Fenway Park, with the All-Star players genuflecting at his wheelchair, illustrated how far the perception had changed. Williams was the greatest modern player. The modern evaluation of statistics proved this. His indifference to defense and baserunning faded in memory, as did his surly attitude. I would be among those to say, "With a .482 on-base, be as surly as you want."

Retroactively recognizing the true level of Williams's greatness was a breakthrough, but it doesn't mean we should ignore what happened on the field. Twenty years after all of these sabermetric advances, I'm barking at Mad Dog Russo about the merits of the all-around player vs. the big hitter. We're talking about Alex Gordon because he's right in front of us night after night, and it has me rethinking DiMaggio. Believe it or not, Gordon *is* a superstar. It's just not obvious. You need to be paying attention to everything in the game, day after day. DiMaggio's hitting was enough to make him a superstar, but to fully *appreciate* his game, you needed to watch him closely. It was the baserunning and fielding—in addition to the hitting—that had people thinking he was the greatest ever.

I *know* Alex Gordon is not Joe DiMaggio. DiMaggio was in a completely different class as a hitter. Even the edge in intensity is stark. While DiMaggio ran the Reds out of the World Series in '39, Gordon coasted to third in the ninth inning of Game 7 of the 2014 Series. This was with the Royals down 4–3 in the ninth against Madison Bumgarner, with a hobbled Salvador Perez on deck. Gordon didn't kick it into high gear until he neared second base, and then held up at third. Maybe that was the smart play. Who wants to be thrown out by 10 feet to end a World Series? But reread DiMaggio's ninth and 10th innings in Game 4 of the '39 Series above.

Despite the differences, though, there is a common thread; both Gordon and DiMaggio did these seemingly "smaller" things on the field that led to winning baseball.

The Dog is saying, "Brian, Brian, Brian! *Hitting* is what matters! Please!"

I used to believe that. But as I studied the game closer and closer, I knew we needed to get beyond the obvious hitting stats, and consider the totality of a player's contribution on the field.

Funny thing was, the pre-war and pre-WAR sportswriters *did* think DiMaggio's overall contribution was better. It was just more difficult to explain, and not possible to quantify.

Now that we have better tools to measure with, it's time to use them and judge two legends during one of the greatest seasons ever.

# Summer of '41

Entire books have been written about each player's 1941 season. Your summer reading list could be completely comprised of what these two ballplayers did this one particular six-month stretch:

*Ted Williams: The Last .400 Hitter* by John B. Holway

*56: Joe Dimaggio and the Last Magic Number In Sports* by Kostya Kennedy

*Joe DiMaggio and Ted Williams: Baseball's Greatest Player and Baseball's Greatest Hitter* by Dom Forker

*Baseball in '41: A Celebration of "The Best Baseball Season Ever"—In the Year America Went to War* by Robert Creamer (Naturally, Joe D and Teddy Ballgame are on the cover of this book)

The titles alone tell us just how impressed the culture was, and is, by this one season, with Williams batting .406 and DiMaggio hitting in a record fifty-six straight games.

Pearl Harbor was attacked just two months after the Yankees beat the Dodgers in the 1941 World Series. Very quickly, the U.S. was launched into a war all over the globe. It was a world seemingly being blasted into hell.

Only a few months earlier, fans checked the newspapers each day to root for Joe D. in his 56-game hitting streak. Or Williams saying a .3995 batting average *wasn't* hitting .400, and deciding to risk it on the final day of the season. Williams went 6-for-8 in that final-day doubleheader. It all seemed so heroic, innocent, and glorious. That summer resonates decades later.

In Creamer's *Baseball in '41*, reporters mentioned to Williams the possibility of being the MVP after that last-day doubleheader. "Do you think there's a chance I could win it?" Williams asked. Yes, it mattered to the legends, too.

Here's what the sportswriters said in the MVP vote:

### 1941 AL MVP

|               | Total Votes | First Place Votes |
| ------------- | ----------- | ----------------- |
| 1. DiMaggio   | 291         | 15                |
| 2. Williams   | 254         | 8                 |
| 3. Bob Feller | 174         | —                 |

Joe D. gets nearly twice as many first place votes. This wasn't close.

In the decades that followed, this result came to be seen as the sportswriters falling in love with their own story; the 56-game hitting streak *dominated* the summer. It had six weeks of drama, and daily tension. You could follow it every day.

DiMaggio not only broke the record, he buried it. Initially the record was 41, held by George Sisler. Then someone unearthed the old records, and out of nowhere came a Wee Willie Keeler 45 game hitting streak from 1896 and 1897. Ole Wee Willie had no idea! But DiMaggio blew right by it, and kept on chugging to 56 in a row. The night it was stopped, there were 67,468 in Cleveland's Municipal Stadium to see it. The Streak was a sensation.

Not only was this seen as an impressive athletic feat, it was seen as a testament to DiMaggio's *mental* fortitude. Every day he had to deal with the pressure, and each day he withstood it. The man initially called the Big Dago (it was a different time) was becoming Joltin' Joe DiMaggio. He was better than good copy, he was front-page news. He deserved to be rewarded.

As the years passed, it started to look like a very sentimental MVP vote.

Chad Finn of the *Boston Globe*: "It was the greatest season for the greatest hitter who ever lived [Williams]. But the Sox finished second in the AL, 17 games back of the Yankees, so you can see how they settled the 'does the MVP have to come from a contender?' debate back then."

Jeff Zimmerman on Beyond the Box Score: "DiMaggio's defense was not even close enough to make up for the almost 40 extra runs Williams' offense created. Williams' OBP and SLG were each about 100 points higher than DiMaggio's."

These comments are from sabermetric baseball writers who approach the game with intellectual rigor and passion. In this time period, I thought the same thing: DiMaggio had the better team, and better story. The perception of '41 is that this was one of the times that Williams was jobbed by the sportswriters.

But who actually had the better year? Let's look at what a sportswriter in 1941 was looking at:

|          | BA    | HR  | RBI  |
|----------|-------|-----|------|
| DiMaggio | .357  | 30  | 125* |
| Williams | .406* | 37* | 120  |

*led league

In the Triple Crown stats, Williams was the better player offensively. That's nearly 50 points in batting average, and seven more home runs. Joe D. had the story, the team, and the headlines. The writers of 1941 likely took 10 minutes to think about it, and hit Toots Shor's for a drink.

The slash line from the stars of '41 make the comparison look even more lopsided:

|  | BAvg/OBP/SLG |
|---|---|
| Williams | .406/.553/.735 |
| DiMaggio | .357/.440/.643 |

Williams's numbers can barely be fathomed. Not just the .406 batting average, but our minds aren't trained to see .553 as an on-base percentage. It's too high. No one does that past high school. It was the all-time single-season baseball record until Barry Bonds found the Fountain of Youth in his late 30s and surpassed it twice.

Remember how powerful the leaderboards are. It sets our thinking before we even begin to do the analysis. Sportswriters saw the batting average leaders every day, but imagine if they were able to see this:

### 1941 AL On-Base % Leaders

| | |
|---|---|
| 1. Williams | .553 |
| 2. Cullenbine | .452 |
| 3. DiMaggio | .440 |
| 4. Keller | .416 |
| 5. Foxx | .412 |

Even with Roy Cullenbine and DiMaggio having big years, Williams has *over 100* points on them. Keep in mind, this list did not exist in the 1940s.

It has also been pointed out that Williams out-hit DiMaggio during DiMaggio's hitting streak. This was, I have to admit, a neat way of looking at it:

### May 15–July 16, 1941

|  | BA/OBP/SLG |
|---|---|
| DiMaggio | .408/.463/.717 |
| Williams | .412/.540/.684 |

While fans were following the Streak, Williams was doing just about the same amount of damage. It's just that Williams did so without having at least one hit spread out over every game.

This also brings up the nineteenth-century nature of a "hitting streak." Why do we care, exactly? It is a fun thing to follow, but once again, it has very little to do with winning. As with batting average, it ignores walks and treats all hits the same. This may have made some sense in the 1800s, when winning was tied closely with stringing together a bunch of singles. By 1941, that game was over.

I know, it's baseball blasphemy, but hitting streaks belong on the Nonsense List with wins, saves, batting average, the Triple Crown, and errors.

In live-ball baseball, 0-for-0 with 3 walks is likely better than a 1-for-5 with a single. In the world of the hitting streak, a 1-for-5 is success, 0-for-0 with 3 walks is failure. But the object of the game is not to *hit*, it's to *score runs*.

Yet even today, hitting streaks are top-of-the-page news, and on-base streaks are for the small type at the end of a notes column. We all know DiMaggio holds the record for the longest hitting streak. Any idea who holds the record for the longest on-base streak?

**Longest On-Base Streak**

| | | |
|---|---|---|
| Williams | 84 | (1949) |
| DiMaggio | 74 | (1941) |
| Williams | 69 | (1941) |
| Williams | 65 | (1948) |

No headlines for that streak. No one wrote a hit song about Ted Williams in 1949 ("Jolting Joe DiMaggio" was a top 20 hit in '41). The day DiMaggio's streak ended, it produced a torrent of print about Ken Keltner. The Indians' third baseman made two outstanding plays at third base to rob DiMaggio and end the streak. Little mention was made of DiMaggio's intentional walk in the fourth inning. The poor walk gets no respect.

With the walk and an ensuing 16-game hitting streak, DiMaggio had, at the time, the longest on-base streak of all-time. It would still be, except for his chief rival.

# Next Level

With a better understanding of what constitutes hitting production, Williams towers over DiMaggio in 1941. It would seem there is no way DiMaggio's season can bridge the gap Williams had with the bat.

Or is there? Let's remember: DiMaggio was an exceptional fielder. DiMaggio *could run.* I'm not going into leadership skills, I want tangible production. DiMaggio—at age 26—had a huge advantage in fielding and base running, which is reflected in AL wins above replacement for 1941:

**1941 AL WAR**

| | |
|---|---|
| 1. Williams | 10.6 |
| 2. DiMaggio | 9.1 |

A decent gap, but it's closer than you might think. A nine-win season is a serious year. As of now, with a separation of 1.5 between the two, you would still have Williams as your MVP.

But WAR is not the end of the conversation. WAR takes park effects into account, but in a broad sense of how the park plays, not the specifics of what the park does to a particular hitter.

Joe DiMaggio, more than almost anyone in the history of baseball, was hurt by his home park. He had great power, but as a right-handed gap hitter, he was hitting into the broad expanse of ground called "Death Valley." In 1941, Yankee Stadium center field was 461 feet away, and left-center was 457.

The deepest left-center-field in a 2014 park is in Houston, at 404 feet. There is nothing like Death Valley in the majors today.

I mean, this is positively unfair. This is what DiMaggio was facing half of his entire career. Here are his home/road splits:

### Joe DiMaggio—Career

|                | OB/Slug   | HR  |
| -------------- | --------- | --- |
| Yankee Stadium | .391/.547 | 148 |
| Road           | .405/.610 | 213 |

Almost all players hit better at home. That DiMaggio slugged 63 points better on the road shows just how much Death Valley dampened his offensive production.

All of this is not Ted Williams's problem. And while Fenway Park is a hitters' park, he personally did not greatly benefit. Here are his home/road splits:

### Ted Williams—Career

|             | OB/Slug   | HR  |
| ----------- | --------- | --- |
| Fenway Park | .496/.652 | 248 |
| Road        | .467/.615 | 273 |

Ted did just fine on the road, actually hitting more home runs away from Fenway. Players are normally better at home, so Williams, at the very least, is not a creation of Fenway Park.

So if we take away *both* home parks from each player, can we learn something about their season?

### 1941 Road Stats

|          | BA/OBP/SLG       |
| -------- | ---------------- |
| Williams | .380/.529/.700   |
| DiMaggio | .369/.457/.667   |

That flattens things out quite a bit. Williams still has an advantage, but now it's 11 points in batting average, and 33 points in slugging. In on-base percentage, though, Williams still has a big 72-point advantage.

Even with making an adjustment for park effects, WAR does not capture how drastically Yankee Stadium affected DiMaggio's hitting. With this said, Williams is still way out ahead.

The first wave of sabermetrics was seemingly conclusive. Williams was the king in 1941.

# Next, Next Level

Sabermetrics, though, was never just about on-base percentage. That was just the most obvious, misunderstood part of a complex game.

As we pointed out in Trout vs. Cabrera (see Chapter 3), there are two basic types of hitting stats when evaluating outcomes: context neutral, and context dependent.

Context neutral is your batting average for the entire year. Everything thrown in together.

Context dependent takes into account your situation: Are the bases loaded or empty? Is it early or late in the game? How much did you change your team's chances of winning with your at bat?

Yes, this is clutch. Clutch does exist. It exists as a part of history. It has been proven, at the major league level, *not* to be predictive of future performance. But it does happen. And there are better indicators of this than our memories. Indicators that came about decades after Williams and DiMaggio duked it out in the '40s: run expectancy and win probability.

Who had more of an effect on their team's chances of run scoring? For every situation, there is an outcome. Williams leads off with a walk. DiMaggio hits a double with two on. Williams hits a three-run home run. DiMaggio hits into a rare double play (a big negative).

Run expectancy measures a change in the team's ability to score runs. At the end of the year, it tells the story of how each player affected either run scoring, or the chances of winning.

So let's start with run expectancy.

**1941 AL Leaders—Run Expectancy (RE24)**

| | |
|---|---|
| 1. DiMaggio | 83.95 |
| 2. Williams | 68.68 |

Okay, this is a stunner. I have to admit, I had no idea this was the case when I was talking Williams vs. DiMaggio with Mad Dog Russo, or when I began writing this chapter. I thought there might be a case for DiMaggio's fielding and baserunning bridging the gap in hitting, much the way Mike Trout's did against Miguel Cabrera in 2013 and 2014.

What I didn't know is that DiMaggio's hitting, in a certain respect, *already was better.*

Even with Ted Williams having the then best on-base percentage of all time, Joe DiMaggio did more to score more runs for his team. When you add up all of his at bats and how he changed the probability of scoring runs, DiMaggio was better. And a gap of almost 15 is not small, it is vast. DiMaggio by a landslide.

Each player has different circumstances. Having more men on base gives you more opportunities, just like RBIs, so it's not a completely fair comparison. But unlike RBIs, every at bat is a chance to move the needle in run expectancy. It's nowhere near as team dependent.

Also, the 1941 Red Sox had the top scoring offense in the American League. The Yankees were number two. So it's not as if Williams was at some vast disadvantage.

# Just Win, Baby

Even measuring clutch hitting, there is another way of measuring the effect of a hitter. The basic question is, How much did you affect the chances of your team winning? The answer comes in the form of win probability added.

Again, each player will face different circumstances, but these are the breaks. A team that is in a position to win more often will bring more of those possibilities, but again, the Yankees and Red Sox went 1–2 that year in wins, so it's not a completely unfair comparison.

A walk-off come-from-behind home run brings a big swing in win probability, but a stolen base in the third inning of a tie game also adds points. The game is always on the line in WPA. If one believes in clutch, this is the clutchiest stat we currently have.

Here are the win probability leaders of 1941:

### 1941 AL—Win Probability Added (WPA)

| | |
|---|---|
| 1. DiMaggio | 7.27 |
| 2. Williams | 6.15 |

Wow, and wow again. In hitting alone, *not counting defense*, DiMaggio changed the probability of his team winning more than Williams did. The game-winning ability spoken of about DiMaggio was—at least for this season—not a by-product of his reputation. He actually did it.

At this point, DiMaggio in 1941 is better than Williams in the field, on the bases, in changing his team's chances to score runs, and changing his team's chances of winning.

Amazingly enough, sophisticated modern baseball math and the 1940s sportswriters are in alignment. In one of the most storied seasons in sports history, Joe DiMaggio was indeed the American League Most Valuable Player.

## Luck or Instinct?

Did the writers get it right for the wrong reasons? Very possibly. Through the years, the Knights of the Keyboard were always unduly influenced by the story line and team result.

The mythmaking of DiMaggio had a lot behind it: his representing

Italian Americans and giving immigrants reason to be proud. His team being immensely successful, and a symbol of power in the country.

Not only did the BBWAA name DiMaggio the MVP, so did the *Sporting News*. DiMaggio was the Associated Press Athlete of the Year. These guys were not looking at run expectancy or win probability added. The hitting streak was the biggest good-news story of a tumultuous world-at-war summer, and DiMaggio obliterated a record while an entire nation watched.

Williams's hitting .400 was remarkable, but it had been done 11 years earlier—Bill Terry in 1930—and had been done eight times in the previous 21 seasons (going back just to the Live-Ball Era, which began in 1920).

Years after he was done playing, DiMaggio was spoken of with reverence. His teammates were in awe while they were playing alongside him. Sportswriters wrote glowing accounts of his play, and mostly kept a respectful distance. His manager, Joe McCarthy, said, "Joe was the one ballplayer who never made a mental mistake." DiMaggio's play was the standard of excellence. This is because of thousands of small acts and habits.

I'm going to give the beat writers at the old stadium some due. They saw greatness, inning to inning, day to day. The Clipper was bigger than the numbers. As it turns out, they got the right guy.

# 15

# Department of Decision Sciences

"Just about all our intuitions are wrong. Modern science comes out of that understanding."

—Noam Chomsky

It's March of 2013, and I'm trying to come up with an absurd number. I said 90 wins, and it worked. The room erupted in laughter. Having lost 100 games for back-to-back years, the idea that the sad-sack Astros would soon be winning 90 and making the postseason seemed comical. I asked, "In five years, would the Houston Astros be winning 90 games a season?"

The crowd laughing wasn't a bunch of rubes. It was the 2013 SABR Analytics Conference, a room filled with analysts, writers, ardent fans, and a whole bunch of young "Baseball Ops" hotshots from every major league team. The panel was made up of Vince Gennaro (SABR president, author of *Diamond Dollars*, an early baseball economics book), Rob Neyer, and Dave Cameron of FanGraphs. I thought the Astros would, in fact, be churning out 90 wins in five years, but was wondering what the intelligentsia thought.

All three on the panel would say yes to 90 wins within five years. I looked out to the audience to Bill James himself. I said, "Bill, will the Astros be winning 90 games within five years?" The Godfather of Sabermetrics, also a Red Sox executive, replied, "95."

In 2012, the Astros front office was seen, depending on your viewpoint, as revolutionary or a joke. New GM Jeff Luhnow was a former engineer who was unabashed in his analytic approach. As the director of player development for the Cardinals, he had been wildly successful. Yet to the outside world, it was difficult to know what came about under Luhnow, and what was a shared result from an outstanding organization. As Luhnow was famously not a "baseball man"—meaning not a major league player, scout, or lifer—there were *plenty* of snickers from within the industry. Many predicted failure.

Luhnow made it clear: The Astros were going to be a pure, data-driven, logical organization. If he was going to fail, it wasn't going to be because he compromised. As good as the Cardinals' front office was—and it was considered MLB's model franchise—this was going to be a sabermetric enterprise from the ground up, a more hard-core version of the Red Sox, and a more structured version of the A's.

It was ballsy and brilliant. With so many teams into analytics, where was a competitive advantage possible? It would come to a team that didn't go halfway. A club that didn't have encumbrances to logical thinking and roster building at any level. The Astros, with new ownership, the right GM, and a chance to do a total rebuild, were just the team to complete the *Moneyball*/Jamesian vision.

It was also clear they were not afraid of looking wonky. In January of 2012, they put out a press release announcing a baseball first: a "Director of Decision Sciences." After years of sabermetricians in hiding, this was in-your-face geeky. There would have been a lot of ways to bring Sig Mejdal over from the Cardinals quietly; who knew who he was, anyway? They could have called him an analyst, or a VP of, well, *anything*. Calling him the director of decision sciences, *and putting out a press release about it,* showed a kind of chutzpah usually absent in a forward-thinking baseball front office. Even smart GMs had chased off the Sig Mejdals of the world in the '80s and '90s, once the press found out about them.

"While it's an unusual title, in my opinion it's the most descriptive of what I do," says Mejdal, "We could have called ourselves analysts. Analysts are looking at numbers, doing their statistical analysis and presenting information, but Jeff [Luhnow] has always wanted a process of what the decision maker is supposed to do once he's received this information."

Even the club long at the front edge of sabermetric thinking wasn't looking for this kind of trouble. "We do [have one] too," said A's general manager Billy Beane. "We just don't call it that. Many organizations have someone functioning in the same role, we probably cloak him with a more traditional title."

"Cloak" is an interesting choice of words. Through the late '90s, teams that built an analytics staff preferred that it stay in the background. Much like in high school, where to be known as a "brain" might bring undue attention and a potential beating, except that these are adults working in a billion-dollar business. Despite what most think because of *Moneyball*, Beane was never looking to be Team SABR. The Astros, coming along more than a decade later, had no such restraint. "I understand it," says Beane. "I think it's a statement saying, 'this is where this organization is going,' which is great."

In an age of information explosion, the competitive advantage will come from those who can figure out which information is helpful, and then what to do with it. Finding out ahead of the curve is vitally important. Some recent examples:

- The Oakland A's found that more and more pitchers were inducing ground balls. They ended up signing hitters with uppercut swings. This gave them power and cut down on double plays.
- The Pirates found, as many did around the same time, that a catcher's ability to "frame pitches," turning close pitches into strikes, is more valuable than previously thought. They made a rare trip to the free agent market, signing renowned pitch framer Rus-

sell Martin to a two-year, $16 million contract. Martin was a foun-
dation player for back-to-back postseason berths.
- Several teams invested heavily in Cuban players. The A's, White
  Sox, and Dodgers got superstar talent for midlevel money (far
  below what a U.S. player would get on the free agent market).

There are several steps in the process: studying information, realizing
what's important, and then deciding what to do about it. There is a sizable advantage to be gained with each decision. But here, the Astros have
taken a quantum leap forward. They are not only attacking the data and
trying to figure out the best possible decisions, *they are studying the process
by which all of their decisions are being made.*

"Human beings have evolved with great capabilities," says Mejdal
"but they did not evolve to be perfect—instead they are just 'good
enough.'" Mejdal studied this specific kind of human deficiency—the
biases in decision making. "Anytime that you have human beings faced
with an overwhelming amount of information, you can expect predictable errors. The more you can learn about those errors, the more you can
take steps to avoid them."

The Astros are getting answers where most teams aren't even asking
the questions.

# Card Counting

One of the more memorable scenes in the movie *Moneyball* is when Brad
Pitt/Billy Beane tells the room filled with scouts that they are now "card
counters at the blackjack table." It's about believing in a process where
information is giving you a small, but meaningful, advantage. It's no surprise then that the Astros' director of decision sciences was a blackjack
dealer. "It was wonderful training. Quite often you are bypassing your
emotions, and often that is the right thing to do." Mejdal was, in this case,
the house, so the odds were actually in his favor from the start. But he

learned to observe what was happening in front of him. "You learn basic strategy, and often a strategy doesn't feel right. But you learn it *is* right."

For Mejdal, it was "practice in divorcing myself from emotional decision making." This dispassionate approach was kept out of baseball for a long time. According to historian John Thorn, "Baseball society figured if you grew up in baseball, you knew all there was to know about baseball." In that world, what *felt* right was what was done, even when it ran counter to the data. "If you go to aviation school, you learn how to do night flying," says Thorn. "The first thing you learn is 'do not trust your eyes, trust the instruments.' So it's very hard for veteran baseball people to trust the instruments and not trust their eyes." So the Astros pay someone to keep their eyes trained on the instruments. "As human beings, you miss subtle differences," says Mejdal. "A dealer will often tell you something wrong. He doesn't do it on purpose, but it's that observational skill and mental math are not adequate to sense nonsignificant differences."

A batter drawing a leadoff walk doesn't seem significant. In fact he has made it 15 percent more likely for his team to score a run. A hitter who is 0 for 3 with two walks doesn't make the TV highlights—he's likely the unnamed player crossing the plate on that "clutch" hit—but from a distance that's a .400 on-base percentage. That's significant. These are the obvious lessons of the '80s and '90s. In today's game, what seems nonsignificant—yet important—might be harder to find. "There just might be something that goes into baseball skill that's invisible," says Mejdal, "that you can't see in a small sample. Whether that's a higher resolution of the guy's contact rate, or his plate discipline. We must admit that there could be something to baseball skill that we can't pick up in a small sample."

While other kids were falling asleep during fourth grade math, Sig stayed focused with visions of baseball players and their numbers. He learned if Hank Aaron had seven home runs in the first month, Sig could use fractions to figure out how many he might have over the 162 games. It's one thing to be a baseball fanatic, though, and another to be one who goes on to get degrees in mechanical engineering, aeronautical engineering, and operations research. "The engineering exposes you to breaking down complex problems into smaller parts and solving each of the smaller parts, one at a time. I think those skills were very useful for baseball."

I know many of us just want to watch baseball and enjoy it. But if you have an emotional investment in a team, there is a great reward in seeing that team win, and you don't win by not paying attention to the details. The new analytical approach is seen by some as dehumanizing, but this is simplistic thinking. It is more of an attack on the unthinking, habitual behavior. An attack on bias, and lazy, irrational decision making. Our day is made up of thousands of decisions. Which food to eat, which road to take, how to spend our time. How are we making these decisions? "It's human nature to jump from what feels right to the conclusion that it is right. I think it's important to stop that leap and question it. If at all possible, to test the thing that feels right."

# The Habit of Bias

In his book *The Power of Habit*, Charles Duhigg goes into exhaustive detail examining habitual patterns that take over our lives. He cites a 2006 study at Duke University that claims 40 percent of our decisions aren't actually decisions at all, but merely habits. Duhigg writes: "When a habit emerges, the brain stops fully participating in decision making. It stops working so hard, or diverts focus to other tasks." Our brains are wired to make things simple. Says Mejdal, "It's human nature to look for evidence that confirms what we already believe in, but it's important to force yourself to look for evidence that's going to contradict what you believe in. Our human nature gets in the way of ourselves."

Duhigg backs up Mejdal's point about making big problems small: "Understanding how habits work—learning the structure of the habit loop—makes them easier to control. Once you break a habit into its components, you can fiddle with the gears."

There are a number of gears to be fiddled with if you are a professional baseball analyst. This is the essence of Mejdal's job. "We have all sorts of blind spots," says Mejdal. "There's recency effects, primacy effects, the anchoring effects, representativeness. There's a whole field related to this. If you first see a player [and he's] good, you're going to be anchored to that. Or if you go in with the expectation that he's good. It's a well-documented inefficiency that you're anchored to your first impression."

Think of how the perception of a free agent is largely tied to his first year. Catfish Hunter was seen as a great signing, Carlos Beltran was seen as a bust. Beltran delivered *much* more to the Mets than Hunter did to the Yankees, but Hunter was a stud in his first season after signing a big free agent deal, while Beltran struggled in his. Perception can become fixed early if a player hits a home run in his first game, or has a good first season. Yet it leads to a misleading valuation, erroneous conclusions, and then more poor decision making.

The cliché is "your mind is playing tricks on you," and economist Daniel Kahneman—cited in Chapter 1—observes just how easily this is done. We no longer need the survival skills of an ancient hunter-gatherer, but the hardwiring is still there. We are built to make incredibly quick decisions based on memories—the information we immediately have on hand. But this "associative memory" is extremely faulty and mostly hidden from our conscious selves.

A scout or coach won't know he favors a player because that player reminds him of an old teammate, or because the scout likes the beautiful ballpark the player plays in. Are the warm breeze and comfortable setting affecting your judgment? The answer is, "of course." It's just a matter of how aware you are of this and how to minimize it. One positive attribute can cause you to think highly of someone in all areas. I'm not saying a scout or a coach is easily fooled by a kid with a firm handshake, but if you go into a situation wanting a player to be special, there are cues that can subconsciously seal the deal for you and you will not even be aware of them.

One psychological effect that has reached the mainstream baseball vernacular is the "Law of Small Numbers," which we now call a "small sample size." We know not to believe in a player's production until he has proven it over a good period of time. But how often do we brand a player as "clutch" after a handful of hits strung together over several Octobers? Our minds are wired to find certainty. The principle of confirmation bias states that we are conditioned to believe in something first, un-believe if necessary. Un-belief takes analysis, which means hard work. And our minds do not like hard work! Writes Kahneman: "many people are overconfident, prone to place too much faith in their intuitions. They apparently find cognitive effort at least mildly unpleasant and avoid it as much as possible."

Representativeness is an especially powerful bias. When you are looking for a baseball player, you are looking for a blend of skill and athleticism. For decades—and still to this day—the physical characteristics of a person play a far greater role than they should. This applies to much more than just baseball, of course.

Back in the days when there was just one small ESPN newsroom, we all sat in close quarters. There were workstations—called pods—of four to six people each. Each show, the 6 p.m. *SportsCenter*, *Baseball Tonight*, the 11 p.m. *SportsCenter*, had its own pod. In its pod, the boss was the coordinating producer (CP). Once, two of the neighboring CPs were having a loud, animated conversation. The producer I was working with, Stu Mitchell, said to me quietly, "Have you noticed all our CPs are the same?" I looked up. There were two big, burly guys with very deep voices, bellowing back and forth about nothing of any importance. I guess I had sort of noticed, but never thought it through. Stu said, "Do you think the executives think that because these guys are big and yell all the time, they should be in charge?" We thought about it. Many of the CPs were exactly this type: alpha males with baritone voices. If you look one by one, it seems like they would rise from the producer and production assistant level because they were "take-charge" guys. But were executives just selecting the candidates who *looked* and *sounded* like take-charge guys?

Think of the job: the ability to coordinate a staff producing television program; editorial judgment in putting together the show rundown. It takes a variety of skills, but the ability to "bust heads" is rarely one of them. Looking like a hard-boiled TV boss had little to do with *being* one, but it sure seemed to help in getting that position.

Players run, and sluggers swing a mighty bat. Muscles matter. But there are skills that come into play to decide the game. The duel between pitcher and batter, played out pitch after pitch, several hundred times in a single game, and several hundred times a season for a single player, is where the game is won and lost. "We were underrating this skill," says A's GM Beane. "Look at a guy like Matt Stairs, who back in the '90s maybe doesn't pass the eye test. He was 5'9", maybe 230 pounds. He wasn't 6'4", didn't look like Adam Jones in a uniform."

Stairs wasn't drafted, played in Japan, and didn't have his first full major league season until he was 29 years old (with the A's). Representativeness cost him his prime. In his first seven full seasons, he slugged .504. "What was interesting about Matt was that he was also a good defender, but he didn't necessarily look like your classic defensive outfielder," says Beane. In the pre-data world, the eye test ruled, and your eyes are more tied to emotion and bias than you think. "We were relying upon our own emotional response to watching a guy play," says Beane, "Aesthetics played a part of that."

Stairs played in the majors until he was 43, but you get the feeling his skills were never fully embraced. Stairs finished with an OPS+ (park-adjusted, league-adjusted on-base plus slugging) of 117, about the same as Steve Garvey, Wally Joyner, and Hideki Matsui. Garvey won an MVP, Joyner and Matsui went to All-Star Games. Stairs bounced around year to year, playing for 12 different teams.

Even the most rational are susceptible to this bias. While with the Cardinals in 2005, Mejdal went to a Stanford game to see the number one player in the country according to his player projection model. "I hadn't gone to a college baseball game sober in my life." Now he was on business, a bona fide scouting trip for a player he had never seen. "I went to see this Paul Bunyan of a second baseman, a Ryne Sandberg man-among-boys."

When Stanford took the field, Sig realized they didn't have names on the jerseys. Here he was scouting for the St. Louis Cardinals, and he's about to bolt to the concession stand to buy a program. He waited to see if he could find his number one prospect. "Here comes the Stanford team—they're a good-looking lot—and then there's this little guy at the end. I'm thinking, oh they must have run out of scholarships and that's probably a chemical engineer who played baseball or something to fill out the team. You could see where this is going. I got the roster and sure enough that number three at the end was Jed Lowrie, the guy who was number one on my stat list."

Sig's training was about to be tested. He was about to go back to the Cardinals with his report, and the sell is easier if you go back with an Adonis-in-cleats. "I remember getting this sick feeling, like, 'this can't be right.' This guy doesn't even look like he belongs on the Stanford team." Sabermetric haters will often rail against "numbers taking over the game," so remember this moment. It's the numbers that make this a meritocracy. Without them, little Jed Lowrie has no shot, and fat Matt Stairs stays in the minors. "I remember imagining going to St. Louis, they're going to see this supposed 'value' of the analytics," says Mejdal, "and they're going to send me right back home."

Representativeness gives the decision maker cover. Even if the player is a bust, it's understandable to others if the person *looks* the part. In the early '90s, Bengie Molina was one of the best amateur hitters in Puerto Rico. For three straight years, he sat by the phone on draft day for a call that never came. He was later signed for a low-end bonus, and only after scouts had come out to see his highly regarded little brother Jose.

Why would one of the most accomplished players in Puerto Rico get bypassed? Likely because Molina didn't *look* like a major leaguer: 5'10", about 220 pounds, not the body beautiful. In his book *Molina*, he describes his first look at the Angels' minor league gathering: "The players in camp looked as if they had stepped out of a baseball magazine; square-jawed, broad-shouldered, long-limbed." When I spoke to Molina, he still clearly remembered being intimidated: "I'd never seen anything like it. It was like a movie. They looked the same, walked the same, even had the same haircut."

Of course, if you get a fair shake, it doesn't matter what you look like. Give credit to the Angels' coaches and scouts for getting Molina through their system. Despite the squatty body, Molina played full time for 11 major league seasons and was the Angels' starting catcher on their 2002 World Series championship team.

Molina, though, cost the Angels only 25 grand. Mejdal was pitching Lowrie for a much bigger investment, and even with his considerable training, he was filled with doubt: "I know what a major league baseball player looks like, and I expect others that are going to be baseball players to look like this." The Cardinals had both the 28th and 30th pick of the draft, and Sig stuck to his guns, making his case to draft Jed Lowrie in the first round. "My brain was telling me this can't be right. But this guy who's too small—even for college—has outperformed every big guy, medium guy, and other small guys for three years."

This has been the baseball battle for decades: "tools" vs. performance. With limited and unreliable data for high school and college players, what an athlete could do physically often trumped what the player was actually doing on the field to win games. Through the years, we heard about players "running like a deer," or having an arm "like a cannon." You rarely heard about a player's "plate discipline" or "pitch recognition."

Lowrie was a two-time First-Team All-American and the Pac-10 Player of the Year. He had a .435 on-base, slugging .551. "Intellectually, you begin to fight this feeling, but that's not an easy battle to win," says Mejdal. "Your emotions and your gut, in my experience, are going to run over the intellect much more often than not."

Sig won the intellectual battle in his own head, but did not convince the Cardinals. St. Louis went with Colby Rasmus and Tyler Greene, the latter a 6'2" college shortstop described by Sig as "uber-athletic." The Red Sox picked Lowrie 45th.

"To be honest when they took somebody else I was relieved. I still have confidence, but I still had a sick feeling." Mejdal wasn't sure he wanted to be on the line for an undersized infielder without speed. "Like 'how dumb is this new guy?'" Mejdal envisioned them saying. "Did he not even see this guy is too small?"

Lowrie has played eight years in the major leagues, providing above-average offense at shortstop, with the ability to also play both second and third base. "Uber-athletic" Tyler Greene played parts of five major league seasons, and hasn't played in the majors since 2013. Sig's system had the right guy.

# Engineering the System

By the end of 2002, the Cards had been to the playoffs three straight years. They had a young Albert Pujols, and had been very successful in making trades, picking up Jim Edmonds Scott Rolen, and Edgar Renteria. Cards owner Bill DeWitt Jr., though, was looking forward, and didn't like what he saw. "After the 2002 labor agreement, the landscape was changing." DeWitt saw increased revenue sharing among the factors that would be leveling the field, and believed the market for picking up free agent talent would be drying up. The Cardinals have a large fan base, but lack the economic might of the coastal teams, and the ability to complete dollar for dollar on the free agent market. "We'd been successful, but I didn't think it would last," says DeWitt. Unable to sway his group into a new way of thinking, he introduced it himself, bringing in a management consultant with degrees in engineering and economics, Jeff Luhnow.

"We had a talented group," says DeWitt, "but it was traditional in a sense that there wasn't a lot of interest in analytics, in different ways of looking at things." Soon the Cardinals had state-of-the-art analysis, and a drafting and development machine that was the envy of the rest of the league. "I bought into that work they were doing. I spent a lot of time with that group. Always challenging and always pushing for the new frontier, for what would give us a competitive advantage."

With no experience in organized baseball, though, Luhnow's presence would cause a divide in the front office. It was exacerbated in 2005 when Luhnow was promoted to VP of player development and scouting. Like many clubs going through this transition, the Cardinals had a split personality—partly data-driven and analytical, partly traditional. The club's informational edge wasn't being maximized.

DeWitt insisted everyone get along, or else. "There was clearly conflict as time went on, and something we had to do was resolve that conflict."

After a 78-win season in 2007—just one year removed from a World Series title—respected GM Walt Jocketty was fired, eventually moving to the Reds. The Cards promoted John Mozeliak to general manager, and Luhnow's place in the game solidified. After decades of ownership backing down in the face of their "baseball people," the Cardinals took the giant leap forward.

Within the game, this was seen as an assault on baseball tradition. Bill Madden of the New York *Daily News* wrote a column titled, "Walt Jocketty Gets Axed from Cards Because of Numbers Crunch." In it, Madden called it part of a "growing trend of meddling owners reducing the powers of the general manager and shifting the emphasis of baseball operations to statistical analysis."

Between 2011 and 2014, the Cardinals made four straight appearances in the League Championship Series, won two NL titles, and a World Series championship. In 2013, 16 of the 25 Cardinals players on the World Series roster had been drafted during Luhnow's tenure.

The "meddling owner" was a unique figure in baseball history. Bill DeWitt Jr. fixed something *before* it was broken.

# The Process

At the time, Luhnow was called a "new wave stat practitioner," so out there he actually "hired a NASA scientist" to help him with data. That former NASA scientist was Sig Mejdal.

You didn't hear about this much, but the Cardinals under Luhnow did something revolutionary at the minor league level: They stopped paying attention to the stats. But only the stats we're used to, what you can call "results data." By "results data," I mean not only batting average, but on-base, slugging, and every other offensive result.

A number of teams are already there, including—of course—the A's. "What we measure is process," says A's GM Billy Beane, "giving credit for a process that consistently led to results as opposed to taking a stat, which is just a result that doesn't tell you how you came to it."

What the Cardinals and other teams had access to was better than stats: the exit velocity, launch angle, and vector of each batted ball. Think about it; what does it matter if a Double-A center fielder tracks down a rocket off the bat of your minor league first baseman? What matters is the skill and consistency of the hitter. When you can calculate some sort of, let's call it "Frozen Rope %," what does it matter if it was caught? Some hits find gloves, others find gaps. By looking at the granular data, rather than results, you strip away a good part of the player's circumstance and boil things down to his skill. "All base hits are not equal," says Beane, explaining that an infield bouncer and a rocket to right field might both be "singles," but do not belong in the same category. "If you consistently hit off of your fists you're going to make outs, whereas if you consistently hit a line drive, you're going come out with a good result over time. So people looking at 'stats' are looking at the wrong thing."

The batting average, doubles and triples don't travel with the player, but his plate discipline and his hitting skills do. Now it was being measured in its purest form. The Cardinals' player development machine under Luhnow (and certainly the rest of the Cardinals organization) became the envy of Major League Baseball. In just three draft classes— Luhnow's first three—the Cardinals' system churned out 24 major league players, by far the most in the major leagues in that span.

Years later, Luhnow was running his own ship, and the amount of data continued to explode. Now every major league stadium is rigged with systems that measure almost all player and ball movement. Player movement is trackable, from the "route efficiency" of the outfielders, to the spin rate of a slider.

"There are few industries as well recorded as to what's taken place as baseball," says Mejdal, "So if you're able to retrospectively gather all the information that you had at the time of the decision, you could look for patterns, you look for which of these attributes should be driving future decisions."

Let's say you're thinking of signing a 31-year-old pitcher. That's past prime, but there are plenty of mitigating factors. What's his track record? How many innings has he pitched? Injury history? Cost? How has he aged? Will his stuff play as he ages? What's the trend of his spin rate? Does he rely on velocity? "We know we are in the probabilistic world so we know sometimes it's going to point 'yay,' and the guy 'nay'd,'" says Mejdal. "But you can begin to learn about which of these attributes is important. And it's nothing that the person doesn't try to do in their head anyway. They're just doing it from memory, experience, and mental math."

"Mental math" is a big expression for Sig. It means we all weigh things very quickly and come up with a gut feeling. Depending on what you believe, it could be what Malcolm Gladwell called a "Blink" moment, where your inner computer makes a sophisticated decision, or it could be just where we wing it, and make a hasty decision that "feels" right or expedient. Guess which way Sig is leaning? "You wouldn't do your taxes in your head, why would you do something much more complicated in your head?" says Mejdal. "You have this mental model how to make sense of all these attributes, but you weren't born with that. That comes with your experience, which is only pretty good. So if we could take all these attributes that you use to make your decision and really analyze them, we could get a data-driven recipe. And I bet you a dollar it's not going to agree with what's in your head entirely."

## Draft Dodging

Nearly three years in, the ground started to look shaky under baseball's Grand Sabermetric Experiment. The hometown *Houston Chronicle* fired the early shot, with a piece in May 2014 entitled, "Radical Methods Paint Astros as 'Outcast.'" The club was characterized as having a "a dehumanizing, analytics-based approach," with an anonymous player claiming the

Astros "take out the human element of baseball." The piece was, by and large, balanced in its treatment of the team, but the headlines create the national perception. The torches were being lit, the mob was assembling. They'd soon have a rallying cry.

For the third straight year, the Astros had the number one pick in the draft, and the most money to spend. Drafting was a vital component to the rebuilding system, and the Astros had orchestrated the previous two drafts to maximize a new system. Compared to other ways of acquiring players, the draft provides an exponential bang for the buck. So gathering extra money is a huge edge in investment.

In 2014, though, there was a problem. After the Astros drafted high school pitcher Brady Aiken with the number one overall pick, a medical report reportedly showed Aiken to have a "small" ulnar collateral ligament. The Astros cut their offer from $6.5 million to $3.1 million. Aiken and his representatives were outraged. Aiken was fine, they said, throwing a free-and-easy 95 mph at the end of his high school season. The Astros weren't even claiming he was hurt, just that they now believed there was a significant risk of injury. It was a tricky spot. The Astros not only had Aiken on the line, but with draft budget limits being tied together, two other high school draft picks were tied to Aiken's signing. The Astros made a final-day offer of $5 million, and said their calls to agent Casey Close went unanswered. The Astros had whiffed on the number one pick in the draft.

A horrible situation obviously for Aiken, it was also a public relations nightmare for the Astros. "Unequivocal draft disaster" and "Hard to overstate repeated failure for Houston" were among the quick reads.

The Players Association blasted the club, with a statement from MLBPA chief Tony Clark: "Today, two young men should be one step closer to realizing their dreams of becoming major league ballplayers. Because of the actions of the Houston Astros, they are not. The MLBPA, the players and their advisers are exploring all legal options."

At the time, the Astros' other top two picks were also far from successful. Two thousand twelve pick Carlos Correa was recovering from a broken leg, and 2013 pick Mark Appel had about a 10 ERA in Class A ball.

The media smelled blood. The high-and-mighty science-loving Astros were now getting their comeuppance. I was crowing about them on MLB Network, gleefully calling them the "Team of the Future." Ben Reiter of *Sports Illustrated* had bought in, putting the Astros on the cover of the magazine only a month before, and calling them "Your 2017 World Series Champs." Now it was written that the cover was "a source of comic gold." Sportswriters and analysts would cackle to me, saying "How's that 'Team of the Future' looking?" in mocking tones. No doubt, it was a low point. By the end of July 2014, the Astros, coming off three straight 100-loss seasons, were 20 games under .500, and had given the brush-off to the number one pick in the draft. What kind of Decision Sciences was this?

"The plan was clear," says Mejdal, "The Astros were going to be rebuilt through the draft and player development. We knew it was going to take a long time. When there was bad press from not signing Aiken, and the *SI* article, that didn't change the time frame at all."

Shortly thereafter, someone who had hacked into the Astros' data system leaked conversations the team had had about trades. A year later, the Cardinals would be linked to the investigation, and they would fire their scouting director. At the time, however, it was all lumped into the summer of embarrassment for the Astros.

Then in September, the Astros fired manager Bo Porter. The week before, Ken Rosenthal had written a piece for FoxSports.com saying, "Those critical of Luhnow say that he keeps a small circle, communicating mostly with director of decision sciences Sig Mejdal and others while rarely consulting the team's on-field staff, executive advisor Nolan Ryan and special assistant to the GM Craig Biggio." The subtext was that the wonks were sticking together, while the "men in uniform" were being kept out of the loop. Through the history of the game, this has often been a fireable offense. With the wolves starting to circle, you had the feeling the winning had better start soon.

But the tide turned in a number of ways in 2015. Not wanting to go to college and delay his professional career three years, spurned number one pick Brady Aiken entered a postgraduate semester at IMG Academy, a private school that features elite athletes. All he needed was some showcase work prior to the 2015 draft. "Brady has been seen by some of the most experienced and respected orthopedic arm specialists in the country, said Casey Close, Aiken's representative, during the clash with the Astros. "All of those doctors have acknowledged that he's not injured and that he's ready to start his professional career."

In his very first IMG game, Aiken tore his UCL. The ligament the Astros believed to be too small snapped 12 pitches into his next game. You can say the Astros couldn't have known that would happen, and yes, they couldn't have. But from the time of the Astros' physical to that UCL giving out, Aiken hadn't lasted for even an inning of competitive throwing. Aiken had Tommy John surgery, and was still a first-round pick that June. Selected 17th by the Indians, he signed for a bonus of $2.5 million, half of what he had turned down from the Astros.

Skewered the year before, the Astros received no apology from the media. The only columns I can find addressing the Astros *possibly* being properly concerned over the state of Aiken's arm came from "Sports on Earth" (oh yeah, that's my column), and Dave Cameron of FanGraphs. To acknowledge that the Astros were—perhaps—not merely heartless and cheap would go against the anti-intellectual narrative, and the usual media depiction of the sabermetrician as a computer-using bloodless freak ready to crush mankind with an army of robots. Maybe in 1980 the idea of "computer knowledge!" would be frightening. Thirty-five years later, when most of us own two or three portable computers, isn't it time to let that go? The Astro's decision making looked sound, but that doesn't mean this wasn't a difficult time. "Perhaps," says Mejdal, "I lost some more stomach lining because of it."

2015 would be year four of the Astros rebuild. The club was still lean; 29th in payroll, outspending only the newly rebuilding Arizona Diamondbacks. Even frugal teams like the Twins, Mets, Royals, and Orioles were outspending the Astros by 50 percent. Houston's payroll was just under $70 million, and six clubs were close to outspending them by *one hundred million dollars.* Yet, on Memorial Day—before they brought up their top prospects and before they made any trades—the Astros were 12 games over .500, and leading the AL West by five and a half games.

Typical of sabermetric teams, they led the AL in strikeouts and were second in home runs. Every team likes home runs, but homers can be bought on the cheap if you buy them via the "flawed" home run–centric player. The Astros had plenty of these all-or-nothing hitters, giving them a lot of pop, and the ability to overcome deficits.

In another example of zigging while others zag, the Astros were decidedly *not* playing the on-base percentage game. Before calling up 2012 number one pick Carlos Correa and making a trade for Brewers center fielder Carlos Gomez, Houston was regularly rolling out *five* regulars with a sub-.300 on-base. Had this happened with the late '90s A's, Billy Beane would've run out of TVs to throw through clubhouse windows. Fifteen years later, on-base was expensive, and the state-of-the-art sabermetric club had to move in another opposite direction.

Along those lines, the Astros also led the American League in stolen bases. This, too, goes directly against the Bill James teachings of the 1980s. However, in the new, lower-run-scoring era, extra bases were vital, and the young Astros were a hard-swinging, big-slugging, high-strikeout, base-stealing outfit. With a high-speed and high-strikeout game, the Astros also hit the fewest ground balls in the league, leading to the second fewest double plays.

With a fraction of the payroll of the elite teams, the Astros had pieced together the sixth highest run-scoring team in baseball. By the stretch run, they had bona fide stars like Correa and Gomez, but their home run leaders right after the trade deadline were Luis Valbuena, Chris Carter, and Evan Gattis, three players not especially expensive ($9 million combined for one year) or difficult to obtain. The roster was young, with just one position player in his 30s (Jed Lowrie, at 31).

Only months after the Grand Sabermetrics Experiment had appeared to be floundering, the Astros emerged as a contender. They would spend most of the season leading the AL West, win 86 games, and take a postseason berth. They would beat the Yankees in the AL Wild Card game, and get within six outs of eliminating the eventual World Series champion Royals in the Division Series. The ridicule and questioning of the Astros' methods had stopped.

What wasn't apparent to the mainstream media for three years became clear in 2015: The Astros were building a sustainable powerhouse. The front office that had drawn ridicule was starting to be seen as state-of-the-art. Before the season was over, the Brewers had hired Astros assistant GM David Stearns to replace their retiring GM Doug Melvin. Only 30, Stearns is the youngest GM in baseball. We'll have to wait to see who the Brewers name as their director of decision sciences.

Stearns' hiring points to the drastic expansion in the Major League Baseball talent pool. A new class of highly educated junior executives is flooding front offices. "Take Farhan Zaidi," says Beane, speaking of his former assistant GM, who is now the general manager of the Dodgers. "A young man whose dad worked for the Asian Development Bank, who grew up in the Philippines following American sports on the Internet." Beane is right, someone like Zaidi had no chance of running a baseball team a generation ago. "Think of the opportunity for every kid who loves sports, that doesn't necessarily have the physical abilities to become a player. They now have a portal to be a part of something they have loved since they were a kid." Of course, competition is rising on all ends. "The same talent that Silicon Valley is competing for, we're competing for on the business side," says Beane. "The advantage we have in sports is that they'll come work for their favorite team for 20 cents on the dollar. Why wouldn't we take advantage of that?"

Mejdal represents that talent pool, and the high level of thinking that will be required to compete in Major League baseball in the future. Armed with an education far beyond that of most baseball executives, Mejdal's broader view carries the torch of the sabermetric founders 35 years earlier: a healthy skepticism of things already taken for granted. "Question the ground rules, question the convention," says Mejdal. "Try to think differently."

# 16

# The Year of Getting Smart

"The whole world is based on utilizing information as quickly and as intelligently as you can. The ones who can do it are the ones who are going to win."

—Billy Beane, Oakland A's

In only the time it took to research and write this book, there has been a stunning change in the baseball landscape. A final tipping point was reached in a very specific and vital place in the baseball machinery—the major league dugout.

After years of illogical obstinance, a wall has come down. A quote like this—"We hang on to tradition. But is it tradition, or is it truth? You've got to seek the truth"—comes not from Bill James or a baseball outsider, but from a 50-year-old baseball manager: Jeff Banister of the Texas Rangers, the 2015 A.L. Manager of the Year. Things are changing right in front of us. Revolutionary thought is now mainstream thought. Even for the manager.

# Lag Time

Let's see if you can spot the trend:

> The live ball is introduced in 1909. The Live-Ball Era begins 11 years later for Babe Ruth, 20 years later for the rest of baseball.
>
> The relief ace is first used in the 1920s, helping the Washington Senators win the 1924 World Series. Relief ace era begins 23 years later.
>
> Lou Boudreau introduces defensive shift in 1946, shutting down Ted Williams. Defensive shifts become widespread 65 years later.
>
> Sabermetric revolution introduces analytics in early 1980s. Adopted league-wide nearly 30 years later, after subject becomes a hit book, and then a hit movie.
>
> Bullpenning used effectively every All-Star Game, often in World Series. Bullpenning comes into widespread use . . .

Athletes train hard for hours every day. Managers plot and plan, losing sleep. Organizations pour money into resources. Given how hard every player, coach, manager, and executive works, wouldn't you think they would *leap* at the chance to gain a tactical edge using information?

We are slow, however, to move against the herd, even if it helps us win. We behave irrationally, out of habit. Despite going after opponents to the point of violence on the field, we actually behave quite politely in a grand strategy sense, as if to keep things "sporting." This goes for more than just baseball.

Imagine if we gave a home run to the opposite field two runs instead of one. You would certainly try to hit to the opposite field, right? You would think coaches would emphasize that type of hitting, and front offices would pay a premium for hitters with opposite field power. But just *how* far would you go? How much would you tailor your team to this obvious gain of opposite field power? This is akin to what the NBA was facing in the 1980s.

# Downtown

There are few competitive advantages as clear as shooting three-pointers in basketball. In the 2015 playoffs, Steph Curry of the Golden State Warriors hit 98 of them. In the first playoffs where there were three-pointers—1979–1980—the NBA playoff leader had just 10.

It's not that the '79 Seattle SuperSonics weren't thinking of taking advantage of the three-pointer, they had a guard named "Downtown" Freddy Brown! Brown led the NBA in three-point shooting percentage that season. What they *thought* was taking advantage, however, was no-where near what they could have been doing. In the 2015 playoffs Curry attempted eleven 3s per game; in '79–'80, Brown was averaging only two. Given an obvious advantage, a chance to get three points a shot rather than two, teams still moved very slowly to maximize the advantage.

In 1985–86, for example, legendary shooter Larry Bird led the NBA with 82 three-pointers. Steph Curry, in 2014–15, made 286. Same deal in the NBA finals. Bird's Celtics, even with another deep threat in Danny Ainge, made 12 three-pointers. Curry's Warriors made 67. Seven years into the three-point era, a team with two all-time great shooters was making only 2 three-point shots per game.

This isn't a quirk. In 1993, the year of Michael Jordan's first three-peat, the Phoenix Suns led the NBA in three-pointers with 398. That figure would be dead last among NBA teams in 2015. Teams have gotten hip—there is a big advantage shooting from three. Shooting *a lot of 3's* gives you a huge edge—much more than teams initially thought, and then thought for a good 20 years.

Teams try something new, and it points to an competitive gain. Other teams follow. But they also follow *very slowly*. This is a normal part of the human learning process.

So.... What if we knew this about herd behavior, realized its inefficiency, and then decided to skip that part of the process?

This could be done in Major League Baseball right now—with

"opening" pitchers, relief aces, bullpenning, and changing the position of manager as we now know it. It's like knowing on-base was king in the 1950s. Everybody *kind of* knows it, but no one is taking it to the fullest advantage. Wins are there for the taking, if anyone is willing to skip the normal 20-year waiting period, and *just get there.*

In 2013, I was the keynote speaker at the SABR Analytics Conference. I advocated bullpenning, Kill the Win, knuckleball academies, and a managerial staff to replace the "manager" position. Once done, I mingled. At the conference were most of the young Turks then working in the analytics, or "Baseball Operations," departments with major league clubs. The place was filled with bright minds, people in their 20s and 30s with economics, mathematics, and various science degrees. I was in a good conversation with one of them, and he laid out his club's vision: integrating starters and relievers, front-loading the lineup with the club's best hitters, and getting more playing time for players with broader skills. I loved all his ideas, and told him so. His club, though, I pointed out, was doing *none* of these things. He told me, "Yeah, I know." Don't they listen to what your guys are saying? He replied, "That's not how it works." I had similar conversations with many of the major league analytics staffers.

*How are ideas not getting to the field?*

It was the final gatekeeper, the man in uniform.

# The Middle Manager

The manager used to be the most important man in a baseball organization. He was a coach, game tactician, team psychologist, and scout. The front office was not always the large operation it is now. There was a team president, a general manager, then the manager. In the 2014 book *In Pursuit of Pennants*, Mark Armour and Dan Levitt trace the evolution of the front office. In 1983—only a generation ago—the San Francisco Giants had six executive positions in what we would now call Baseball Operations. In 2014, they had 35.

The man known as "The Skipper" has become a middle manager. I often wonder why the man in this position, in such plain sight, could make so many suboptimal decisions. Whether it be batting a weak hitter at the top of the lineup or bunting in the first inning, how could a professional who's lived his whole life devoted to a sport be doing things people *in the stands* know is counterproductive? Sabermetric pioneer Dick Cramer thought this was precisely why they did so: "It's a goldfish bowl, people are watching your decisions. I think so much of the decision making in sports is hard because everyone *is* watching you."

This leads to a lot of decisions based on blame avoidance. Bunting shifts the pressure to the hitters. You've traded three chances for two, and if those two batters fail, the onus is on them. If you leave in your starting pitcher while he's fatiguing, *he* becomes the one who "let the game get away," not the manager. Even if the manager had a variety of options with his eight—eight!—bullpen pitchers. "Generally, in anything," says Billy Beane, "if you do things the traditional way and fail, you kind of get to shrug your shoulders. It's an easy out. If you fail in a nontraditional way, you leave yourself open to criticism."

I ran my managing theory of blame avoidance by Hall of Fame manager Tommy Lasorda. I braced for a possible volcanic reaction. Tommy was always friendly to me, but a "who the hell is this guy telling me about managing" response was clearly in play. He instead said, "Did you know I had nine Rookies of the Year?" I didn't make the immediate connection. "When you play the veteran and he doesn't perform, it's *his* fault," said Lasorda. "When you play the rookie and he doesn't perform, it's *your* fault. That's why most managers don't play their young players. I *always* played my young players." I had always given the Dodgers' player development group credit for that incredible talent pipeline, and clearly they deserve most of the credit. But *nine* Rookies of the Year? Lasorda had a huge edge in that era by not being afraid to take the short-time hit for the long-term gain.

In the late first decade of the 2000s, front offices may have been revolutionized, but many of Lasorda's big-name colleagues were still in the saddle. Men with large personalities and reputations. Then, between the end of 2010 and 2013, the following managers left the dugout: Jim Leyland, Dusty Baker, Tony La Russa, Davey Johnson, Charlie Manuel, Jack McKeon, Jim Tracy, Ron Gardenhire, Joe Torre, Bobby Cox, Lou Piniella, and Cito Gaston.

That's an entire generation of the old guard checking out. Some were good, some all-time great, some were stuck in dead-ball mud. On the whole, the problem was not that they were relics but that they were *powerful*. Coming from the '70s or '80s, they had built up years of equity and credibility. The game had changed drastically, but because of the nature of the job and its varied demands, a powerful figure could still be effective, even when ignoring tactical advantages and helpful information. Managing people is a big part of the job. As long as these imposing figures were in the dugout, the smart-ass baseball ops kid can drop off his info packet down in the manager's office, but then he'd better keep walking. Uniformed personnel only, son. But with the old guard gone, and more information pouring in, the next phase was rapid.

"It's a redefinition of how things are done," says Billy Beane. "There's so much information now. That has changed the position. Getting that info down to the dugout and making sure it's implemented." Beane, of course, has been accused of "interfering" with his manager. My question to that has always been, why shouldn't he? Shouldn't the utilization of personnel and resources be something that's subject to an organizational discussion, not just a manager's whim? The game is filled with too many options to be left to one person's point of view. "There's a real synergy between the dugout and the front office," Beane adds, "making it a real part of game planning, and game management."

A shift in how a culture thinks—a paradigm shift—doesn't happen in a linear fashion, bit by bit, each year. Many a player had told me "If you tried to mess with Jimmy Leyland's lineup card, you'd better duck." That's a funny story, but why wouldn't Leyland—or any manager—want the maximum information available? You'd figure Leyland, La Russa, Cox, and most of these successful managers had daily sessions with their coaching staff, going over options. Why wouldn't you want to go over those options with a staff devoted to dissecting the questions you're asking? Because the old guard—with all their success—just didn't have to. Once they cleared out, as Thomas Kuhn writes, "one conceptual world view [was] replaced by another." The Major League Baseball manager, after years of stagnancy, changed his thinking in 2015. Here are a few examples of the new world view:

- The Pirates are a new model of excellence. Manager Clint Hurdle and his staff, having seen the light, made the postseason for the third straight year. The old-school manager turned the Pirates into a model integration of analytics, scouting, and coaching, going all-in on the information brought to him by an analytics team led by Dan Fox and Mike Fitzgerald. Old-schoolers could write off the A's and Rays as desperate and the Yankees and Red Sox as big-money, but there was no ignoring the worst-to-first Pirates with all their defensive shifting.

- Buck Showalter's success. Maligned as a "micromanager" 15 years earlier, Showalter was now seen as the game's best strategist. Micromanaging was in, and with a 96-win season in 2014, Showalter won his third Manager of the Year Award.

- The Dodgers make Rays GM Andrew Friedman an offer he can't refuse. New ownership looks to exploit a market inefficiency: below-market-pay for the best baseball executives. They bring in Friedman, A's assistant GM Farhan Zaidi, and former Padres GM Josh Byrnes (from the Indians Cradle of GMs). Friedman gets a five-year deal for $35 million. Big money? Sure, about what the Dodgers were paying Alex Guerrero, their backup utility infielder. This, for the man overseeing a roster of $300 million.

- The Cubs pounce on Joe Maddon. The Rays' skipper was allowed out of his deal if Friedman left, and the Cubs raised his $1.8 million salary to $5 million. Maddon, a top-notch motivator and leader, was also the best example of a manager as extension of a forward-thinking front office. The marketplace was speaking, and it was saying a new wave manager gets paid.

- The Rays replace Maddon with Kevin Cash. The former Indians bench coach is analytically inclined, leading the league in taking out starters after going twice through the lineup (bullpenning). Rather than wait for the ninth inning, he sometimes uses his "closer" in the eighth to face the heart of the order, and he throws two "bullpen" games when playing interleague.

- The Rangers hire Jeff Banister as manager. Having served on the Pirates' forward-thinking coaching staff, Banister immediately announces the club has no set batting order, that it'll be changed day to day, depending on matchups and what will maximize the chances of scoring in any given game. Claims to be up on Bill James. "If the numbers say the same thing year after year," said Banister, "There's gotta be some truth to it, right?"

- The Astros hire A. J. Hinch as manager. The Stanford psychology grad has an analytic mind-set, locking him into the hard-core data-driven front office.

- Theo Epstein's Cubs break out. Boy Wonder GM could be easily dismissed as a Pedro/Manny creation if he flopped in Chicago. The former Red Sox GM was in year four of Chicago rebuild and the grumbling had begun. That's all forgotten as the Cubs bring up a bumper crop of talent from the farm system, and win 97 games in 2015.

How did everyone get so smart in one year? "I don't know if they all got so smart, or if they just now have enough cover," says Rob Neyer. "Managers now know that this is what their owners want. Their owners are businessmen, they understand the use of data. They also have plenty of places, like FanGraphs and other websites, that won't crush them for making decisions for data-driven reasons." It's not that the managers are necessarily smarter, it's that the entire *culture* is. The herd has moved so it is now safe to move with it.

So with all these advances, how did the 2015 season end? With a manager ignoring evidence and allowing his actions to be dictated by emotion.

In Game 5 of the World Series—with the Royals leading three games to one—Matt Harvey had thrown eight shutout innings, helping the Mets to a 2–0 lead. They were three outs from sending the Series back to Kansas City. Relief ace Jeurys Familia—a 1.85 ERA in the regular season and a 0.71 ERA in the postseason—was warm in the bullpen. When Terry Collins and pitching coach Dan Warthen told Harvey he was done for the night, Harvey insisted Collins send him back to finish the game. The crowd was chanting Harvey's name, calling for him to return. So what's wrong with a manager letting his stud pitcher take the mound for three more outs?

Here's what wrong: A mountain of evidence that pointed to Harvey's fatiguing late in games. The immediate prior performance does not matter. Shutout and dominance aside, Harvey has a fairly clear fatigue point. It's exactly the fatigue point that Grady Little ignored when he left in Pedro Martinez in the 2003 ALCS. It's the same fatigue point that has become the generic statistic for starter fatigue: 100 pitches.

To that point in his career, in pitches 1–100, major league hitters hit an anemic .206 against Harvey. After Harvey reached 100 pitches, they hit a robust .373, with a Hall of Fame–level .440 on-base percentage. Harvey, after eight innings against Kansas City, was at 102 pitches.

Beyond that data, Harvey had a history of hitting a wall. In 2013, he had started a fresh inning having thrown 99 pitches or more six times. *In five of those six games* he had to be rescued for a relief pitcher, and in the sixth such game he labored and gave up a run. In 2015, Harvey was coming off Tommy John surgery, so the Mets limited his pitch count. In seven games they sent Harvey out for another inning when he was past 90 pitches. *In three of those seven games* he had to be rescued or gave up a run. It's fair to say the Mets were faced with the "Should we let Matt Harvey pitch another inning" question 13 times, and nine times he ran into trouble. Down three games to one in a World Series, the Mets could not afford to have him run into trouble.

You'd have to be deliberately obtuse to ignore the pattern: One of the top pitchers in the game quickly goes from great to mediocre at a point of fatigue. That had been the case throughout his major league career.

On what basis did Collins decide to stay with Harvey? In the post-game press conference he said, "When you looked in this kid's eyes, when he came off that inning—and I mean, he's been through a tough summer; he's been beaten down—and I just trusted him."

Armed with experience and evidence telling him that Harvey was done for the night—with his club's season on the line—a professional baseball manager *looked in his player's eyes* and changed his mind.

Collins even acknowledged his player's "tough summer." Harvey had been branded a quitter for wanting to limit his innings the first year off of elbow surgery. This was a great pitcher with a bruised psyche wanting to redeem his own personal reputation. This is his right and he's not to be blamed for it. A warrior is trained to compete beyond his levels of normal effectiveness. But it's his manager's job to know those limits and to stop him from harming the team because of his personal goals and ego. As for the crowd? Some writers would later state Collins was just listening to his fan base, but there's a reason why the people in the stands are having a beer and a bratwurst while the people in the dugout are wearing a uniform. The guy in the uniform is a professional. A professional is paid to make an informed, rational decision unmoved by emotion and mob rule.

Matt Harvey and the crowd would get their way. Collins sent Harvey to the mound, to an immense roar from the crowd. In the stands, Royals GM Dayton Moore told the Kansas City fans around him, "Get ready, we're going to win the World Series."

At the start of the inning, the Royals' win expectancy was 14 percent. After a walk to Lorenzo Cain and a double to Eric Hosmer, Collins predictably—*this was predictable*—came out to rescue Harvey. It was now 2–1 Mets. The Royals' win expectancy was now 35 percent.

When Hosmer later scored on a mad dash to the plate, the pro-Harvey crowd was silenced. I was up the third base line in the MLB Network suite, but I could hear individual Royals players cheering across the field in their dugout. The score was 2–2. Here come extra innings. The long Mets death march was on. The Royals would score five runs in the 12th, and later celebrate a World Series championship on the Mets' field. There would be no trip back to Kansas City, no Jacob deGrom in Game 6 or Noah Syndergaard in Game 7.

After the game, Terry Collins would have the good grace to say he had made a mistake in letting Harvey go back out for the ninth. Unlike Grady Little, he understood his mistake. The mainstream media, though, almost universally defended Collins for "going with his heart over his gut." Nowhere that I can recall did anyone wonder where brains fit into this equation. Beyond questioning the moves of any individual manager, can we just admit something? The job is too big for one person. As I said in "Good Looking Beats Good Pitching," the game often moves too quickly for sound decision-making. Mike Matheny and John Farrell both did excellent jobs leading their clubs to league titles, so why leave them hanging when they needed tactical help? What's needed is a managerial staff. Keep your large, ruggedly handsome ex-player in place. He is now freed up to do what he's good at—be a leader, maximize performance, and keep a regular check on the energy and esprit de corps of the club. Pitching fatigue, pinch-hitting, pinch-running, defensive shifting, double switches, and bullpen usage can now all be monitored by your managerial staff, with much more relevant information. Reduced velocity and spin rate can tell you fatigue level before a pitcher's mechanics break down, and certainly before he will tell you. If you feel the need to hide your brain trust, stick them right behind the dugout off the tunnel. Sound crazy? That's where the video guy now sits for most clubs. When you see a hitter bolt from his at bat to the tunnel, that's usually where he's going. Steps from the dugout, the hitter can get instant feedback on the at bat.

What was the pitch sequence? What pitch got him? It all can happen before the hitter has to go back onto the field. Your staff can sit there, or you could stick uniforms on your wonks and call them bench coaches.

This is where Billy Beane sees it going. "At some point there's going to be an IT coach in the dugout," says Beane. "Not a guy out there hitting fungoes, but a guy who is out there giving real-time info after every single pitch." Think about something simple, like knowing the leverage of any at bat. Knowing that with a four-run lead, a bases loaded situation in the sixth *is* the time for your closer. A managerial staff, or IT coach, will have that information the instant the situation presents itself. An IT coach will also know your pinch hitters and how they perform not only against the pitchers in the opposing bullpen, but pitchers with a similar arm slot or repertoire.

The manager can always reject the information—he might know a player didn't sleep or has a stomach bug—but in a postgame review, as Sig Mejdal showed us, even these decisions can be measured and stored for future evaluation. "Think about real-time information and moving players on every pitch," says Beane. "We're going to have real-time dashboards you can access as to where you're going to set your infield, where the pitch is going to go, based on the hitter, the ump, everything, maybe the atmospheric conditions." This is possible right now. "Something like that will happen," says Beane.

This is not just a sabermetric pioneer, this is the VP of baseball operations of the Oakland A's. So I asked him, Billy, why aren't you doing this? "Haha, I'm too old! I'm more interested in what fly to use up on the Deschutes River at a certain time of year. Someday soon I'm going to be guest hosting on your show. At some point you turn into a consultant as opposed to an operator." Beane knows better than most the trouble that comes with being the first one out in front. There is a price, after all, for straying from the herd.

# Epilogue

In the ESPN newsroom, my co-workers would come over to my desk and run potential trades by me for their fantasy teams. My colleague Michael Kim, sitting next to me, would watch them leave, shake his head, and say, "When did *you* become the math guy?" It has been an unexpected path.

No matter how many World Series I attend, or Hall of Famers I meet, my favorite moments in baseball will always be coaching my own boys—Lucky and Peter—in Little League. (For the record, I did not impose sabermetric principles on the Rockies of the Kingston Colonial Little League.) Our competitive advantage was teaching our boys that we would be only as good as our weakest players. Our star kids learned to embrace and encourage the kids that could barely catch the ball. It worked. We won back-to-back league titles those years. It might not sound like much but those neighborhood titles meant as much to us as any World Series title means to Joe Torre.

My love of baseball revolves around the history of the game, and our family's vacations often revolved around trips to its ancestral home. When my wife, Nicole, and I were first married we had planned a winter trip to Cooperstown. A huge storm was moving in and I knew that she—being the responsible one—would want to cancel. The night we were supposed to leave she called the newsroom and my heart sank. "We better leave right after your show so we can stay ahead of the weather!" That's my girl! Five hours later we were on Main Street, Cooperstown, as the snowstorm that would strand us for three days roared into town. These are the times you live for.

As the years passed and our family grew, Hall of Fame Induction Weekend became de rigueur. The crowds, the history, the pageantry of it all is in our bones. These days Nicole and I still go back there, still in love, still cherishing the whole mystique of it all. We're not alone.

One day I was sitting on the set of *MLB Now*, arguing with columnist George Will about Yasiel Puig's "comportment." I'm in favor of players showing their individuality, but I'm pretty sure Will was winning this one. Mid-show, I get a text from our oldest daughter, Alexandra, who had been scouting locations for her wedding. "Sooo . . . I want to get married at the Otesaga in Cooperstown." I turned to George to tell him. "My daughter is getting married in Cooperstown!" He said, "You can do that?" Why, yes you can, George. Without changing expression, he said, "Well, it doesn't get any better than that, does it?" No, George, it doesn't. Months later I was having dinner with ESPN's Tony Kornheiser and mentioned Alexandra was getting married at the Otesaga in Cooperstown. Tony, no stranger to the finer things in life, stared at me in disbelief. "That's my favorite hotel in the world. In the world!" Yes, there is something about this game of baseball that even my statistics can't quantify.

Through baseball I learned to look for the difference between what is apparent and what is actually happening. I slept through Voltaire and the Socratic method in school, but when Bill James asked, "Everybody is always saying this. Is any of this true?" a whole new world opened up. Ask a question, get your answer, and ask the next question. Think critically, and independently. Avail yourself of bright people and new ideas.

Had I mentioned a club putting together an "analytics department" in 1999 when I was hosting *Baseball Tonight* on ESPN, I would've been mocked. Now the Cardinal's owner points to it as the pivotal moment in the Cards becoming baseball's model organization.

As a man who has endured the slings and arrows of being known as a stat geek, I ask you to indulge me for a moment:

> When I predicted the Red Sox' hiring of Bill James would put an end to the Curse, people laughed. The Sox went on to win three World Series titles in ten years.
>
> When I predicted in 2013 that the Astros would be winning 90 games within five years, people laughed. Three seasons later, they went to the postseason.
>
> When I said shifting would revolutionize defense, I was told shifting didn't work.
>
> When, in the '80s, I said players were juiced up on steroids, I was asked if I also had a theory on the Grassy Knoll.
>
> When I said we should listen to what Jose Canseco was actually saying, I was told he was "only in it to sell books."
>
> When I said the Angels were ignoring the lessons of history in signing Albert Pujols long term, I was told that my stupid numbers didn't apply to Hall of Famers.
>
> When I said the Nationals would win 105 games in 2015—OK, I was wrong about that.
>
> When I now say starting pitchers will blend into the bullpen, managers will turn into a management staff, and ninth-inning closers will turn into high-leverage firemen, I'm sure it'll be dismissed as well. Feel free to run with the herd. You will never be alone.

The best thing about the sabermetric revolution is that the pioneers of the movement weren't looking to run teams, they were fans of the game. For most fans, guys who loved baseball and were forced to watch from a distance, the sabermetricians proved that we can see much more when we take a wider view. We have outlived the snickers and dismissals to see baseball—and most other sports—swept up in an analytics revolution.

I had already learned to believe little of what was handed to me, but there is a difference between a cynical mind and a critical mind-set. It's through sabermetrics that I was better able to understand the world and to continue to evolve. It's true that the only constant is change, and through baseball I've learned not to fear it, but anticipate, understand, embrace, and enjoy it.

In *Moneyball*, Billy Beane famously says after a postseason loss, "My [stuff] doesn't work in the playoffs." As it happens he's wrong. He's allowed to be wrong once in a while. This stuff works all the time.

# Afterword

## The Future Is (Almost) Here: The 2016 World Series

I don't see as well as I used to. I should probably have glasses for distance. At Game 6 of the World Series in Cleveland, I squinted to make out who Joe Maddon had just put into the game. I didn't know the Cubs had another tall, skinny black left-hander in their bullpen besides, of course, Aroldis Chapman. Sitting in a sea of celebrity Cubs fans, I turned to the guy next to me and asked, "Who is that?" John Cusack—a bit faster than Eddie Vedder—shot back, "You mean Chapman?"

My eyes had seen Chapman, but my brain could not process it. There was no way that could be Aroldis Chapman. The Cubs led Game 6 of the World Series 7–2 in the 7th. Chapman had been ridden hard two nights earlier in Game 5; 42 pitches over 2 ⅔ innings—way beyond his normal workload. A five-run lead with 2 outs in the 7th meant Chicago had a win probability of 96 percent. If I'm managing in this situation, I already have Chapman watching the game back at the team hotel in a robe and fuzzy slippers. It never entered my mind that Chapman would be in if the game wasn't close. Joe Maddon would later offer a compelling reason for bringing in his relief ace: "There's no Game Eight." He was correct on that. I'm not saying he made a terrible choice. The Cubs were down three games to two, so even with a 7–2 lead, a loss ends your season. Even the remote chance of losing that lead cannot be risked.

The bill, however, came due the next night. After throwing 20 pitches in Game 6, his velocity was down more than two miles per hour, Chapman was not the same pitcher for Game 7. Maddon brought him in with 2 outs in the 8th with a two-run lead. Like a starter going over his fatigue point, he still may have looked like the man with the best fastball in the game, but the action on his pitches told a different story. Chapman immediately gave up a double and then the game-tying home run to Rajai Davis. It was one of the most stunning turn-arounds in the history of the World Series. Maddon was right about having to win Game 6, but to win the World Series he needed to win two games, not one. Maddon would be heavily criticized, but then essentially forgiven when his team would go on to win in extra innings.

Buck Showalter got no such reprieve. Weeks earlier, in the American League Wild Card Game, the Orioles manager made an even more stunning decision. In a tie game going into the bottom of the 9th and facing the end of their season, the Orioles had the option of going with a pitcher who had just finished the year with the lowest single-season ERA in baseball history. We might not all be stat geeks, but most anyone who has ever seen a box score knows that Zach Britton's 0.54 ERA was an absurdly low number, signaling an all-time great season. Britton was sitting in the Orioles bullpen, about to get bypassed in favor of four teammates.

You could argue in favor of Showalter's choice of hard-throwing Brad Brach to start the 9th. Brach had just finished the 8th, and was also coming off an excellent regular season (2.05 ERA, 92 strikeouts in 79 innings). You could also make an argument in favor of his next choice of Darren O'Day, a righty killer with a lifetime 2.41 ERA.

What you cannot argue—successfully—is not using Britton to start the bottom of the 11th. Brian Duensing seems like a perfectly nice fellow, but he had thrown just 13 innings for the O's in 2016 and over the last six seasons owned an ERA of 4.66. That he struck out his one and only batter is just a fortunate result. But it's one out, and the top of the Blue Jays order was coming up. Showalter wisely pulled Duensing.

Britton stood in the bullpen. Showalter brought in Ubaldo Jimenez.

Once an excellent starter, Jimenez had been a disastrous signing for the O's. Erratic and unreliable, he had a 4.77 ERA in his three years in Baltimore. As bad as he was starting, he was even worse in relief. In 2016, he had thrown 10 innings out of the pen and had given up 10 runs. This pitcher known for his complicated mechanics was also about to face two of the top ten hitters in the American League, Josh Donaldson and Edwin Encarnacion. I'm not nitpicking. There was very little reason to think Jimenez would be successful in that situation.

The Jays quickly smacked back-to-back singles against Jimenez, setting up first and third with one out. What the Orioles then needed most was either a strikeout or a ground ball for a double play. If these are the two things you require, the very first major league pitcher you should want is Zach Britton.

Britton has an excellent strikeout rate, and a best-in-baseball-by-a-wide-margin 80 percent ground-ball rate. Here was one last chance for Buck Showalter to go with his relief ace. Instead, he stubbornly and inexplicably stuck with Jimenez. The first pitch to Encarnacion landed in the upper deck. Jimenez had thrown five pitches, giving up three hits, three runs, and not recording an out. Twitter was blowing up, the Rogers Center was going berserk, and the Orioles were done for the year.

Everyone was asking me, "What's with your boy?" (Buck was the one manager I asked to contribute a blurb for this book). My answer is this: Showalter made a mistake, but he did what most every other manager of this generation does.

Even the most brilliant of baseball minds is susceptible to herdthink and prone to old habits. In 2016, there were 374 games where a team on the road faced a sudden death loss (a tie game in the 9th inning or later). In only 27 percent of those games, did that road team use their closer. Just over a quarter of the time. Managers in this generation are almost all willing to do basically the same thing that brought national scorn and embarrassment to Showalter: risk the end of the game with the club's best pitcher sitting in the bullpen.

In this book, I discussed some of the last remaining options for a team looking to seize a competitive advantage. I suggested replacing the solo manager job with a managerial staff. I went over the obvious suboptimal choices made by the ruggedly handsome managers of the 2013 World Series, Mike Matheny and John Farrell. It may have seemed like I was picking on two guys who were slightly overwhelmed in new situations. What we saw in the 2016 postseason, however, should make this completely clear: The job is too big for any one person, even the most talented. We're now talking about two of the top skippers in the sport facing intense criticism. Buck Showalter is not only one of the most highly regarded managers in the game, he is widely considered to be the very best at the specific skill of using a major league bullpen. And in his two years with the Cubs, Joe Maddon won 97 and 103 games, culminating with his club's first World Series title in 108 years. Both are clearly exceptional managers, yet both needed help at the biggest moments. A team that goes with a managerial staff helping their manager with real-time options will have a decided advantage.

But while that idea has yet to seized upon, we did see major advancements in two other areas: bullpenning and the use of a relief ace.

Ironically, in the year of the Zach Britton disaster, Terry Francona of the Indians showed a wider audience what a relief ace could do. In the opening game of the Division Series against the Red Sox, Francona stunningly brought Andrew

Miller out of the pen in the 5th inning. Through the three rounds of playoffs, he would use Miller in the 5th, 6th, 7th, 8th, and 9th, pitching anywhere from 4 to 8 outs. For the most part, Miller set up the capable late-inning duo of Bryan Shaw and Cody Allen. In Game 3 of the ALCS, though, Francona switched up, using Shaw and Allen for the 7th, and going to Miller in the 8th and 9th. The Indians refused to be tied to convention, won 7 of 8 games in the American League playoffs, and went all the way to Game 7 of the World Series. It was a managing tour de force.

Miller-mania would have an immediate effect on other managers in the playoffs. After a season of conventional (9th inning only) usage, both Aroldis Chapman of the Cubs and Kenley Jansen of the Dodgers started to come in as early as the 7th, with both throwing multiple innings.

This is a perfect example of baseball's herd mentality, as detailed in Chapter One. As long as no one is getting "cute," you can lumber along as inefficiently as you like with no repercussions. Terry Francona though, strayed from the herd and was starting to make his fellow playoff managers look like prime candidates for Mamaluke of the Year. Anyone watching the playoffs would ask, "Why don't we use our closer like that?" And there would be no justification not to.

Turning a closer into a relief ace is a relatively quick fix. Bullpenning is a tougher concept, yet the game inexorably continues toward it. For the first time in World Series history, no starter would record an out in the 7th inning. Despite the fact that both clubs had excellent rotations. The Cubs starters led their league in ERA, the Indians were second in theirs. The two clubs had three of the top five starting pitchers in park-adjusted ERA (Kyle Hendricks, Jon Lester, and Corey Kluber). This was a case of managers—backed by astute analytics staffs— no longer waiting for starter failure to make a move to the bullpen. Maddon and Francona weren't alone. Starters throughout the postseason were coming out earlier:

| Average Innings per Start/Postseason | |
|---|---|
| 1986 | 6.2 |
| 1996 | 6.0 |
| 2006 | 5.2 |
| 2016 | 5.0 |

This change was not due to a high-scoring World Series; this was two teams consistently making a preemptive strike. The numbers make it clear that being proactive makes sense. Not only do pitchers get hit much harder when they go through a lineup for the third time, we are also in an era where the bullpen alternative is better than ever before:

**Number of Relief Pitchers with Sub-3.00 ERA**
**and 9 Strikeouts or More per 9 Innings**

| 1996 | 11 |
|------|----|
| 2006 | 15 |
| 2016 | 35 |

There are more flame-throwing bullpen guys than ever. Not that pitching as a craft has improved, just that there are more pitchers who can smoke three hitters than ever before. Hence there is an added incentive to go the bullpenning route.

Of course, sportswriters are still sportswriters, and even the combination of visual and statistical evidence was not enough. Unable to deny the effectiveness of the Indians' usage of Andrew Miller, sportswriters did the next best thing: deny it would work for anyone *other* than Andrew Miller. An Associated Press column had this headline, "Don't Expect Bullpen Bingo from Playoffs to Become the Norm." Paul Hoynes of cleveland.com wrote a column headlined "Want to Start a Bullpen Revolution? Just Clone Cleveland Indians Lefty Andrew Miller." I've explained the natural human resistance to change, so this sort of reaction has to be expected. What the Miller exceptionalists are missing is that most every club has a pitcher who is a bit better than everyone else—out for out. This person is normally called "the closer." Francona was letting that guy roam for key moments, rather than having him sit and wait for the final three outs.

The question now is whether any other manager will jump in and grab the advantage. Or will Terry Francona have to embarrass the rest of the league again? Nationals manager Dusty Baker, evidently forgetting how relievers were used when he was a major league player himself, commented, "It's not a trend that I'd like to be a part of any time." Brad Ausmus of the Tigers said, "If you can find me another Andrew Miller, let me know." But A. J. Hinch of the Astros might be ready: "In the playoffs we ended up seeing what baseball would be like in a very short series, in a very short time frame. The goal now is how can we apply that to games that count in April just as much as they do in September." Lag time in grabbing a competitive advantage is shrinking. There's no time to wait.

# Glossary

**BABIP—Batting Average on Balls in Play** The batting average *only* on balls put into play. By excluding the Three True Outcomes—strikeouts, walks, and home runs—we pare things down and see the variance of the batted ball (luck, if you prefer). Not all BABIPs are created equal. Both a pitcher and hitter will have a BABIP baseline based on performance over previous seasons. Once this baseline is established, however, we can see how hit-lucky or unlucky a pitcher or hitter has been.

**Context Neutral vs. Context Dependent Hitting Statistics** A vitally important distinction. *Context neutral* is what the hitter does all the time, regardless of situation. Batting average, for example, is a context neutral stat. If you "hit .300," you have a .300 batting average in all situations: bases loaded or nobody on; no outs or two outs; in the first inning or in the eighth inning.

*Context Dependent* takes the situation into account. A two-out, two-run double in the eighth down 2–1 is a much bigger hit than a single in the third, leading 10–0. This is the "clutch" that clutch fans have been craving for decades. There are two main ways to determine clutch hitting: changing the chances of scoring a run (run expectancy), and changing the chances of your team winning (win probability).

**DRS—Defensive Runs Saved** The state-of-the-art defensive metric, as measured by Baseball Info Solutions. Calculated by sabermetric pioneer John Dewan, DRS assigns a specific run value to the defensive performance by a player. Similar in concept to UZR (below) but differs in how the data is collected and how run values are calculated. Also now features intensive video review of all defensive plays.

**ERA+ Earned Run Average Plus**  Park- and league-adjusted ERA. A great tool in comparing pitchers of different areas, in that it adjusts for the run-scoring environment of the particular season. Bob Gibson's record-setting 1.12 ERA in 1968 reads better than Pedro Martinez's 1.74 in 2000. Pedro, though, was pitching in a hitter's park in a high-run-scoring season. His ERA+ that year was 291—the best in the modern era—while Gibson's was 258. (Unlike ERA, a higher number is better.) Martinez had the better season, relative to the run scoring of the time.

ERA+ is also scaled to 100 being league average. If league ERA is 3.80, then a pitcher with a 3.80 ERA in a neutral offensive park will yield an ERA+ of 100. Remember, being described as "league average" is not an insult. A league average pitcher is worth about $10–12 million a year (in 2015 money) on the open market.

**FIP—Fielding Independent Pitching**  Measures strikeouts, walks, and home runs from a pitcher in a formula that converts these statistics into a number comparable to ERA. This statistic is based on Voros McCracken's breakthrough work in *Baseball Prospectus* in 2001. This theory has taken many shapes since its inception, but the basic premise is still this: A pitcher is *most* responsible for the Three True Outcomes: strikeouts, walks, and home runs. Everything else is highly dependent on the defense behind a pitcher and the random variance of the batted ball. To a certain degree pitchers influence the level of contact from a batter, but to a much lesser degree than most thought prior to McCracken's work.

FIP is most valuable as a projection tool. It has been shown to be a more accurate indicator of future performance than ERA.

**FIP–Fielding Independent Pitching Minus**  Park-adjusted FIP. It's scaled so that league average equals 100, with below 100 being better than average. It is similar in concept to OPS+, except that in FIP-, a lower number is better than a higher one. It differs from FIP in being park and league adjusted.

**OPS—On-base Plus Slugging**  An offensive statistic combining two stats that measure distinctly different things. On-base percentage is the percentage of a player's plate appearances in which he safely reaches base via hit, walk, or hit by pitch. Slugging percentage is total bases divided by at bats, a measure of a player's power. Though OPS undervalues on-base percentage, it gives a rough idea of the best hitters in the league. In a typical year, an OPS near .800 means you're above average, near 1.000 means you're an MVP candidate.

**OPS+ On Base Plus Slugging Plus** Park-adjusted and league-adjusted OPS. If you're going to be using OPS, you might as well use OPS+. Set to a scale where league average is 100, it allows you to quickly analyze team offense by scanning the starting players' OPS+ column. A team with every hitter over 100 is extremely deep and will score loads of runs. Here's a quick guide:

100: League average, productive
110+: Above average, a good season
120+: All-Star level
130+: Excellent production
140+: High level, possible MVP candidate
150+: Top 10 bopper, likely MVP candidate
170+: Historically high production, the place of Hall of Famers

As with ERA+, OPS+ is an excellent tool for comparing eras. Forty home runs in the late 1960s is a great achievement. In the late 1990s it's almost commonplace. OPS+ lends instant context.

**RA/9—Runs Allowed Per Nine Innings** The average number of runs a pitcher gives up over every nine innings pitched. Differs from ERA by including unearned runs.

**RA/9 WAR** The runs allowed per nine innings, with innings pitched mixed in. Extremely useful in Cy Young Award analysis. Despite the wonky-sounding name, this is very basic: How many innings did you pitch, how many runs did you allow?

**Run Expectancy (RE24)** This measures the change of probability of a team scoring runs event to event. Sometimes called RE24, it comes from the run expectancy in the 24 base/out states. There are 24 different base and out possibilities, from no one on and no outs to bases loaded and two outs. Let's say you single with a man on first, nobody out. You have then changed the run expectancy of a man on first and no outs to the run expectancy of men on first and third and no outs. RE24 measures that change based on average number of runs you would score in each of these situations.

This stat measures not only clutch, but all offensive actions. A leadoff walk increases the expected number of runs that inning from .54 runs to .94 runs, so the batter is given credit for increasing run expectancy by .4 runs. If the leadoff man makes an out, the expected runs that inning have decreased from .54 runs to .29 runs, so the batter is charged with decreasing the run expectancy by .25 runs. All these differences are tallied through the season, then added up for a final total.

The one downside for comparative analysis is that this is not a completely "fair" measurement. A hitter can have a larger effect on run scoring when he has more chances with men on base; therefore a hitter on a powerful offensive club may have a higher RE24 than a better hitter on a weaker club. On the whole, though, this is a very useful stat, and reflects "clutch" hitting through the season.

**SIERA—Skill Interactive ERA** FIP, with a groundball component mixed in. On the whole, ground balls do less damage than fly balls. Therefore, a high-strikeout pitcher who also induces ground balls is an extremely valuable player. This is not an absolute requirement, though. A pitcher *can* be great without a high ground ball rate. By and large, however, it's better to have a ball put into play be a groundball. SIERA tells you who has the best mix of these skills.

**UZR—Ultimate Zone Rating** A measurement of defense kept by FanGraphs. com. Devised by sabermetrician Mitchel Lichtman, it divides the field into zones, and compares a fielder's performance to league-wide averages.

**WAR—Wins Above Replacement** WAR measures the totality of a player's contribution, boiling things down to one number. No other stat forces us to confront a quantifiable contribution of baserunning and fielding as well as hitting in measuring the value of the player. Because it is one number, it enables us to make a reasonable, quantifiable comparison between pitchers and position players.

WAR, as a number, is an economic model. It measures how a player compares to low-cost, available talent. A "replacement" player is basically a bench player or minor league player making the league minimum salary. According to FanGraphs, a leading sabermetric website: "WAR offers an estimate to answer the question, 'If this player got injured and their team had to replace them with a freely available minor leaguer or a AAA player from their bench, how much value would the team be losing?'"

The WAR number is an approximation. In an MVP debate, the difference between an 8.3 and an 8.1 is not especially important. The difference between an 8.3 and a 5.0 is significant.

Hitting statistics are very accurate. Baserunning stats are reasonably accurate. Fielding stats need to be examined closely, neither taken at face value nor dismissed. The defensive part of WAR can be eyed warily, but critics of WAR dismiss the measurement entirely if they don't agree with the defensive metrics. You know the saying, "Don't let perfect be the enemy of the good." Defensive stats are not perfect, and even with MLB's new Statcast, they may never be. That doesn't mean we shouldn't try to measure defense the best we can, and it doesn't mean we shouldn't attempt to measure the total contribution of a player, including defense.

There are multiple versions of WAR, from Baseball-Reference, FanGraphs, and from another leading sabermetric website, Baseball Prospectus (where it is called VORP). The key WAR difference is that Baseball-Reference WAR uses runs allowed for pitching and defensive runs saved for defense, while FanGraphs uses fielding independent pitching for pitching, and ultimate zone rating for defense. They still operate on the same theoretical principles.

**oWAR—Offensive WAR** A calculation of wins above replacement that accounts only for a player's offensive production. While WAR estimates the value of a player's entire game, oWAR measures only what a player does offensively.

**VORP—Value over Replacement Player** Baseball Prospectus's version of WAR. It has recently become WARP, wins above replacement player. Because the anagram sounds like a planet in *Star Trek*, it is more easily mocked by baseball writer/comedians.

**bWAR Baseball-Reference's** calculation of the WAR statistic. BWAR calculates pitching value from runs and innings pitched. It is rooted, then, in the actual runs allowed by the pitcher, while making an adjustment from the pitcher's team defense. The defensive component comes from defensive runs saved, which is figured by Baseball Info Solutions, run by sabermetric pioneer John Dewan.

**WHIP—Walks plus Hits per Inning Pitched** A WHIP at or below one implies dominance. A pitcher approaching 1.5 WHIP is going to give up a lot of runs.

**Win Probability** At any point in a baseball game, there is a precise probability percentage that a team will win. This probability percentage is based on the results of thousands of previous games. For example, in Game One of the 2015 World Series, the Royals were down 4–3 to the Mets with one out in the ninth inning. The Royals had just an 11 percent chance of winning—that is, their Win Probability was 11 percent because only 11 percent of teams in their situation win that game. When Alex Gordon homered to tie the game at 4, the Win Probability changed to 58 percent because in a tie game in the ninth inning with one out and playing at home, the team in that situation will win 58 percent of the time.

Win Probability is a team statistic. Win Probability Added is an individual statistic.

**WPA—Win Probability Added** Similar to run expectancy, but measures how each hitting result changes the probability of the team winning. The name explains it: Over the course of a game, what did a player *add* to the *probability* of his team *winning*?

At any point in a game, one can calculate the probability that either side will win, based on the average team in similar situations. WPA calculates the effect that each individual batter or pitcher has on his team's chance of winning the game, both negative and positive, during every at bat.

A solo home run in a scoreless game in the first inning does not sway the probability of winning nearly as much as a solo home run in a tie game in the ninth. This is also not a completely "fair" stat in terms of comparative analysis, given that some players will have many more opportunities to make big changes in the win probability. Knowing this, this stat rewards the player who repeatedly comes through with big, "clutch" moments.

**wRC+—Weighted Runs Created Plus** The most accurate context neutral hitting stat. Very similar to OPS+, it measures offensive production, adjusting for park effects, and scales to a league average of 100. The difference is that wRC+ uses the relative value of each offensive event as the components of the final statistic, rather than on-base plus slugging. For instance, on average, hitting a single will lead to .47 runs, and a home run 1.4 runs. Weighted runs created plus measures this difference, as well as all negative run events (making outs).

Weighted runs created plus is useful in comparison to OPS+ because it is more accurate in terms of valuing offensive production. For instance, OPS+ treats slugging percentage and on-base percentage as equally valuable, but on-base percentage plays a larger role in run scoring. wRC+ eliminates this discrepancy, valuing all offensive events as precisely as possible.

**XBT%—Extra Bases Taken** How often does a player take the extra base, that is, go from first to third on a single, second to home on a single, or first to home on a double? Great base runners like Willie Mays, Rickey Henderson, and Mike Trout will exceed 60 percent in their best years, while 50 percent is still an excellent percentage. This stat is an excellent way of discerning the excellent base runners who might not have the obvious stolen base numbers. Alan Trammell, Keith Hernandez, Joe DiMaggio, and Roberto Clemente did not steal bases but were still outstanding baserunners. The XBT% reflects this.

**xFIP—Expected Fielding Independent Pitching** Similar to FIP, but with the difference that a player's FIP is calculated with a league average HR/FB (home runs per fly ball) ratio. This statistic is based on observation that an individual's HR/FB ratio is prone to large fluctuation and may be more a product of luck than skill by the pitcher. A pitcher can limit home runs by inducing ground balls, but over a larger sample about 10–12 percent of fly balls will turn into home runs for almost all pitchers. This is not a tool to be used for, say, Cy Young Award voting: A home run should not be eliminated because it may have been "lucky." However, just as FIP has been found to be a better indicator of future performance than ERA, xFIP has been found to be a better indicator of future performance than FIP. Really.

# Acknowledgments

Most of the fun on the project has been spending time with my son Peter—researcher, social scientist, and companion through this process. Our road trips and late-night writing sessions are something I'll always remember and treasure. He also asks that if the book bombs, he be completely disassociated from the project. Noted.

To the rest of my beautiful and fascinating children, Alexandra, Lucky, Clare, and Camille, I love you all so much. To my father and mother, Charlie and Cathy Kenny, thank you for your unfailing support and a lifetime of love.

Those who took the time to be interviewed for this book make up quite an incredible group: Bill James, John Thorn, Pete Palmer, Dick Cramer, Peter Gammons, Michael Lewis, John Dewan, Sig Mejdal, Bill DeWitt Jr., Rob Neyer, Billy Beane, Paul DePodesta, Dan O'Dowd, Dr. Joel Fuhrman, and John Sawatsky. I am fortunate to have had access to such an array of distinguished thinkers.

And thank you to those who helped shape my thoughts about life, baseball, and this book: Marc Adelberg, Greg Amsinger, Sanford Appel, Marc Appleman, Teddy Atlas, Perry Lee Barber, Lou Barricelli, Johnny Bench, Carter Berardi, Al Bernstein, Yogi Berra, Bruce Bochy, George Bodenheimer, Jim Bouton, Larry Bowa, Jim Bowden, Scott Braun, Jim Breuer, Lou Brock, Jackie Brown, Eric Byrnes, Dave Cameron, Marc Capalbo, Rod Carew, Sean Casey, Gerald Celente, Fran Charles, Albert Chen, Marc Ciafa, Nick Ciminello, Jane Forbes Clark, Joey Cora, Bob Costas, Keith Costas, John Daly, Ron Darling, Ryan Dempster, Mark DeRosa, Marc Desy, David Dinkins Jr., Greg Dowling, Jim Duquette, Gregg Easterbrook, Dennis Eckersley, John Entz, Michael Epstein, Lorraine Fisher, Carlton Fisk, Tim Flannery, Cliff Floyd, Bill Francis, Vince Gennaro, Bob

Geren, Ken Gold, Goose Gossage, Jim Gray, Mitch Green, Butchie Guido, Tony Gwynn, Daryl Hamilton, Jay Harris, Thomas Hauser, Jon Heyman, Brad Horn, Jeff Idelson, Tom Ingram, Rich Isakow, Ben Jedlovec, Richard Justice, Jim Kaat, Elliot Kalb, Al Kaline, Micah Karg, Jeff Katz, Michael Keaton, Max Kellerman, Kostya Kennedy, Jonah Keri, Pastor Earl Kim, Jee Ha Kim, Tim Kirkjian, Ethan Kleinberg, Mike Konner, Tony Kornheiser, Mark Kriegel, Tony La Russa, Tom Lasorda, Al Leiter, Joe Lemire, Ben Lindbergh, Mike Lowell, Zach Lupica, Joe Magrane, Rob Manfred, Bruce Markusen, Chris Martens, Wayne Martin, Buck Martinez, Pedro Martinez, Voros McCracken, Rob McGlarry, Michael McKee, Bryan Meyers, Kevin Millar, Theresa Misasi, Bengie Molina, Paul Molitor, Scott Mondore, Marty Montalto, Joe Morgan, Craig Muder, Phil Mushnick, Eric Nehs, CJ Nitkowski, Jack Nugent, Dan Okrent, Keith Olbermann, Adam Ottavino, Dave Patterson, Carlos Pena, Tony Petitti, Dan Plesac, Joe Posnanski, Maury Povich, Jere Powers, Nate Purinton, Gus Ramsey, Ed Randall, Ben Reiter, Harold Reynolds, Rich Rinaldi, Bill Ripken, Cal Ripken Jr., Brooks Robinson, Chris Roenbeck, Ken Rosenthal, Christopher "Mad Dog" Russo, Joan Ryan, Barry Sacks, Matt Sandulli, Mike Santini, Rich Savino, Tom Scheiber, Mike Schmidt, Howie Schwab, Tom Seaver, Joe Sheehan, Joel Sherman, Buck Showalter, Bill Simmons, Ozzie Smith, John Smoltz, Jerry Springer, Sylvester Stallone, Jayson Stark, Erik Strohl, Rick Sutcliffe, Don Sutton, Frank Thomas, Barry Tompkins, Joe Torre, Bobby Valentine, Dave Valle, Matt Vasgergian, Tom Verducci, Suzyn Waldman, Marc Weiner, Justin White, Karen Whritner, Steve Wilkos, George Will, Mitch Williams, Norby Williamson, Juan Woodson, Robert Wuhl, Brian Yu, and Don Zimmer.

Baseball-Reference.com is one of the greatest innovations in baseball history. Without it, a project of this type is not possible. Thanks to Sean Forman and everyone who makes Baseball-Reference.com such a resource. My thanks as well to FanGraphs.com, and WhatIfSports.com.

A tip of the cap to the Cardinals fans at the Cooperstown Diner who gave this book its title.

Thank you to David Vigliano for your belief in the project and the subject matter. This wouldn't have happened without you.

And to Bob Bender, a true gentleman who edited this book with great care and expertise. I am also indebted to ace copy editor Fred Chase for his outstanding, meticulous work.

And a final thank-you to my true friend and agent Nick Khan, who is always in my corner.

# Sources

## 1. The Herd

5  *Run expectancy charts:* http://tangotiger.net/re24.html.

8  *"I'll leave it up to Grady":* Theo Epstein quoted in Sean McAdam, "Red Sox Going with the Closer-by-Committee Approach," ESPN.com, March 13, 2003, http://sports.espn.go.com/mlb/columns/story?id=1489225.

9  *"Anybody who thinks"* and *"Tell Bill James to come":* Troy Percival and Rick Peterson quoted in Steve Goldman and *Baseball Prospectus, Mind Game: How the Boston Red Sox Got Smart, Won a World Series, and Created a New Blueprint for Winning* (Workman Publishing Company, 2005), pp. 69–70.

9  *"I think if it was any other city"* and *"We are going to get":* Theo Epstein and Chad Fox quoted in Peter Schmuck, "Without a True Closer, Red Sox Look for Relief," *Baltimore Sun,* April 11, 2003, http://articles.baltimoresun.com/2003-04-11/sports/0304110131_1_boston-red-red-sox-closer.

14  *"It was bad execution":* Theo Epstein quoted in Rob Bradford, "Ten Years Later, Revisiting Merits of Closer-by-Committee Approach," WEEI.com, April 2003, http://www.weei.com/sports/boston/baseball/red-sox/rob-bradford/2013/04/25/ten-years-later-revisiting-merits-closer-comm.

16  *"That's the first time I've seen":* Nick Swisher quoted in Adam Berry, "Rays Redefining Defense with the Shift," mlb.com, April 26, 2012, http://mlb.mlb.com/news/print.jsp?ymd=20120426&content_id=29715994&vkey=news_mlb&c_id=mlb.

17 *"They're not above the game":* Kevin Long quoted in Marc Topkin, "Yankees Hitting Coach: Rays 'Not Above the Game,'" *Tampa Bay Times,* May 8, 2012, http://www.tampabay.com/blogs/rays/content/yankees-hitting-coach-rays-not-above-game/2088422.

23 *Those who study the "Hiddink Syndrome" note that a coach:* Naami Lee, Stephen Jackson, and Kuenmo Lee, "South Korea's Glocal Hero," *Society of Sport Journal,* 2007.

24 *"supported by a powerful professional culture":* Daniel Kahneman, *Thinking, Fast and Slow* (Farrar, Strauss, and Giroux, 2013), p. 217.

25 *"Humans are a social animal":* author interview with Dr. Joel Fuhrman.

26 *"The orthodoxy still believes":* author interview with Bill James.

26 *"law of least effort":* Daniel Kahneman, *Thinking, Fast and Slow* (Farrar, Straus, and Giroux, 2013), p. 35.

## 2. Good Looking Beats Good Pitching

35 *In multiple studies, people were shown pictures:* Gabriel Lenz and Chappell Lawson, "Looking the Part: Television Leads Less Informed Citizens to Vote Based on Candidates' Appearance," *American Journal of Political Science,* Vol. 55, No. 3, July 2011.

43 *"Baseball's Last Gunslinger":* Peter J. Schwartz, "Baseball's Last Gunslinger," *Forbes,* May 21, 2008, http://www.forbes.com/2008/05/21/baseball-twins-morris-biz-sportscz_pjs_0521morris.html.

43 *"Coming at Ya":* Dennis Brackin, "Comin' at Ya: Winning Is Everything for Ultra-Competitive Morris," *Minneapolis Star and Tribune,* February 6, 1991, p. 1C.

43 *"The 100 Manliest Moustaches":* "The 100 Manliest Moustaches in Sports History," http://www.brobible.com/life/article/the-100-best-sports-mustaches-in-sports-history/.

44 *"Fat Man on the Mound":* "Fat Man on the Mound," *Time,* June 19, 1972, p. 92.

44 *"When Fat Is Beautiful":* Ira Berkow, "When Fat Is Beautiful," *The New York Times,* August 7, 1989.

44 *"Carrying Their Weight":* "Carrying Their Weight," *The Washington Post,* April 9, 2006, http://www.washingtonpost.com/wp-dyn/content/article/2006/04/08/AR2006040800906.html.

47 1990 Topps Jack Morris DET #555, 1979 Topps 251 Jack Morris Detroit Tigers baseball card, http://3.bp.blogspot.com/_D84Z7vc38Aw

/S5viomAH_RI/AAAAAAAAFac/zC1-S43c8wA/s320/76topps3
85.jpg.

## 3. The Will to (Not) Win

56  *"President Branch Rickey":* Frank Eck, Associated Press, September 23, 1947, https://captnsblog.wordpress.com/2011/03/28/was-branch-rickey-the-father-of-sabermetrics/.

56  *"Numbers Nonsense":* Stanley Frank, "The Numbers Nonsense," *Sports Illustrated,* November 1958.

57  *Cook followed up with* Percentage Baseball and the Computer *in 1971:* Earnshaw Cook, *Percentage Baseball and the Computer* (Waverly Press, 1971).

58  *In a letter to the Baseball Hall of Fame in 1975:* "Earnshaw Cook Letter to Hall of Fame," 1975, accessed courtesy of Giamatti Research Center at Baseball Hall of Fame.

58  *"Computerball Is Here":* Joe Klein, "Computerball Is Here," *Sport,* April 1983.

58  *"The Computers of Summer":* "The Computers of Summer," *Newsweek,* May 23, 1983.

58  *"It's the Apple of His Eye":* Ray Kennedy, "It's the Apple of His Eye: A's Manager Steve Boros Is Helping Lead Baseball into the Computer Age," *Sports Illustrated,* June 6, 1983.

58  *"Steve Boros woke one morning":* Alan Schwarz and Peter Gammons, *The Numbers Game: Baseball's Lifelong Fascination with Statistics* (Macmillan, 2005).

59  *"a computer-savvy Ed Norton":* Rob Neyer, "The Rise and Fall of Mike Gimbel," espn.com, November 6, 2002, http://static.espn.go.com/mlb/columns/neyer_rob/1456677.html.

59  *"As the Red Sox were losing":* Paul Doyle, " 'Stats Man' Only Adds to Discord," *Hartford Courant,* March 20, 1997.

62  *"sounds as unappealing as":* Fuhrman Bisher, "Sabermetricians, Let's Try to Keep It Simple," *The Sporting News,* May 28, 1984.

63  *"This is the new romance":* Bruce Jenkins, "New Baseball Stats Designed for Nerds," *Herald-Journal,* April 22, 1990, https://news.google.com/newspapers?nid=1876&dat=19900422&id=xdIpAAAAIBAJ&sjid=Ms4eAAAAIBAJ&pg=5152.1497536&hl=en.

63  *"Go ahead, disappear":* Bruce Jenkins, "Stupid Comments Are Up," *San*

*Francisco Chronicle*, September 14, 2005, http://www.sfgate.com/sports /jenkins/article/Stupid-comments-are-up-2569796.php.

63　*"Oh, and let's not forget"*: Dan Shaughnessy, "Lackey Starts Season with Loss—of a Few Pounds," *The Boston Globe*, February 15, 2011.

63　*"I mean, did you do the math"*: Mitch Albom, "The Eyes Have It," *Detroit Free Press*, November 16, 2012, http://archive.freep.com/article/20121116 /COLO1/311160108/detroit-tigers-miguel-cabrera-mvp-award.

65　*"Everybody outside of baseball"*: author interview with Michael Lewis.

66　*"The game itself"*: Michael Lewis, *Moneyball* (W. W. Norton and Co., 2004), p. 287.

68　*"computer nerd" who "speaks in megabytes"*: T. J. Simers, "Dodgers Come Up Short on New General Manager," *Los Angeles Times*, February 17, 2004, http://articles.latimes.com/2004/feb/17/sports/sp-simers17.

68　*"Google Boy"*: T.J. Simers, DePodesta's Computer Must Have a Bad Virus, *Los Angeles Times*, January 4, 2005, http://articles.latimes.com/2005/jan/04 /sports/sp-simers4.

68　*"Doogie Howser"*: Bill Plaschke, "With Luck, the Dodgers Won't Crash," *Los Angeles Times*, February 17, 2004, http://articles.latimes.com/2004/feb /17/sports/sp-plaschke17.

71　*"To me, VORP epitomized the new-age nonsense"*: Murray Chass, "As Season Approaches, Some Topics Should Be Off Limits," *The New York Times*, February 27, 2007, http://www.nytimes.com/2007/02/27/sports /baseball/27chass.html?_r=3&ref=baseball&oref=slogin&oref=login&.

74　*"Roth is the figure filbert"*: Steve Snider, United Press, December 28, 1950, https://captnsblog.wordpress.com/2011/03/28/was-branch-rickey-the -father-of-sabermetrics/.

76　*"In a few years, maybe the data"*: author interview with Rob Neyer.

# 4. The Epiphany

80　*In the 1980s, the stance of the American College of Sports Medicine:* Michael Kremenik et al., "A Historical Timeline of Doping in the Olympics: Part II—1970–88," *Kawasaki Journal of Medical Welfare*, Vol. 12, No. 2, 2007.

82　*When I was in junior high, our school board found several books:* Herbert N. Foerstel, *Banned in the U.S.A.: A Reference Guide to Book Censorship in Schools* (Greenwood) 2000.

90　*In a 2006 ESPN* The Magazine *column:* Bill Simmons, "I See Dead People," *ESPN The Magazine*, March 17, 2006.

# 5. The Godfather

97   *"Bill James changed my life:* Scott Gray, *The Mind of Bill James: How a Complete Outsider Changed Baseball* (Doubleday, 2006).

98   *"Jack Kerouac contributed a column in 1962 for* Writer's Digest*":* Jack Kerouac, "Are Writers Born or Made?" *Writer's Digest,* January 1962.

104   *"Red Sox failures":* John Thorn quoted in Gregory F. Augustine Pierce, *How Bill James Changed Our View of Baseball* (ACTA Publications, 2007).

105   *"In the wake":* Jim Baker quoted in Scott Gray, *The Mind of Bill James: How a Complete Outsider Changed Baseball* (Doubleday, 2006).

# 6. The Tyranny of the Batting Average

112   *"The game was one of advancing":* author interview with John Thorn.

113   *"Throughout most of the history of baseball":* Bill James, BillJamesOnline .com.

117   *He even tried Winter Baseball—on skates:* "Chadwick Had Baseball Tried on Ice Skates," *Brooklyn Eagle,* January 22, 2009.

118   *"The first offensive statistic to consider":* John Thorn and Pete Palmer, *The Hidden Game of Baseball* (Doubleday), 1984.

123   *Baseball Info Solutions counted up nine:* "Ryu Stacks Cards Deck with Soft Stuff," Defensive Misplays, ESPN Stats and Info Blog, http://espn .go.com/blog/statsinfo/post/_/id/75488/ryu-stacks-cards-deck-with -soft-stuff.

# 7. Kill the Win

140   *The official scorer, however, deemed David Robertson:* David Brown, "Mariano Rivera Gets Win in Save Situation After Official Scorer Calls David Robertson 'Brief and Ineffective,'" yahoo.com, September 13, 2013, http:// sports.yahoo.com/blogs/mlb-big-league-stew/mariano-rivera-gets-win -save-situation-official-scorer-155210509—mlb.html.

# 8. Kill the Save Too

150   *Tom Tango, Mitchel Lichtman, and Andrew Dolphin point out:* Andrew Dolphin, Tom Tango, and Mitchel Lichtman, *The Book: Playing the Percentages in Baseball* (Potomac Book), March 2007.

# 9. Bullpenning

162 *"We talked all winter":* Joe Lemire, "For Many Yankee Pitchers, It's Going, Going Gone—But Not for Long," *USA Today,* August 25, 2015, http://www.usatoday.com/story/sports/mlb/2015/08/25/yankees-roster-shuffle-designate-assignment-chris-capuano/32340855/.

164 *"This is what the Rockies' season":* Troy E. Renck, "Reeling Rockies Go with Unconventional Four-Man Rotation," *The Denver Post,* June 19, 2012, http://www.denverpost.com/ci_20895136/reeling-rockies-go-unconventional-four-man-rotation.

165 *"When I first heard the Colorado Rockies' ":* Scott Nulph, "Rockies Have Become a Joke,"*Wyoming Tribune Eagle,* June 28, 2012, http://www.wyomingnews.com/articles/2012/06/29/sports/20sports_06-29-12.txt#.VeNxlEIbBE4.

165 *"were throwing in the towel on 2013":* Gabe Lacques, "Rockies Commit to Unique Pitching Plan in 2013," *USA Today,* August 30, 2012, http://content.usatoday.com/communities/dailypitch/post/2012/08/rockies-pitching-plan-four-man-rotation/1#.VeNy50IbBE4.

168 *"Why save your closer":* Billy Martin quoted in Bill Pennington, *Billy Martin: Baseball's Flawed Genius* (Houghton Mifflin Harcourt, 2015), p. 279.


# 10. When Bad Contracts Happen to Good People

181 *"According to sports economists":* Edward Moran, "Egad, A-Rod! $252m Deal with Rangers Sends Shockwaves A-Lot of Trouble? Observers Call Rodriguez Deal Ominous Sign," *Philadelphia Enquirer,* June 12, 2000, http://articles.philly.com/2000-12-12/sports/25579212_1_rangers-owner-tom-hicks-sports-contract-franchise-values.

184 *Hampton cited the Denver School System:* Bob Kimball, "Lefthander Mike Hampton Retires—Finally," *USA Today,* March 27, 2011, http://content.usatoday.com/communities/dailypitch/post/2011/03/lefthander-mike-hampton-retires—finally/1#.VdvSwkIbBE4.


# 11. Hall of Fame

201 *The people in Cooperstown had their beautiful little village:* Dennis Corcoran, *Induction Day at Cooperstown* (McFarland, 2010).

201 *There was a Centennial Commission in charge of the whole probject:* Zev Chafets, *Cooperstown Confidential* (Bloomsbury USA, 2010).

202  *Walter Johnson was just 51:* Jim Reisler, *A Great Day in Cooperstown* (Carroll & Graf, 2006).

202  *Hall of Fame founder Stephen Clark, ably assisted:* Ken Smith, *Baseball Hall of Fame* (Grosset and Dunlap, 1952).

204  *They use statistics as a club:* Bill James, *The New Bill James Historical Abstract* (Free Press, 2001).

## 14. The 1941 MVP — Blind Squirrels Find Nut

261  *"I knew I had to do it for Joe":* Dennis Gaffney, "What Made DiMaggio a Great Player?" PBS.org, http://www.pbs.org/wgbh/amex/dimaggio/sfeature/essay .html.

265  *In 1969, he was famously voted:* Richard Ben Cramer, *The Hero's Life* (Simon & Schuster, 2001).

270  *"It was the greatest season":* Chad Finn "Ted Williams, Joe Dimaggio, and 1941," *The Boston Globe*, September 24, 2011, http://www.boston.com /sports/touching_all_the_bases/2011/09/ted_williams_joe_dimaggio _and.html.

270  *"DiMaggio's defense was not even close":* Jeff Zimmerman, "Reward Retrospective: 1941 AL MVP," *Beyond the Box Score*, January 6, 2010, http:// www.beyondtheboxscore.com/2010/1/6/1231697/reward-retrospective -1941-al-mvp.

272  *Any idea who holds the record for the longest on-base:* Herman Krabbenhoft, SABR Baseball Records Committee, June 2003, http://sabr.org/cmsFiles /Files/ACF1FBA.pdf.

## 15. Department of Decision Sciences

284  *"When a habit":* Charles Duhigg, *The Power of Habit* (Random House, 2012), Chapter 1.

286  *"Many people are overconfident":* Daniel Kahneman, *Thinking, Fast and Slow* (Farrar, Straus, and Giroux, 2013), p. 45.

288  *In his book Molina:* Bengie Molina with Joan Ryan, *Molina: The Story of a Father Who Raised an Unlikely Baseball Dynasty* (Simon & Schuster, 2015).

291  *Bill Madden of the New York Daily News:* Bill Madden, "Walt Jocketty Gets Axed from Cards Because of Numbers Crunch," *NY Daily News*, 10/7/2007 http://www.nydailynews.com/sports/baseball/walt-jocketty-axed-cards -numbers-crunch-article-1.230511.

293 *"a dehumanizing, analytics-based approach":* Evan Drellich, "Radical Methods Paint Astros as 'Outcast,'" *Houston Chronicle,* May 23, 2014, http://www.houstonchronicle.com/sports/astros/article/Radical-methods-paint-Astros-as-outcast-5501982.php.

294 *"Unequivocal draft disaster":* Jeff Passan quoted in Mike Oz, "Astros Fail to Come to Terms with No. 1 Overall Pick Brady Aiken, Two Others," yahoo.com, July 18, 2014, http://sports.yahoo.com/blogs/mlb-big-league-stew/astros-fail-to-come-to-terms-with-no--1-overall-pick-brady-aiken--two-others-215717197.html.

294 *"Hard to overstate":* Brett Dolan, "Astros Strikeout with Aiken," CBS Houston, July 18, 2014, http://houston.cbslocal.com/2014/07/18/astros-strikeout-with-aiken/.

294 *"Today, two young men":* Tony Clark quoted in Mike Oz, "Astros Fail to Come to Terms with No. 1 Overall Pick Brady Aiken, Two Others."

295 *Ben Reiter of* Sports Illustrated *had bought in:* Ben Reiter, "Your 2017 World Series Champs" *Sports Illustrated,* June 30, 2014.

295 *"a source of comic gold":* David Coleman, "What Failing to Sign Top-Pick Brady Aiken Means for the Astros," SB Nation, July 18, 2014, http://www.sbnation.com/mlb/2014/7/18/5917355/astros-brady-aiken-2014-mlb-draft-jacob-nix.

295 *"Those critical of Luhnow":* Ken Rosenthal, "Tension Growing Between Astros Manager, GM," Fox Sports, August 29, 2014, http://www.foxsports.com/mlb/just-a-bit-outside/story/tension-growing-between-astros-manager-gm-082914.

## 16. The Year of Getting Smart

299 *"We hang on to tradition":* Jeff Banister quoted in Kevin Sherrington, "How Rangers Manager Jeff Banister Plans to Meld Baseball Tradition with Analytics," *The Dallas Morning News* March 11, 2015, http://www.dallasnews.com/sports/columnists/kevin-sherrington/20150310-sherrington-how-new-rangers-manager-jeff-banister-plans-to-meld-tradition-with-analytics.ece.

301 *Freddy Brown:* Fred Brown, Basketball Reference Page, http://www.basketball-reference.com/players/b/brownfro1.html.

301 *Steph Curry:* Steph Curry, Basketball Reference Page, http://www.basketball-reference.com/players/c/curryst01.html.

301 *Larry Bird:* Larry Bird, Basketball Reference Page, http://www.basketball-reference.com/players/b/birdla01.html.

301  1986 NBA Finals, Basketball Reference Page, http://www.basketball-refer
     ence.com/playoffs/1986-nba-finals-rockets-vs-celtics.html.

301  1992–93 NBA Season Stats, Basketball Reference Page, http://www.basket
     ball-reference.com/leagues/NBA_1993.html.

301  2014–15 NBA Season Stats, Basketball Reference Page, http://www.basket
     ball-reference.com/leagues/NBA_2015.html.

302  *In the 2014 book:* Mark Armour and Daniel R. Levitt, *In Pursuit of Pennants*
     (University of Nebraska Press, 2015), pp. 372–73.

# Index